'BEYOND THE DEAD HORIZON'
STUDIES IN MODERN CONFLICT ARCHAEOLOGY

edited by

Nicholas J. Saunders

OXBOW BOOKS
Oxford and Oakville

Published by
Oxbow Books, Oxford, UK

© Oxbow Books and the individual authors, 2012

ISBN 978-1-84217-471-5

Front cover image: Photograph credit to Steven Whitehead
A German naval observation tower at Noirmount on the south west coast of Jersey
Back cover: copyright Nicholas J. Saunders

This book is available direct from:

Oxbow Books, Oxford, UK
(Phone: 01865-241249; Fax: 01865-794449)

and

The David Brown Book Company
PO Box 511, Oakville, CT 06779, USA
(Phone: 860-945-9329; Fax: 860-945-9468)

or from our website

www.oxbowbooks.com

A CIP record for this book is available from the British Library

Library of Congress Cataloging-in-Publication Data

Beyond the dead horizon : studies in modern conflict archaeology / edited by Nicholas J.
Saunders.
    p. cm.
  Includes bibliographical references.
  ISBN 978-1-84217-471-5
  1. Military archaeology. 2. Archaeology and history. 3. World War, 1914-1918--
Antiquities. 4. World War, 1939-1945--Antiquities. 5. Military history--20th century. I.
Saunders, Nicholas J.
  CC77.M55B48 2012
  930.1--dc23

                            2012026114

Printed and bound in Great Britain by
Short Run Press, Exeter

Contents

Contributors

Deborah A. Atwood B.A., M.A., is a graduate student in the Department of Archaeology and Anthropology at Bristol University, UK. She has worked at the National Museum of Bermuda (incorporating the Bermuda Maritime Museum), and carried out archaeological and archival research with the Bermuda National Trust. Her current research interests include conflict archaeology, confinement art, and cultural heritage tourism. She took the M.A. in Historical Archaeology at Bristol University, where she is now studying for a PhD in Archaeology and Anthropology. Email: debatwood@gmail.com

Margaret Bagwell B.A., M.A., is a graduate student at Wesley Theological Seminary, Washington, DC, USA. She took the M.A. in Historical Archaeology at Bristol University, and has carried out archaeological research in England. Her current research interests include heritage preservation issues during times of natural disaster. email: mnellbagwell@gmail.com

Esther Breithoff B.A., M.A., took the M.A. in Historical Archaeology at the University of Bristol, where she is now a postgraduate student. Her PhD research focuses on the material culture and conflict landscapes of the Chaco War (1932–5) between Bolivia and Paraguay. Her wider research interests include Latin American dictatorships, wars, and indigenous struggles. email: esther.breithoff@hotmail.co.uk

Martin Brown B.A., MiFA, FSA, is a professional archaeologist working for the UK Ministry of Defence. He is a founder member of No-Man's-Land, an international group involved in archaeological research on sites of the Great War. His current research interests include past and current training landscapes, and the role of cultural heritage as it interacts with the military, both in conflict and as a manifestation of military ethos. He is currently studying for a PhD in Archaeology and Anthropology at Bristol University.

Susannah Callow B.A., M.A., took the M.A. in Historical Archaeology at the University of Bristol, where she is currently PhD student. Her research interests focus on the concepts and uses of human and animal bones and body parts in recent conflicts.

Paul Cornish is a Senior Curator in the Department of Exhibits at the Imperial War Museum, London. He has a longstanding interest in the material culture of conflict, and is currently involved with the regeneration of the IWM aimed to coincide with the 2014 centenary of the First World War. He has published widely on various aspects of modern conflict, and his two most recent books are *Machine Guns and the Great War* (2009), and with Nicholas J. Saunders, *Contested Objects: Material Memories of the Great War* (2009).

Julie Dunne MSci, took her Master's degree in Archaeological Science at Bristol University, where she is now conducting PhD research in the Organic Geochemistry Unit. She is currently studying the effects of climate and environmental change on Holocene subsistence strategies in Libya. Her current research interests also include the archaeology of conflict and modern day burial grounds. email: julie.dunne@bristol.ac.uk

Charles Donald Eavenson II A.A., B.A., M.A., is an independent scholar. His current research interests include American culture in modern wars. He earned an A.A. at Modesto Junior College, California, and a B.A. in Anthropology at the University of Hawaii at Hilo. He took the M.A. in Twntieth-Century Conflict Archaeology at the University of Bristol. email: Charles. Eavenson@bristolalumni.org.uk

Emily Glass B.Sc., M.A., took the M.A. in Historical Archaeology at Bristol University, from where she currently divides her time between PhD research and professional archaeological work. She has been involved with numerous national and international fieldwork projects, including 10 seasons at the UNESCO World Heritage Site of Butrint in Albania. It was this experience which led to her doctoral research into the materiality and conflict landscape of Communist Albanian Defences. emilyglass@yahoo.com

Niamh Keating B.A., M.A., is an independent scholar. She took her M.A. in Historical Archaeology at Bristol University, and currently works in the Education and Outreach Department of Wandsworth Museum, London. Her current research interests include war memorialisation in conflict situations, institutional archaeology in colonial and neo-colonial contexts, and the archaeology of medicine. email: niamh360@hotmail.com

Matthew Leonard B.A., M.A., took his M.A. in Twentieth-Century Conflict Archaeology at the University of Bristol, where is currently undertaking PhD research into the First World War's subterranean landscapes along the Western Front. He is also carrying out broader archaeological and anthropological Great War-related research in Belgium and France. email: mgpleonard@ aol.com

Gunnar Maus M.A., is a graduate student in the Department of Geography at Christian-Albrechts-Universität zu Kiel, Germany, where he also teaches Human Geography. His PhD is concerned with memory, heritage, and militarized landscapes of the Cold War. He took the M.A. in Historical Archaeology at Bristol University. email: maus@geographie.uni-kiel.de

Cassie Newland B.A., M.A., PhD, is part-time lecturer in the Department of Archaeology and Anthropology, University of Bristol, where she recently completed her doctoral research on the archaeology of telecommunications. She also works as a freelance archaeological consultant. Her recent projects include the archaeology of mobile phones, the telegraph, and 'In Transit', the excavation of a 1991 Ford Transit Van. She is also an on-screen archaeologist for Channel 4's *Time Team*. email: cassie.newland@bris.ac.uk

Liam J.S. Powell B.A., M.A, is an independent scholar. He has carried out archaeological research in the UK and the United States. His current research interests include landscapes of modern conflict, and the relationship between modern heritage management and homelessness and squatting. He gained his B.A. (Hons) in Theology and Religious Studies, and his M.A. in Twentieth-Century Conflict Archaeology at the University of Bristol.

Philip R. Rowe B.A. (Hons), M.A., PiFA, is currently an Archaeological Landscape Investigator, based in the Department of Archaeology and Anthropology, University of Bristol, UK. His main research interests are the social archaeology of modern conflict, especially of Britain's home defences of the early to mid-twentieth century. His PhD at Southampton University focuses on Britain's Second World War anti-invasion defence network. email: philip.r.rowe@bristol.ac.uk

Nicholas J. Saunders is course director for the M.A. in Twentieth-Century Conflict Archaeology in the Department of Archaeology and Anthropology, University of Bristol, and Honorary Reader at University College London. He is currently engaged in investigating First World War battle-zone landscapes in Jordan and also in Slovenia. His recent publications include *Trench Art* (2003), *Matters of Conflict* (2004), *Killing Time: Archaeology and the First World War* (2007), and with Paul Cornish, *Contested Objects: Material Memories of the Great War* (2009).

Gabriella Soto B.A., M.A., took the M.A. in Twntieth-Century Conflict Archaeology at the University of Bristol. She is currently a doctoral candidate at the University of Arizona, USA, where her research focuses on the archaeology of transient peoples and cultures – particularly the modern refugees and undocumented migrants travelling to the USA across it southwest border. She has worked at the Harris Environment Group in Tucson, and has carried out archaeological fieldwork in the American southwest, Honduras, and in northern France. email: Gabriella.soto@gmail.com

Chantel Summerfield B.A., M.A., took the M.A. in Twentieth-Century Conflict Archaeology at the University of Bristol, where she is currently an AHRC-funded PhD candidate, researching the relationship between nature (especially trees and wood) and modern conflict. She has worked in France and Belgium, and has always had a keen interest in industrialised warfare. email: chantel_summerfield@hotmail.com.

John B. Winterburn BSc., M.A., C.Eng., is a graduate student at the University of Bristol. Following a career in the telecommunications industry, he took the M.A. in Landscape Archaeology in 2004, and has undertaken landscape research in the UK and Jordan. His PhD focuses on the conflict landscapes of southern Jordan, and his other interests include First World War training landscapes in Wiltshire, and the industrial landscape of south-east Wales. email: John@Winterburn.Info

Melanie Winterton B.A. (Hons), M.A., took the M.A. in Twentieth-Century Conflict Archaeology at Bristol University. Her M.A. dissertation was on the cultural associations and legacies of the Second World War's Lancaster Bomber, focusing on ritualisation, memorials, crash sites, and the sensorial experiences of air crew. Her AHRC-funded PhD research at Bristol focuses on First World War aviation, and in particular on the sensory 'pilot body' experiences of airscape.

Foreword

Nicholas J. Saunders

Few enjoy the privilege of contributing to the birth of a new sub-discipline – in this case the multidisciplinary, anthropologically-informed endeavour known as 'Modern Conflict Archaeology'. While at University College London, my own British Academy-sponsored research into the material culture of the First World War (1998–2004) afforded the opportunity to create links with at the Imperial War Museum in London, the In Flanders Fields Museum in Ypres, Belgium, and the Historial de la Grande Guerre in Péronne, France. It quickly became apparent, to colleagues at these institutions, and elsewhere, as well as to myself, that in the conceptual space between military history, cultural history, museum studies, and traditional battlefield archaeology, something new was stirring.

A move from UCL to Bristol University allowed for the teaching of this nascent sub-discipline to be included in the well-established M.A. in Historical Archaeology. Such was the interest generated, that many postgraduate students opted to write their essays, and sometimes their dissertations, on one aspect or another of the archaeology of modern conflict. Several of these students later returned to Bristol to undertake doctoral research on the same or similar themes. In subsequent years, many others have followed them.

It was, in part, this student-led enthusiasm which led to the redesign of an earlier M.A. configured for UCL in 2002 into the M.A. in *Twentieth-Century Conflict Archaeology* at Bristol. It is taught by a panel of international experts, and includes also a professional placement in the UK or abroad. With its focus solely on conflicts of the twentieth and twenty-first centuries, and with an avowedly anthropological approach, the Bristol M.A. was and remains fundamentally distinct from other postgraduate degrees that espouse more traditional 'Battlefield Archaeology' values, and that are concerned mainly with pre-twentieth century wars.

As momentum gathered, the students inaugurated an annual 'Postgraduate Conference in Modern Conflict Archaeology' in 2009, to provide a forum for international discussion and co-operation, and to provide an intellectual centre of gravity for the interdisciplinary study of modern conflict.

It is worth saying here, that none of the Bristol students to date have been motivated by a predominant interest in military history or traditional battlefield archaeology – subjects that are well served by other UK universities. The Bristol students are primarily interested in an interdisciplinary approach where they can move across traditional subject boundaries, conceptualise their own multidisciplinary research agendas, and innovate their own methodologies. This intellectual excitement and vigour draws its theoretical inspiration from 'material culture anthropology' – the hybrid approach developed in the Department of Anthropology at UCL during the 1990s, and refined internationally ever since.

It soon became apparent that the quality and diversity of Bristol postgraduate work was such that it deserved an afterlife in print, and that a volume of edited papers could be produced solely from this corpus. *Beyond the Dead Horizon* is the fruit of the decision to do so. Its aims are not only to bring exciting new research into the public arena, but also to provide a new generation of researchers with the opportunity to write an academic paper to professional standards, and to suffer the inevitable shock of 'first contact' with the editorial and peer-review process.

This volume also aims to demonstrate the vitality and huge potential of modern conflict archaeology at a time when such an interdisciplinary approach is sorely needed. Veterans of many twentieth-century conflicts are passing away; the First and Second World Wars are being increasingly memorialised and commemorated; archaeological research is being recognised and accepted as a legitimate investigation of recent times; traditional battlefield archaeology has been revealed as an empirical and theoretical cul-de-sac; and the world seems increasingly afflicted with ever-more deadly, technological, and complexly-globalised conflicts – most of which are not formal wars in the traditional sense.

This volume is written by and for the next generation of archaeologists and anthropologists interested in modern conflict in all its bewildering manifestations. Nothing in war or more generalised conflict is certain, and truth is always the first victim. These disturbing realities appear to be self-perpetuating, and can be verified by anyone, everyday, on any news bulletin.

The conflict-archaeology strata of the future are being laid down today, before our eyes – not only in the physical remains of destruction, but also in new and rejuvenated monuments and landscapes of commemoration, new museological engagements with conflict, the agendas of the media in re-presenting war, new ideas of war heritage, and a burgeoning multi-million dollar commerce in tourism to places associated with conflict.

It is clear that we are rapidly moving away from an approach based on the digging up of 'buttons and bones' on battlefields, and into a more intellectually grounded multidisciplinary future. It is the younger generation of scholars, such as those in this volume, which will take us there.

Introduction: Engaging the Materialities of Twentieth and Twenty-first Century Conflict

Nicholas J. Saunders

None of the contributions in this volume can be described in any sense as traditional 'Battlefield Archaeology'. Each author has, in their own way, taken theoretical inspiration and general approach from modern interdisciplinary archaeology, and material culture anthropology. In other words, every paper here is located firmly within what is called 'Modern Conflict Archaeology' – a hybrid sub-discipline which draws on the knowledge and insights of a diversity of academic subjects that, besides anthropology, includes cultural studies, cultural geography, military history, art history, museum studies, and tourism and cultural heritage studies. Diversity is strength in this approach – which, rather than privileging one or other kinds of knowledge, seeks instead to draw on each as appropriate in order to respond to the complex challenges of investigating conflict in the modern world.

* * * * *

Modern conflict archaeology is 'modern' in several ways. First, it deals only with conflicts of the twentieth and twenty-first centuries, and second, it is an anthropologically-informed multidisciplinary endeavour, concerned with the social, cultural, psychological, and technological as well as military complexities of recent conflicts, and their powerful and unpredictable legacies.

Modern conflict archaeology takes a radically different approach to that of traditional battlefield archaeology, and is a necessary response to dealing with the complex nature of historically recent conflicts. These complexities are generated partly by the nature of modern wars as conflicts of industrialised intensity, and partly because they incorporate political and nationalistic motivations, and notions of ethnicity and identity. Many of these conflicts are often within living memory, and so demand an increased level of sensitivity in their investigation. Many conflict locations have become (or are becoming) 'sites of memory', politically contested and economically important places of cultural heritage and, increasingly, of tourism. This multitude of issues makes modern conflict sites, in effect, highly sensitised multilayered landscapes that require a robust, interdisciplinary approach, far beyond the ability of traditional, single-event-oriented, battlefield archaeology to deliver.

Modern conflict archaeology focuses on the idea of conflict as a multifaceted phenomenon, which may leave a variety of physical traces in many different places, all or most of which can possess multiple meanings that may change over time. Conflict generates new experiences and ideas for soldiers and civilians alike, and these may vary for men, women, and children – all of whose material worlds are transformed to a greater or lesser extent. This fact alone brings the archaeological study of modern conflict into the realm of anthropology.

Conflict archaeology, crucially, is not restricted to battlefields, nor to large-scale wars between nations, but embraces any kind of (often, but not exclusively, armed) conflict (and its wider social and cultural correlates and consequences), at any level, within a single nation, or between nations. In this view, the constantly-shifting multidimensional aftermaths of conflict are as important as the conflicts themselves. The scale of potential research topics is vast, and the topics themselves are not always obvious. They may be half a world away, perched on a mountainside, laying on the seabed, seen everyday on the way to work, or packed in a box in the attic.

Illustrating this point, a random selection of research topics includes: First World War training trenches, the shrapnel collecting habits of Second World War British children, the material culture produced in prisoner-of-war and internment camps from the Boer War to today, the 'ghost villages' of western Turkey abandoned during the 1922 exchange of populations with Greece, 3-D artworks produced by Vietnam veterans, the wearing of war medals, the exhumation of Spanish Civil War victims, the effects of modern wars on indigenous peoples, the material heritage of the Cold War, the effects of the 1992–5 ethnic cleansing on the traditional craftworks of the Balkans, the devastation of Iraq's peerless museum collections during the Second Gulf War, the investigation of post-conflict 'killing fields' represented by unexploded munitions, the 'disappeared' of Argentina and Chile, the genocide of Rwanda, the conflict in Gaza, the remains of the uprisings of the so-called Arab Spring, and the 'sensual worlds' of front-line soldiers and home-front civilians.

All of these, and more, are consequences of conflict – but the majority do not involve formal battle-events. Adopting an interdisciplinary approach, and an integrated archaeological and anthropological perspective, it is clear that we have hardly begun to investigate modern conflict.

* * * * *

This unique collection of papers is a snapshot of current research. It demonstrates the vitality and energy of this new engagement with the material remains of recent conflict. The overarching anthropological framework allows for a diversity of topics to share a common theoretical outlook, and thereby contribute to refining this new sub-discipline in ways that are relevant to a younger generation of scholars and the public alike.

The range of topics is impressive, and forever breaks the mould of common assumptions about what such activities should look like. The reader will search in vain for papers detailing the opportunistic digging of battlefields, the counting of musket balls, the search for First World War cap badges or altimeters and propellers from crashed Second World War aeroplanes. Instead, we see a broad range of challenging new engagements with the material culture and landscapes of conflict in its widest sense.

In this volume, a critical analysis of the use and infinite meanings of body parts over the last 100 years (Callow) sits alongside a study of the sensual terrors of First World War trench life (Winterton), and an exploration of the personalised objectification of that war's dead, known as the 'Dead Man's Penny' (Dunne). Two heirloom diaries (Bagwell; Leonard) provide family insights into how long departed relatives can be embodied in evocatively textured objects, and Boer War prisoner-of-war memorabilia are shown to mark the gendered tensions of camp life in Bermuda (Atwood).

Modern conflict archaeology sees objects and landscapes not as separate entities, but as complexly embedded and inter-connected materialisations of the human experience of conflict. The investigation of linear features in conflict landscapes allows Hadrian's Wall to be compared to the early twentieth-century Hejaz Railway in the Middle East (Winterburn). On a different scale, trees and their arborglyph carvings mark human presence in times of war – living memorials to the dead that blur the distinction between nature and culture (Summerfield). Miniature First World War terrain models are investigated for their military, social, and memorial aspects (Brown), and the virtually unknown conflict landscapes of the Chaco War in South America are subjected to a sustained archaeological and anthropological study for the first time (Breithoff).

Memorials to the First World War 'Doughboys' lay bare the still political and contested nature of that conflict in the American psyche (Eavenson), just as the investigation of (apparently mundane) Second World War air-raid shelters in rural England unexpectedly connect to personal attitudes and memories through their surviving wartime graffiti (Glass). Hidden away in still more rural settings, is a seemingly innocuous garden shed, whose role in the archaeology of the Imperial Wireless System has been revealed (Newland). The complex meanings of Irish commemorative architecture illustrate the tensions of Ireland's political dynamic after the First World War (Keating). Britain's coastal landscape was transformed by the war against Hitler's Germany (Rowe), and the illegal disposal of that conflict's legacy of unexploded munitions created a deadly conflict landscape beneath the Baltic Sea (Soto).

The investigation of the Cold War early warning radar station at Wasserkuppe in Germany (Maus) shows how an innovative approach can reveal positive multiple 'social lives', whereas the similarly Cold War nuclear landscape of the Nevada Test site in the USA embodies seemingly endless negative qualities (Powell).

These important contributions to modern conflict archaeology have been written by a new generation of scholars. The range of topics and levels of engagement that they represent are a refreshing and promising departure from previous approaches, most of which have been, and to some extent continue to be, dominated by a view of archaeology as but a handmaiden to military history.

One indisputable fact emerges from these papers. It is that the names 'Modern Conflict

Archaeology' and 'Battlefield Archaeology' are neither coterminous nor interchangeable. They embody quite different approaches and agendas, both to the empirical data, and to the presence or absence of an acknowledged theoretical sophistication concerning the nature and meaning of objects and landscapes, and their relationships to people in the past and the present.

Simply by using the term 'Conflict Archaeology' instead of 'Battlefield Archaeology' changes nothing if it is not accompanied by a broader, anthropologically-informed, and theoretically aware approach aimed at capturing many different kinds of evidence concerning modern conflict and its legacies.

Over the previous decade, this new and wide-ranging approach to conflicts of the last hundred or so years, has rather too often been obscured by the headline-grabbing activities of First World War battlefield archaeology projects, supported, on occasion, and to varying degrees, by television companies. These have been driven, to a considerable extent, by the belief that a century of modern conflict's material legacies in all their diversity can be reduced in time and space to – and can only be 'discovered' by – digging up the Western Front battlefields of France and Belgium as if they were simply modern versions of pre-twentieth century battlefields. The general public, the media, students and enthusiastic amateur archaeologists, and historians are thereby presented with a distorted view of what such activities should look like, and are left with little or no idea of the rich and varied kinds of work that are being carried out, and that are so well represented in this volume and elsewhere.

Digging another First World War trench, searching for unusual or well-preserved artefacts of war, being the first to dig here or there, finding more human bones than one's 'rivals', or looting memorabilia for sale on the internet does not constitute meaningful archaeological research – in fact it is the polar opposite.

Confronted with such activities, one is entitled to ask who is doing this and why? Who is paying for it and why? What are the archaeological research questions? What does it add to the developing multidisciplinary archaeology of modern conflict? And, when and where will it be published? With a few excellent and notable exceptions – where human remains have been identified and respectfully reburied with family participation – the answers are often depressingly similar. There is usually little academic, intellectual or moral justification, and the results (such as they are) will mostly never be published in the rigorously peer-reviewed academic literature which is the foundation of serious research, and the wellspring of public confidence in such activities.

This is even more serious than it first appears. Modern battlefields – particularly of the First and Second World Wars – are often full of the dead. Sometimes they are arranged in formal cemeteries, but often they are randomly dispersed across the landscape as undiscovered bodies. Yet, beyond this, the power of modern technological weapons guarantees that a major battle-zone vista will contain vast quantities of unseen body parts, from hundreds (maybe thousands) of recognisably human remains, to millions of microscopic bone fragments.

Apart from economic motives, there may well be a philosophical, perhaps almost spiritual justification for returning the surface of such landscapes to agriculture, but there can surely be no excuse for purposefully digging deep without powerful and convincing intellectual and ethical agendas, or legal requirement to do so. Excavating battle-zone conflict sites is not entertainment, and should not be treasure hunting dressed up as archaeology. For the twentieth and twenty-first centuries, at least, Battlefield Archaeology is a truly dead horizon, and it is time we moved beyond it.

* * * * *

Over the last decade, modern conflict archaeology has developed into an increasingly sophisticated interdisciplinary endeavour, and has at last begun to cast off the straitjacket of previous attitudes and practices. The papers in this volume show beyond doubt that a new generation of scholars are engaging with the archaeology of modern conflict on a global scale, and with a sophistication which demonstrates the vast potential of such an approach to alter our views of and relationship with recent conflict.

Archaeology is concerned with the long afterlife of places and things – multivalent legacies that stretch out into the future, and which change their form and meaning as they collide with new social, cultural, political, economic and ideological realities. Nowhere is this more apparent than in the physical consequences of industrialised conflict – the force which has shaped, and continues to shape the modern world.

Acknowledgements

I would like to thank all my postgraduate students, past and present, who have contributed to this volume, and who have made it in my view such a valuable addition to the developing field of modern conflict archaeology. I hope that their efforts here will inspire others to follow. I am especially grateful, at the University of Bristol, to Professor Leon Horsten (Philosophy) and Professor Robert Bickers (History), who between them raised funds to cover the cost of the colour images that add such a visual dimension to the publication. And of course, my thanks go to Oxbow's editorial team whose professionalism (and patience) have made this book possible.

Nicholas J Saunders, July 2012

1

'Dead Man's Penny': a biography of the First World War bronze memorial plaque

Julie Dunne

Over the last two decades, there have been fundamental changes in the way that material culture has been studied, with a general acknowledgement now that objects or 'things' can be transformed by their relationships with people, and vice versa (Miller 1994; 2005; Pels 1998). In this new interdisciplinary interpretative analysis of material culture, we recognise that, as Kopytoff (1986) proposed, artefacts can carry lengthy biographies encapsulating various meanings that have accumulated through their production, use and deposition.

However, Kopytoff (1986) focused more on how the economic or exchange value of objects shifts as a culture changes. It was Gosden and Marshall (1999) who suggested that, through social and cultural processes, objects gather multiplicities of meanings, which may change in significance through time, place, and ownership, and that of course, the transformations of objects and people are inextricably entwined (*ibid*.: 169).

Illustrating this liberating but complex realisation was Strathern's (1988) observation that in Melanesian culture a person is ultimately composed of all the objects they have made and transacted, and that these objects represent the sum total of their agency. Gell (1998), similarly, recognised that objects can have agency and can be construed as 'social actors'. It has been argued that material culture has the potential to shape our experiences of the world, not just in terms of physicality or 'being' – the moving through and negotiating with material forms in everyday life – but also, symbolically, as metaphor (Cochran and Beaudry 2006: 196). The application of these anthropological ideas to modern conflict archaeology is in its infancy, yet the significant potential of such an approach is revealed in one small kind of object explored here.

* * * * *

During the Great War of 1914–1918, the British government recognised the need to both honour the fallen and show some form of official individual (rather than collective) gratitude to the deceased's next of kin. This personalised commemoration of the dead took the form of a Bronze Memorial Plaque that became known, variously, as the 'Dead Man's Penny', the 'Next-of-Kin Plaque', or the 'Death Plaque' (Dutton 1996: 63).

For the bereaved, these plaques, sometimes displayed in domestic shrines, would have been anchoring points for emotion, memory, and meaning, and may have come to render 'present' those who were so painfully absent. This entanglement and association with the deceased acted to sustain their social presence but also accumulated layers of meaning which, as Joy (2002: 132–133) suggests, can have greater strength and significance where they relate directly to warfare. For me, the Dead Man's Penny also has a strong resonance as what Sherry Turkle (2007) calls an 'evocative object', something which, as an 'emotional and intellectual companion', can fix memory. Indeed, Turkle argues that thought and feelings are inseparable, and that 'we think with the objects we love, we love the objects we think with' (*ibid.*).

However, with the passage of time, these artefacts, like many small-scale war memorials, passed out of memory and became largely forgotten and unnoticed. Today, the Death Plaque is part of the material culture that has come to symbolise the enormous trauma, destruction, and loss which marked the devastating experience of the world's first global industrialised war. These objects are now accumulating further multifaceted layers of meaning as they are collected, researched, traded, and displayed in public and private collections. In this biography of the Dead Man's Penny, the complex process of transformation and entanglement between people and objects which sees meaning given to inanimate things is revealed as the same process by which meaning is given to human lives.

'Memento of the Fallen: State Gift for Relatives'

The start of the Great War was marked by a mood of great optimism, and a surge in patriotism, which saw queues of volunteers at military depots eager to join the 'just and noble cause' of making the world safe for democracy. By 1916, however, people at home in Britain were becoming aware that a new kind of industrialised warfare had arrived. The first mass global war of the industrial age saw both sides inhabiting endless miles of warren-like trenches, and fighting a war of stasis and attrition; images of the Western Front portrayed uncanny and desolate landscapes, thick mud, endless craters, blasted trees and barbed wire (Saunders 2001: 37–39).

When the Battle of the Somme began, on 1 July 1916, the lifeblood of young British men began pouring onto the landscape of the Western Front (Dutton 1996: 62). Soon, telegrams began arriving from the British War Office in London, and across Britain, and whole streets and entire towns suddenly found that they had lost great numbers of young men.

These telegrams, and the depressing daily casualty lists, came to represent the wastefulness and futility of the war to many British soldiers and civilians. By the end of 1916, as the Somme Offensive was coming to an end, David Lloyd George, the Secretary of State for War, recognised the need to show some form of official gratitude to the next of kin of the soldiers and sailors who had died on active service, and set up a committee to decide what form the memorial should take.

The decision was announced in *The Times* on 7 November 1916, under the headline 'Memento of the Fallen: State Gift for Relatives'. The newspaper article stated that the precise form of memorial was under consideration, but that it had been initially accepted that it should be a small metal plate recording each man's name and services, and paid for by the state. Bearing in mind that the war was not going well for the Allies at this time, the decision manifests a spirit of grim optimism (despite its tragic overtones), and also implied an intractable faith in ultimate victory (Dutton 1996: 63).

Included on the committee were two peers, six members of parliament (two of whom held military rank), and representatives from the Dominions, the India Office, the Colonial Office, and the Admiralty. Sir Reginald Brade, Secretary of the War Office and Army Council, was appointed Chairman, and Mr W. Hutchinson, also of the War Office, was made Secretary. A specialist sub-committee was set up to deal with technical and artistic detail. This was composed of Sir Charles Holmes, Director of the National Gallery, and Sir Cecil Harcourt-Smith, Director of the Victoria and Albert Museum, along with George Frances Hill, Keeper of the Department of Coins and Medals (and later to become Director) at the British Museum. It was Hill, a renowned expert in the cast metal works of the Italian Renaissance, who took overall responsibility for managing the design and production of the plaque (Dutton 1996: 63).

The official instructions regulating the *Competition for Designs for a memorial plaque to be presented to the next-of-kin of members of His Majesty's Naval and Military Forces who have fallen in the war* were published in *The Times* of 13 August 1917, some nine months later. The committee announced that the form of the memento would be decided upon as a result of a public competition, with prizes for the best designs totalling £500 (in proportions to be subsequently decided) (Anon. n.d.a).

The committee decided that the commemoration plaque, which would be cast from bronze and must be 'finished with precision', should cover an area as near as possible 18 square inches (*c.* 45.7 cm²), which could be either a circle of 4¾ inches (11.4 cm) in diameter, a square of 4¼ inches (39.8 cm), or a rectangle of 5 inches by 53/5 inches (12.7 × 14.2 cm). The design should be simple and easily understood, and include a subject, preferably some symbolic figure, and incorporate the inscription *HE DIED FOR FREEDOM AND HONOUR*. Space must be left for the deceased's name either in a circular design (around, or partially around the margin), or a square or rectangular form at the base (Anon. n.d.a).

Further instructions stated that all competitors 'must be British born subjects' and that the models, which should be made of wax or plaster, should be packed in a small box and delivered to the National Gallery in London no later than 1 November 1917. Works were not to be signed but marked on the back with a pseudonym, and accompanied by a sealed envelope bearing the same on the cover, and containing the competitor's name and address. Finally, it was stated that the artist's signature or initials would appear on the finished plaque (Anon. n.d.a).

Interest in the competition, particularly from overseas entrants, was considerable, as just four weeks later, on 10 September; it was announced in *The Times* that the closing date for submissions had been extended to 31 December 1917. Details of this extension were repeated in the paper the following month, together with a report of the scheme's good progress. The article also stated that:

> In addition to the plaque, a scroll with a suitable inscription will be given. This is being designed at the present moment and it is hoped that it will be possible to put printing in hand in less than a fortnight. (Dutton 1996: 64)

Unfortunately, this proved to be hopelessly optimistic, as manufacture of the scrolls did not begin until January 1919, having been beset both by technical problems and also shortages of paper and ink (*ibid.*).

The competition was popular, with over 800 designs being received from all over the Empire, the old Western Front, the Balkans, and the Middle Eastern theatres of war, as well as from many artists based at home in Britain (*ibid.*). Sadly, it seems likely that some of the competitors may themselves have 'passed out of the sight of men' and had their own names recorded on the memorial plaque.

On 24 January 1918, the committee, and its specialist 'artistic' sub-committee, met to judge the entries, although the results of the competition were not announced until 20 March 1918. The day after this, the Germans launched the Spring Offensive or *Kaiserschlacht* (Kaiser's Battle) on the Western Front, in a last attempt to defeat the Allies before the United States' forces were deployed against them (Dutton 1996: 65). However, the early dramatic German successes might have led many to feel that issuing a memorial plaque showing the British lion defeating the German eagle was hubristic at best.

The winning entry, *Pyramus,* was submitted by sculptor, painter, and medallist Edward Carter Preston of the Sandon Studios Society, Liverpool, who received a prize of £250. The second prize of £100 was awarded to *Moolie* – produced by the sculptor and medallist Charles Wheeler. Third prizes of £50 each were issued to *Zero* by Miss A.F. Whiteside, *Weary* by Sapper G.D. MacDougald, and *Sculpengro* by William McMillan (who later designed the Allied Victory medal). Nineteen other competitors were deemed 'worthy of honourable mention'. The King approved the design as did the Admiralty and the War Office (Dutton 1996: 64–65), although clearly G.F. Hill was not overly impressed, as he remarked in his (unpublished) autobiography 'no-one of which (design) could be regarded as of outstanding merit' (Anon. 1986: 25). The prize-winning designs were exhibited at the Victoria and Albert Museum in London during the spring and early summer of 1918 (Dutton 1996: 69).

The winning design depicts Britannia, classically robed and helmeted, and supporting a trident, respectfully bowing her head whilst granting a crown of laurel leaves, symbolic of triumph, onto a rectangular tablet bearing the full name of the dead soldier (Figure 1.1). No rank is shown, as it was intended that no distinction would be made between the sacrifice made by officers and other ranks.

The stylised oak leaves are symbolic of the distinction of the fallen individual. The dolphins represent Britain's naval power, and the lion, originally described as 'striding forward in a menacing attitude', represents Britain's strength. Interestingly, the proportions and unusually low profile of the male lion were queried by Sir Frederick Ponsonby on behalf of King George V, and also caused some controversy among the public, in particular, deeply upsetting the officials at Bristol's Clifton Zoo.

In a letter to *The Times* on 23 March 1918, the zoo's Honourable Chairman, Mr Alfred. J. Harrison, and the Head Keeper, Mr J.F.

Figure 1.1: First World War Bronze Memorial Plaque commemorating the author's great-grandfather, William James Collins. (© author)

Morgan, forcefully attacked the lion as 'a meagre big dog size presentation', and as 'a lion which almost a hare might insult'. They argued that Carter Preston's lion could not have been modelled from real life, and certainly not from the 'fine male specimen in Clifton Zoo!' Within the exergue, in symbolic confrontation, another lion, a symbol of British power, is shown defeating the German eagle. The committee had some concerns over this as it was felt that the eagle should not be shown to be too hopelessly humiliated as this would not bode well for future post-war relations (Dutton 1996: 65–66). A prescient sentiment indeed!

Manufacture of the plaques did not begin until December 1918, as the project was beset with numerous problems relating to the mass production of the pieces. It began in a disused laundry in Acton, London, supervised by an eccentric American engineer and entrepreneur called Roy Manning Pike, who was later to be responsible for printing the limited subscribers' edition of T.E. Lawrence's *Seven Pillars of Wisdom* (Anon. 1985: 25). Aptly-named 'The Memorial Plaque Factory', it was mainly staffed by women, some of whom, as a local Acton newspaper reported 'had sadly to make the memorial plaques for their own (deceased) husbands' (Anon. n.d.b).

Later, production at Acton (and Manning Pike's contract), was abruptly terminated and transferred, ironically, to the Royal Arsenal at Woolwich in south London, and subsequently to other former munitions factories (Dutton 1996: 69). The reason for this seems to be surrounded by intrigue and mystery. In his unpublished autobiography, Hill suggests that the War Office deliberately built up a case for poor business management against Manning Pike in order to move production to Woolwich, and thus give employment to ex-servicemen. Despite this, when production at Woolwich foundered due to technical problems with casting, it was Manning Pike who was recalled to complete the operation (Anon. 1986: 25).

It is hardly surprising that there were numerous technical problems involved with mass production of the plaques; casting over 1 million medals, each containing a different name (in relief), must have been onerous and time consuming. Unsurprisingly, it was Hill who was adamant that the names on the plaques should appear as lettering in relief, rather than being engraved, as he wanted them to harmonise with the lettering of the plaque itself. Luckily, Harold Stabler (who, together with his wife, Phoebe, also designed a series of war memorials, including the Durban cenotaph in South Africa), recommended Manning Pike to Hill as an 'engineer with some training and great ingenuity' (Anon. 1986: 25). Certainly Manning Pike's solution to the casting problem was ingenious.

The names of each of the fallen, set up in a font similar to that of the plaque, were impressed onto a thin slip of steel, roughly the size of a razor blade, which exactly fitted the blank panel on the plaque. This was held in place by an electro-magnet on the model; the whole was then pressed into the casting sand and withdrawn, leaving the mould ready for use. The magnet was then switched off, the thin strip of steel consequently fell off, and the next name would take its place (Anon. 1986: 25). Although this allowed mass production of the medals, the typesetting of individual names onto the steel slips was time-consuming (and prone to operator error).

The plaques bear Edward Carter Preston's initials embossed above the lion's right forepaw, and those cast at the Woolwich Arsenal bear 'WA' on the reverse. On the Acton plaques, there is sometimes a number stamped behind the lion's rearmost leg, whereas on the Woolwich variety the number is found between the lion's leg and tail. It is not known what these numbers signify, but it may be assumed that they relate to foundry workers, or perhaps are a Ministry of Munitions factory number (Anon. n.d.c).

There do not seem to be any records of production numbers of the plaque, although Hill originally estimated that 800,000 would be manufactured (Dutton 1996:70). However, later estimates suggest that a total of approximately 1,150,000 plaques were produced (Dutton 1996: 70), although other sources have suggested figures as high as 1,355,000 (Anon. 2010). According to the government's own HMSO publication, *Memorial Plaque and Scroll: Regulations Regarding Issue,* the plaques were to be issued for those who died between 4 August 1914 and 10 January 1920 for Home Establishments, Western Europe, and the Dominions. The final date for those who died subsequently of attributable causes of service, and in other theatres of war, including Russia, was 30 April 1920 (Dutton 1996: 70–71).

Nonetheless, there are many examples of plaques issued in commemoration of men who died after this date, for example, Malcolm Douglas Crawfurth-Smith, who passed away on 1 March 1922, and it is thought plaques may have been issued as late as 1930

(Anon. n.d.c). Around 600 plaques were issued to women who had served under direct contract with the War Office, such as in 'Queen Alexandra's Imperial Military Nursing Service' (Q.A.I.M.N.S.), and Queen Mary's Army Auxiliary Corps (Q.M.A.A.C.), as defined by Army Order 206 of 1919, which specifies classes of women eligible for the 'King's Certificate on Discharge'. These bore the wording *SHE DIED FOR FREEDOM AND HONOUR* (Dutton 1996: 71).

The design and production of the scroll (Figure 1.2) was supervised by the Central School of Arts and Crafts in London (Dutton 1996:64). The motif on the scroll was printed using a woodblock cut by Noel Rooke (Anon. n.d.b), who had a profound influence on the modernist movement in wood engraving (Peppin and Micklethwait 1983:260). He was regarded as one of the finest craftsmen of his generation, as was William Graily Hewitt who produced the calligraphy for the scroll (Anon. n.d.d).

The search for some elegiac couplet that would sum up the gratitude of the country for the ultimate sacrifice that the fallen and their loved ones

HE whom this scroll commemorates was numbered among those who, at the call of King and Country, left all that was dear to them, endured hardness, faced danger, and finally passed out of the sight of men by the path of duty and self-sacrifice, giving up their own lives that others might live in freedom. Let those who come after see to it that his name be not forgotten.

Pte. William James Collins
Royal Welsh Fusiliers

Figure 1.2: The Memorial Scroll for the author's great-grandfather, William James Collins. (© author)

had made proved difficult. Contributions from some of the greatest writers and poets of the age, such as Rudyard Kipling, Henry Newbolt, Laurence Binyon, and Robert Bridges (the Poet Laureate), were deemed inadequate. Apparently, it was the Admiralty representative on the committee, Sir Vincent Baddeley, who suggested consulting Dr James Montague Rhodes, provost of King's College, Cambridge, and Director of the Fitzwilliam Museum (Dutton 1996: 64). Rhodes was not only an outstanding scholar of medieval literature and palaeography, but was also revered then (and still today) as the prolific author of such chilling ghost stories as *A Warning to the Curious* and *Casting the Runes* (Pfaff 2004). Rhodes' original draft, which he apparently produced by return of post, was:

> He whom this scroll commemorates was numbered among the sons of the British Empire who at the bidding of their country left all that was dear to them, endured hardness, faced danger, and finally passed out of the sight of men by the path of duty and self-sacrifice giving up their own lives that others might live in freedom. (Dutton 1996: 70)

The first sentence of this original draft was altered (Figure 1.2) as a result of King George V's wish that the sovereign be specifically mentioned, and a final sentence 'Let those who come after see to it that his name be not forgotten' was added by Charles F. Keary, the novelist and historian (Dutton 1996: 64). Nevertheless, it seems likely that the committee recognised immediately that this text encapsulated the mood of respect and gratitude that the people might want to convey to the families of those who had made the ultimate sacrifice.

Each scroll was individually hand printed using the wooden block prepared by Noel Rooke on good quality paper, sized 11 by 5 inches (27.9 × 12.7 cm), and contained the handwritten name, rank, and regiment of the deceased, using Graily Hewitt's font. Blue ink was used to write the names of Naval and Mercantile Marine casualties and red ink for all other services including the Royal Flying Corps (by then the Royal Air Force). The government paid 1½d for each scroll (Anon. n.d.c).

The plaques and scrolls were sent out separately to the families of the fallen, each package including a letter with a facsimile signature from King George V which read 'I join with my grateful people in sending you this memorial of a brave life given for others in the Great War' (Dutton 1996: 70).

After the war, the plaques and scrolls, along with the deceased's medals, were commonly displayed in homes throughout the country, many in the form of small domestic shrines (Dutton 1996: 70). Some companies marketed display cases for the plaques, although this did not please Hill who, rather snobbishly remarked, 'As to the frames, anyone who pleases can put on the market … such things. Of course if we had a proper 'Committee of Taste' such things could not happen' (Dutton 1996: 70).

Often, a home-made, lovingly prepared frame would be produced to house the plaque (Anon. n.d.c), and occasionally they were affixed to the headstone of the named individual, although inevitably many of these were stolen (Anon. 2010).

Once these objects had passed into the domestic sphere there would surely be routine cleaning and polishing which would inevitably be traumatic at first but may later have metamorphosed into a comforting ritual of remembrance (Saunders 2004: 15). Hill had something to say on this: 'All the poor people will scrub the plaque to keep it bright like soldiers' buttons (doesn't the thought make you shiver?)' (Dutton 1996: 70).

The intervening years

After the Great War, the Death Plaque, like many smaller war memorials, passed out of memory and became largely forgotten and unnoticed. Some remained on display in the home, although it is more likely that many languished, overlooked, in drawers and cupboards, suffering what Hallam and Hockey (2001: 8) call a 'social death'. Others were discarded as being worthless, and many were sold for their scrap value, alongside other campaign medals (Richardson 2009: 112–113). Today, with the surge of interest in the First World War that has occurred since the early 1960s, a vast international trade in militaria has developed, and objects such as the memorial plaque, together with trench art and other ephemera from the conflict, are now accumulating further multifaceted layers of meaning as they are collected, traded, and displayed in public and private collections (Saunders 2003: 160).

Many plaques are exhibited in regimental collections as well as in museums, for example, the Museum of the Manchester Regiment holds over 100 such 'Pennies'. Each memorial plaque is being researched by the museum's curator and volunteers with the aim of creating a biography of the soldier's life and experiences, which, once complete, will be placed in a 'Roll of Honour' in the Museum's Ladysmith Gallery (Anon. 2010). Here, we see the Death Plaque, once inhabiting a 'domain of subjectivity' and used in the fashioning of personal memory, has now been assigned 'object status' for viewing in the public domain as an aspect of national cultural heritage (Hallam and Hockey 2001: 8).

There are many postings on internet forums (for example, 'The Great War Forum', 'The British Medal Forum') in which family members have rediscovered their plaques, and are seeking information as to both the history of the plaque and further details on how to research the military careers of their relations. This often invokes a reconnection with both the object and their long deceased relatives, thus creating new biographies that link across the generations, and also renewing their life histories as evocative objects.

There is a flourishing market for the plaque on internet auction sites where they may be traded singly or as 'lots' together with any campaign medals the serviceman may have received. It is poignant that objects which were once precious heirlooms sometimes now only possess commercial value. However, these are bought by collectors, many of whom own hundreds of plaques (Anon. n.d.b.), often in order to research and recreate the biographies of the individuals named on them. Thus the plaques are actively resurrected, and are accruing new layers of memory and meaning.

William James Collins

In the spirit of these small metal memorials, I will briefly share the biography of my own 'evocative object', the Memorial Plaque which commemorates the death of my paternal great-grandfather, William James Collins, who died on 24 November 1916 (Figures 1.1 and 1.3). He died in a field hospital of wounds received at the Battle of the Ancre, which began on 13 November 1916, as the final act of the Battle of the Somme. Tragically, the day of his death marked the second birthday of his only daughter, my

Figure 1.3: The author's great-grandfather, William James Collins, holding his baby daughter, Elsie Kate, the author's grandmother. (© author)

grandmother, Elsie Kate Codd, *née* Collins (Figure 1.3). Her mother, Kate Collins, had died giving birth to her, and thus the death of her father when she was just 2 years old left her an orphan of war.

Despite this, my grandmother had a happy childhood, being raised by her father's mother, Eliza Collins, and his sisters, May and Edie Collins. However, my grandmother did not often speak of her father, except to say that she had never known him, and seemed to know little about his military service. Today, information about those who served can be accessed in various places such as the Commonwealth War Graves Commission website (www.cwgc.org), an organisation which maintains the 'Debt of Honour Register' which lists the 1.7 million men and women of the Commonwealth Forces who died during the two world wars, and the 23,000 cemeteries, memorials, and other locations worldwide where they are commemorated.

Ninety-five years after William's death, in an act of renewing and recreating his biography linking across the generations, my family identified his name on the 'Debt of Honour Register', the record for private 54853 William James Collins, son of Samuel and Eliza Collins of Roborough Cottages, Ashburton, Devon, of the 10th Battalion, Royal Welsh Fusiliers. He was recorded as having died, aged 27, on 24 November 1916 and is commemorated at the Etaples Military Cemetery in northern France.

Memory and meaning
The Dead Man's Penny was on display on my grandmother's mantelpiece for over 70 years. As a child, visiting my grandparents, I remember it as an object of curiosity, looking nothing more than like the giant (old) penny for which the 'Tommies' had named it. Although a constant presence, it was also, as are many of the objects that

we choose to ornament our homes, both seen and unseen, a 'thing' that hovers on the periphery of our vision, both present and absent – invisible in plain view.

For my grandmother, however, as she polished the plaque – a fortnightly job according to my father – the physicality of the object and the cleaning action may have come to constitute and represent her father as a person, creating for him an enduring sense of personhood, and sustaining his social presence. The plaque may have gained the status of what Hoskins (1998) identifies as a 'biographical object', a thing which transgresses the boundary between people and objects, and becomes imbued with the characteristics of people. Thus, the embodied action of polishing the plaque may have become a 'sacred act' (Saunders 2004: 15) – an act of remembrance, where loss, grief, and memory-making were revisited and reworked each time the object was cleaned.

As Daniel Miller (1994: 417) argues, material forms are one of the key media through which people conduct their constant struggles over identity, and it may be that her performative actions may have allowed my grandmother to recreate and renegotiate her own identity, for, as Driver (1991: 37) points out, 'to ritualise is to make oneself present' (cited in Reimers 1999: 148). Perhaps, though, we should also remember that, as Forty (1999: 9) comments, there is a tension present in all effective works of commemoration. For my grandmother, and the other families of the war dead, forgetting may sometimes have been as important as remembering.

Today, each of these Memorial Plaques, as repositories for numerous stories, and as once precious heirlooms that helped make present those who were absent, demonstrate how objects are 'active life presences' that help us navigate grief, loss, and emotion across the generations, and are still today accumulating rich, multifaceted layers of meaning and memory. They have become 'semantically dense' objects, in which the sensory interaction between people and things is retained as an accumulated 'emotional and historical sedimentation' (Seremetakis 1994, cited in Hallam and Hockey 2001: 11). These tokens of remembrance for individual families, now part of the *matériel* remains of the devastating collective experience of industrialised warfare, are part of the narrative carrying the weight of millions of deaths not only in the Great War, but in all other conflicts since.

Acknowledgements

I would like to thank Nick Saunders both for introducing me to the compelling topic of modern conflict archaeology and also for sharing his endless and inspiring enthusiasm for and knowledge of the subject. This article is dedicated both to the memory of my grandmother, Elsie Kate Codd, *née* Collins, who died in 2010, aged 95, and to her father, William James Collins 'who passed out of the sight of men by the path of duty and self-sacrifice'. I hope that I have helped to 'see to it that his name be not forgotten'. Finally, thanks go to my parents, Ray and Brenda Codd, who are always there.

Bibliography

Anon. (1986) G.F. Hill and the Production of the First World War Memorial Plaque. *The Medal* 8: 25.

Anon. (2010) Museum of the Manchester Regiment Object Focus. *www.tameside.gov.uk* Accessed 27 October 2010.

Anon. (n.d.a) Bronze Death Plaques or the Soldiers Penny. *www.epsonandewellhistoryexplorer.org. uk* Accessed 28 November 2009.

Anon. (n.d.b) Great War Forum. *www.1914-1918.invisionzone.com/forum* Accessed 28 October 2010.

Anon (n.d.c) Bronze Memorial Plaques: Notes on Origins, History and Identification. *The Campaign for War Grave Commemorations 2009.* http://www.cwgc.co.uk/Plaque-history. htm Accessed 28 November 2009.

Anon. (n.d.d) Visual Arts Data Service. www.vads.ac.uk Accessed 18 November 2009.

Cochran, M.D. and Beaudry, M.C. (2006) Material culture studies and historical archaeology. In D. Hicks and M.C. Beaudry (eds), *The Cambridge Companion to Historical Archaeology*, 191–204. Cambridge: Cambridge University Press.

Driver, T.F. (1991) *The Magic of Ritual. Our Need for Liberating Rites that Transform our Lives & our Communities.* San Francisco: Harper.

Dutton, P. (1996) The Dead Man's Penny: a short history of the Next of Kin Memorial Plaque. *The Medal* 29: 62–71.

Forty, A. (1999) Introduction. In A. Forty and S. Küchler (eds), *The Art of Forgetting*, 1–18. Oxford: Berg.

Gell, A. (1998) *Art and Agency: An Anthropological Theory.* Oxford: Clarendon Press.

Gosden, C. and Marshall, Y. (1999) The cultural biography of objects. *World Archaeology* 31: 169–178.

Hallam, E. and Hockey, J. (2001) *Death, Memory and Material Culture.* Oxford: Berg.

Hoskins, J. (1998) *Biographical Objects: How Things Tell the Stories of People's Lives.* London: Routledge.

Joy, J. (2002) Biography of a medal: people and the things they value. In J. Schofield, W.G. Johnson and C.M. Beck (eds), *Matériel Culture: the Archaeology of Twentieth Century Conflict*, 132–142. London: Routledge.

Kopytoff, I. (1986) The cultural biography of things: commoditization as process. In A. Appadurai (ed.), *The Social Life of Things: Commodities in Cultural Perspective*, 64–91. Cambridge: Cambridge University Press.

Miller, D. (1994) Artefacts and the meanings of things. In T. Ingold (ed), *Companion Encyclopaedia of Anthropology*, 396–419. London: Routledge.

Miller, D. (ed.) (2005) *Materiality.* Durham: Duke University Press.

Pels, P. (1998) The spirit of matter: on fetish, rarity, fact and fancy. In P. Spyer (ed.), *Border Fetishisms: Material Objects in Unstable Spaces*, 91–121. London: Routledge.

Peppin, B. and Micklethwait, L. (1983) *Dictionary of British Book Illustrators: the Twentieth Century.* London: John Murray.

Pfaff, R.W. (2004) James, Montague Rhodes (1862–1936), *Oxford Dictionary of National Biography.* Oxford: Oxford University Press.

Reimers, E. (1999) Death and identity: graves and funerals as cultural communication. *Mortality* 4: 147–166.

Richardson, M. (2009) Medals, memory and meaning: Symbolism and cultural significance of Great War medals. In N.J. Saunders and P. Cornish (eds), *Contested Objects: Material Memories of the Great War*, 104–118. Abingdon: Routledge.

Saunders, N.J. (2001) Matter and Memory in the Landscapes of Conflict: The Western Front 1914–1999. In B. Bender and M. Winer (eds), *Contested Landscapes: Movement, Exile and Place,* 37–53. Oxford: Berg.

Saunders, N.J. (2003) *Trench Art: Materialities and Memories of War.* Oxford: Berg.

Saunders, N.J. (2004) Material culture and conflict: the Great War, 1914–2003. In N.J. Saunders (ed.), *Matters of Conflict: Material Culture, Memory and the First World War,* 5–25. London: Routledge.

Seremetakis, C.N. (ed.) (1994) *The Senses Still: Perception and Memory as Material Culture in Modernity.* Chicago: University of Chicago Press.

Strathern, M. (1988) *The Gender of the Gift: Problems with Women and Problems with Society in Melanesia.* Berkeley: University of California Press.

Turkle, S. (2007) Introduction: the things that matter. In S. Turkle (ed.), *Evocative Objects: Things We Think With,* 3–10. Cambridge (MA): MIT Press.

The Poppy and the Harp: contested meanings at 'The Oratory', Dun Laoghaire, Ireland

Niamh Keating

Prologue: April 1916

At the end of April 1916, the centre of Dublin lay in ruins. The Easter Rising, a challenge by Irish republicans to British rule, was over. The rebels were defeated, and marched to prison through hostile crowds, many of whose relatives were fighting in the First World War. Their leaders were captured and would soon be executed. In the aftermath of the Rising, a British officer tore down a copy of the *Proclamation of the Irish Republic* which had been pasted up by the rebels outside their headquarters at the General Post Office (GPO) in the centre of Dublin (Horne 2008: 11).

This copy of the *Proclamation*, one of about 50 surviving copies, may be found in the library of Trinity College, Dublin. It differs from the other surviving copies. For, as it was torn from the wall of the GPO, recruiting posters for Irishmen to fight in the war came away with it. The copy preserved in Trinity College still adheres to and overlays the recruiting posters produced by the Department of Recruiting for Ireland.

The *Proclamation of the Republic* superimposed on Great War recruiting posters illustrates the contested nature of the public space in Dublin in the spring of 1916, with competing views of nationhood and of how best to achieve the ideal of national self determination. Many of the estimated 200,000 Irishmen who fought in the Great War volunteered to further the rights and liberties of small nations, including Irish Home Rule. After 1916 they became increasingly viewed in Ireland[1] as the agency of an imperial war machine which denied the Irish impulse to self determination.

By the end of the Great War, some 30,000–35,000 Irishmen had perished in the conflict. Their families, friends, and communities faced the issue of preserving their memory and making sense of their sacrifice in an Ireland which now had an ambivalent attitude to their role in the world's first global conflict. As the Irish politician and academic, Tom Kettle, who was killed at the Somme in September 1916, wrote after the Easter Rising, 'These men [the leaders of the Rising] will go down in history as heroes and martyrs; and I will go down – if I go down at all – as a bloody British officer' (Jeffrey 2000: 61). Irish war memorials became the tangible evidence of how Kettle and the others who died were subsequently remembered.

The poppy and the harp

By the end of the First World War, the poppy and the harp had become powerful symbols of competing assessments of Irish participation in the conflict. The Canadian soldier-physician John McCrae's brief and haunting poem *In Flanders Fields* served to make the poppy a powerful symbol of remembrance of the war (Gardiner 1992: 102–103). In Ireland, the poppy came to have further significance as a symbol of British identity in a time of conflict. A considerable section of the population throughout the country, but especially in the north-east, enthusiastically adopted the poppy as a symbol of their adherence to the United Kingdom.

However, an increasing number of Irish people who identified with cultural nationalism and with the Gaelic revival movement rejected the poppy in favour of the harp. Prior to 1916, such symbols of Britishness and Irishness were not seen as mutually exclusive. Until 1917, Sinn Fein, (literally 'Ourselves Alone'), the Irish political party which became synonymous with the Easter Rising and Irish Republicanism, advocated a dual monarchy on the lines of the Austro-Hungarian Empire, with the British monarch as head of state of an independent Ireland (Davis 1974: 96, 107; Feeney 2003: 37, 68), providing the potential for a harmonious coexistence of the poppy and the harp. Only after the Rising did this harmony between Imperial and Irish symbolism turn to widespread conflict in the south of the country.

This changed popular mood in the south of Ireland created problems about how to commemorate the Irish who fell in the Great War. The final stanza of McCrae's poem throws down a challenge to the survivors: 'If ye break faith with us who die, We shall not sleep though poppies grow' (Gardiner 1992: 103).

In 1919, one community just south of Dublin sought to keep faith with those who died by erecting 'The Oratory' in Dun Laoghaire. Rainbird (2003:32) notes that 'All monuments have biographies …[that]… can involve movement, despoliation, removal, reconstruction and its current role …'. The Oratory has its own particular biography which involves not only its initial construction, but its altered meaning for successive generations, leading to its contemporary significance in the Ireland of the twenty-first century. Through a series of metamorphoses unique for an Irish war memorial, The Oratory came to symbolise reconciliation between the traditions of the poppy and the harp which had been sundered in the aftermath of Easter Week 1916.

Before addressing The Oratory directly, it is necessary to place it in the context of Great War memorialisation in Ireland. I will then trace its origins and symbolism as expressed by its location, iconography, and associated artefacts. Finally, I will examine the transformation of The Oratory almost from the moment of its inception, and its shifting interpretation during the second half of the twentieth century. This interpretation of The Oratory mirrors the wider political and societal reworking of the relationship between the poppy and the harp in contemporary Ireland.

Memorials of the Great War

Writing of 'statuomanie', King (2001: 147) notes that commemoration of the dead of the First World War was probably the largest and most popular movement for the erection of public monuments ever known in western society.

One reason for such opposition was widespread pro-Boer sentiment in Ireland, epitomised by the Irish who fought with the Boers during the conflict (Gooch 2000: 146). Just over a decade later, opposition in Ireland to First World War memorials stemmed from different causes. Pro-German opinion in Ireland during the conflict was extremely limited as is seen by the abject failure of Roger Casement to recruit volunteers to fight on the German side (Doerries 2000: 9–12). Opposition to war memorials after 1918 stemmed from opposition to the continuing British presence in Ireland, and was strengthened by the formation of the illegal First Dail (Parliament) and the outbreak of the Anglo-Irish War in January 1919 (Foster 1988: 494, 613).

Yet these adverse conditions did not prevent commemoration of the war dead. The Irish War Memorials Project (Pegum 2010) lists almost 700 Great War memorials in over 300 locations in Ireland, of which most are in the Republic and over 150 in Dublin.

Public space and private space

The north of Ireland, both before and after partition of the country in the aftermath of the Great War, proved comfortable with the symbolism of the poppy as reflected in its war memorials. A total of 62 such monuments were erected on behalf of particular towns and villages (Switzer 2008). The War Memorial at 'The Diamond' in the centre of Derry City illustrates how a war memorial can dominate the public space. This 1927 memorial stands in the very centre of the city, with its winged Victory and its representation of the army and the navy leaving the viewer in no doubt that it stands for a celebration of sacrifice leading to victory. It symbolises the views of the government and majority of the population of Northern Ireland who stressed membership of the United Kingdom and loyalty to the Crown.

By contrast, in the south, public space was often unavailable for Great War commemoration. Although a commemorative obelisk was erected in the South Mall, Cork, in 1925 – having been granted planning permission by Cork Corporation (Johnson 2003: 98) – such high profile commemoration was the exception rather than the rule. More typical was the reaction of the Executive Council of the Irish Free State who in June 1928 rejected a proposal for a commemorative arch at the entrance to Dublin's Phoenix Park (Jeffrey 2000: 116), possibly because it had triumphalist echoes of 'Traitor's Gate'.

Most memorials occupied private space as seen in the Irish War Memorials Project (Pegum 2010). Thus, schools such as Belvedere College and Wesley College in Dublin commemorated past pupils fallen in the conflict, while Sir Patrick Dun's Hospital memorialised former students who had perished. Protestant churches accounted for a significant proportion of the memorials with no fewer than 16 monuments, mainly plaques, located in St Patrick's Cathedral, Dublin. Plaques at the Royal St George Yacht Club in Dun Laoghaire and the Freemasons' Hall in the centre of Dublin city demonstrate that a significant proportion of the southern Irish Protestant community remained loyal to the poppy. As the 1920s progressed, Great War memorialisation in the south of Ireland largely[2] retreated to the private and mainly Protestant space.

In this context, the inhabitants of Kingstown created The Oratory to remember their loved ones who had fallen in 'The Great War for Civilization'.

Origins of 'The Oratory'

The Oratory was built in the grounds of St Mary's Dominican Convent in Dun Laoghaire, a seaside suburb just south of Dublin, known until 1920 as Kingstown. Although records are preserved of eight buildings on the site erected between 1851 and 1930 (Irish Architectural Archive 2008), no architect's plans of this edifice survive. Similarly, its origins are absent from the historical record. Fortunately, Sister Frances Lally, who campaigned for preservation of The Oratory (O'Reilly 2001: 77), has preserved the oral record of its origin, drawing on the memories of Sister Joanna Tutty who was born in 1913 and entered the convent in the late 1920s (Sr F. Lally, pers. comm.).

According to this record, a small chapel which had stood within the Dominican Convent grounds suffered severe storm damage. As the nuns considered its replacement, the Great War came to an end with a tragic aftermath for the people of Kingstown. Many young men from the borough had gone to fight on the Western Front and Sister Frances relates that of an entire class of school leavers who enlisted from the local Christian Brothers' school, not one returned. According to the custom of the time, these young men had previously been pupils at the Dominican Convent school until they went to the Christian Brothers at the age of seven (V. Heywood, pers. comm.). The initiative for The Oratory as a war memorial originated with the superior of the Dominican Convent, Mother Laurence Byrne (Little 1961: 21). However, Sister Frances notes that a public subscription was raised to fund The Oratory indicating that the initiative also enjoyed popular support.

'The Oratory' and its symbolism

The Oratory was originally a small plain building, 5.6 m by 3.6 m. As 'a memorial to the very many young men from the area who died in the First World War' (O'Reilly 2001: 72), its location and description are revealing. Far from being a socially unifying act, the act of commemoration, and deciding what to erect as a war memorial could be contentious, even acrimonious (King 2001: 158–159). Locating The Oratory in a secluded site hidden behind the walls of a convent of enclosed nuns suggests that the commemoration was almost clandestine.

Dun Laoghaire harbour, which already boasted a monument to King George IV, the imposing Catholic Church in the centre of the town, and the Christian Brothers' school where the young men had completed their education offered more public sites. However, the oral tradition records that the local parish and the Christian Brothers' school were reluctant to be associated with war commemoration, and so it was left to the sisters to construct The Oratory (V. Heywood, pers. comm.). Subsequently, the public space in Dun Laoghaire remained closed to First World War commemoration until a commemorative plaque on an anchor was unveiled in 1996 to commemorate passengers, crew, and postal workers who perished when the mail boat *Leinster* was sunk in October 1918. Clearly postal workers were a safer group to commemorate in public than soldiers.

However, the nuns were not deterred in their aim to commemorate the soldiers. The oral record says that the sisters agreed with the families of the young men who died that the focus of the memorial would be thanksgiving for the end of the war (Lally 2008: 16). King (2001: 148) notes that 'many participated [in memorial building] for the more personal purpose of making sense of the impact of war on themselves ... and to resist the unspeakable prospect that the pain and loss of war might ultimately have been worthless'. The idea of a peace memorial makes sense in a culture which saw the First World War as 'the war to end all wars'. Such a memorial would have helped families to make sense of the loss of their loved ones.

The only external ornamentation is an inscription in Irish over the east facing door which reads *Togadh Seipeal an Criode Naomhta, 1919,* ('Chapel of the Sacred Heart, built 1919') (Figure 2.1). This inscription conveys the same message as a large statue of the Sacred Heart, imported from France for the opening of The Oratory. The oral

Figure 2.1: The Sacred Heart statue on the altar opposite the entrance to the The Oratory. (© author)

tradition records that the statue came from the village where the young men from Kingstown were billeted and from which they went one morning to perish in the poisonous gas clouds of the Western Front.

Tarlow (1999: 159–165) argues that provincial war memorials are expressions of local community interest in having a place for mourning as an aid to the grieving process. The Oratory conforms to this view, being a way to come to terms with loss rather than a glorification of nationalism or the nation state. Yet this coming to terms was tempered by the lack of official support for commemorating the soldiers. Unlike memorials in many other countries, The Oratory was erected to satisfy the needs of those in the local community who had suffered a loss largely unacknowledged by the wider society. Although the population contained a significant proportion of Unionists in 1919, Kingstown was not immune from the disruption of the War of Independence. Significantly, the name of the town was changed back to Dun Laoghaire in 1920, signalling that public space was being reinvented, distancing it from any aspects of monarchy.

Further evidence of the prevailing ambivalence about the role of the young men from Kingstown is contained in the absence from The Oratory of a list of those who died.[3] On the one hand, grieving families wanted their loved ones commemorated. On the other, official Ireland did not acknowledge the role of those who had fought in the war. Thus, both the location of The Oratory and its iconography reflect wider issues of individual loss, public commemoration, and making sense of the war in a particular context.

The Oratory-as-memorial contrasts with Protestant places of worship which frequently contain brass plates listing the fallen with inspiring inscriptions such as '*their glory shall not be blotted out*' or '*greater love hath no man than this*'. The Protestant community was comfortable with such overt commemoration. By contrast, The Oratory conveys commemoration in a much more oblique way by the presence of the Sacred Heart statue and the inscription over the entrance as its only ornamentation.

Devotion to the Sacred Heart is a particularly French Catholic feature which was introduced to Ireland in the late 1880s. By the time The Oratory was built, the devotion had spread countrywide (Morrissey 2008: 9). The practice of consecrating the family to the Sacred Heart was widespread in Ireland until the 1960s. Families placed a picture of the Sacred Heart before which a lamp was kept constantly burning in some prominent place in the home. This was the centre of the family's spiritual life (Fuller 2008: 14). The Oratory therefore fitted perfectly into one of the most popular Catholic devotions of the day. The symbolism is coded. Rather like clandestine Catholic symbolism at the time of the Penal Laws, The Oratory reveals its message to those in the know. The Sacred Heart statue, imported from France, links the devotions of the faithful with the death of 'the boys' on the Western Front.

The symbolism becomes more complex when we consider the inscription over the entrance. Why is it in Irish, not English? The Irish inscription is a powerful statement that, contrary to some popular views, the soldiers from Kingstown did not fall fighting for an alien cause. They went to fight for the rights of small nations. Their sacrifice entitles them to a place in the new nation being born in Ireland. It was a statement that the poppy was not incompatible with the harp.

In its original form, The Oratory provides a fascinating glimpse into how the Catholic working class boys of a seaside town near Dublin were remembered. It was dedicated in a culturally appropriate way at a time when loyalties in Ireland were fracturing and the official discourse of the legitimacy of war commemoration was being challenged. As such, it would have been an interesting but obscure memorial to a little remembered group in Irish history. However, shortly after its erection, The Oratory experienced a fundamental transformation which altered its symbolism to the community at large for the next half century.

'The Oratory' and neo-Celtic art

Publications on The Oratory have focused largely on the significance of the neo-Celtic art on its internal walls (Rynne n.d.; Dominican Sisters n.d.; Little 1961; O'Reilly 2001; Lally 2008). The change in its perceived meaning from its origins as a First World War memorial is illustrated by publications which refer to it as the Celtic Oratory (Kealy 2007: 169, 171). The art developed The Oratory's significance and meaning. As background, it is necessary to consider the place of neo-Celtic Art in national consciousness in early twentieth century Ireland.

The Gaelic League, founded in 1893, initially aimed to revive the Irish language but quickly extended its range of activities to other aspects of Gaelic culture (Curtis 1994: 161, 164). These included neo-Celtic Art, harking back to the golden age of monastic art made famous in works such as the *Book of Kells*. This romantic dream of a golden age of Celtic culture became identified with the impulse towards Irish independence to such an extent that the Gaelic League was banned as a subversive organisation by the British authorities in 1918 (Mandle 1983: 107–108).

Neo-Celtic art became synonymous with the separatist movement which repudiated the memory of the Irishmen who had fought in the Great War. It is therefore ironic that within a few years of its construction, the original symbolism of The Oratory was overlain by such a powerful motif, just as the *Proclamation of the Republic* was posted over First Wold War recruiting posters.

Transformation of 'The Oratory'

On its completion, The Oratory was a bare windowless building. Mother Laurence Byrne, who had overseen its construction, suggested to Sister Concepta Lynch, art teacher in the Dominican school, that she should decorate the wall behind the Sacred Heart statue. Sister Concepta was an accomplished neo-Celtic artist in her own right,[4] having trained in her father's studio before she entered the Dominican Convent in 1896 (Little 1961). Her original design behind the altar is plain, not neo-Celtic but almost Islamic in its non-representational motifs (Rynne n.d.: 8) (Figure 2.1). However, after completing the initial wall, Sr. Concepta's art took a radically new turn, and so began 16 years of work which resulted in a 'shrine of Celtic Art' (Sr F. Lally, pers. comm.) (Figures 2.2–4).

Figure 2.2: Neo-Celtic artwork on rear wall of The Oratory. (© M. Pegum)

Figure 2.3: Unfinished ceiling of The Oratory contrasted with completed walls. (© M. Pegum).

Eventually, every inch of the walls was filled with intricate neo-Celtic art, inspired by the Books of Kells and Durrow but of original design (Figure 2.2). The work was painstaking; Sister Juliana Tutty recalled Sister Concepta showing her a miniscule section containing dots and saying that it took her two hours to complete (Sr F. Lally, pers. comm.; O'Reilly 2001: 73). The ceiling designs are marked out in a light gold colour but not completed (Figure 2.3) since Sister Concepta was unable to continue the work due to ill health after 1936 (Lally 2008: 17).

Figure 2.4: Eucharistic Congress Cross on side wall of The Oratory. (© M. Pegum)

At first sight, the nationalist symbolism of the neo-Celtic art displays a new and different meaning and significance – literally painted over the original conception of The Oratory as a memorial to the fallen and a monument to peace after the First World War. However, closer analysis reveals that inextricably intertwined with the neo-Celtic motifs are references to the Great War. A panel with the colours of the French flag brings to mind those who fell in Flanders (O'Reilly 2001: 77). The original building was windowless, but Sister Concepta arranged for the insertion of five small stained glass windows from the school of Harry Clarke. Two of these make explicit reference to the purpose of The Oratory: the 'Rosary Window' on which is written 'Pray for all the donors of this Oratory, 1919' and, more explicitly, the 'Our Lady of Good Counsel' window, inscribed in memory of Joseph Walsh who died in the Great War on 26 April 1918.

As recalled by Sister Juliana, Sister Concepta arranged for one of the lay teachers in the convent school to buy household paint from a local hardware shop. Local merchants were part of the enterprise and took a keen interest in the progress of the work. This conjures up the image of grieved families participating in the act of adapting their loved ones' memorial to the contemporary iconography of an Ireland which treasured its Celtic past. Thus, Sr Concepta drew her inspiration both from Celtic art and from the original purpose of The Oratory. As her designs progressed, she also drew on current events. One example is the Celtic Cross of the 1932 Eucharistic Congress which features prominently on the side walls (Figure 2.4). While the majority of war memorials remained frozen in time, The Oratory evolved organically with the artist incorporating new motifs while retaining reference to the original purpose of the memorial.

After its original conception as a war memorial, The Oratory evolved in an unplanned way. The coded significance of the Sacred Heart inscription and statue was enhanced by the plain decoration created by Sr Concepta behind the altar. Within a short period, neo-Celtic art came to predominate, due largely to Sr. Concepta's genius for its creation, but also with the knowledge of relatives of the fallen. However, over time, the original identity of The Oratory as a war memorial was obscured to the general public. Over the next half century, it became identified as 'a Shrine of Celtic Art'. Although this change was not designed by its creator to deny the significance of The Oratory as a First World War memorial, the vibrancy and visual impact of the art and its cultural and political connotations came to obscure The Oratory's original meaning.

Saving 'The Oratory' as a shrine of neo-Celtic art

The Dominican Convent was demolished in 1995 to make way for a shopping centre, and if it had not been for the quality of its neo-Celtic art, The Oratory would almost certainly have shared the same fate. However, it remains, preserved and secured on the initiative of the Dominican Sisters and with local public backing. The sisters insisted on its preservation as part of the deal when the convent was sold (Sr F. Lally, pers. comm.) – an act which subsequently involved the wider community.

At the time of its threatened demolition, local artists became involved in an application for European Union funding under the 'European Architectural Award Scheme' to preserve and safeguard the building (V. Heywood, pers. comm.). The grounds for application provide an insight into the meaning and value of The Oratory as it appeared to the applicants: 'this is a unique and personal tribute to Ireland's Medieval Golden Age … it represents the artist's lifelong association with the location' (Application for European Architectural Award, 1995). Its origins as a war memorial were not referred to, but rather its religious purpose and links to the early twentieth century Celtic revival were stressed in the supporting documentation (Letter from Dr Brian Kennedy, National Gallery of Ireland to Veronica Heywood, 1995).

In the course of its preservation, the lens through which the meaning of The Oratory was viewed shifted yet again when planning for the space in front of its entrance (V. Heywood, pers. comm.). The Parks Department of Dun Laoghaire Rathdown County Council undertook the landscaping work in cooperation with those committed to the structure's preservation. The obvious option would have been to emphasise the neo-Celtic art on the application for preservation. However, the first view the visitor now encounters on approaching The Oratory is a garden laid out so that the plants spell out the words *SIOCHAIN – PEACE* (Figure 2.5).

'The Oratory' today

Rainbird (2003: 23) states 'the richness of meaning presented by a monument is myriad and changing, some meanings may become hidden, and others accentuated, while other meanings may compete for the dominant reading'. The Oratory reveals such changes. Despite its appearance today as a shrine of neo-Celtic art, long buried meanings remain and compete for attention. The original meanings of The Oratory as a coded tribute to the fallen, a monument of thanksgiving for peace and evidence of early twentieth century Catholic piety persist, intertwined in the richness of the neo-Celtic art. The involvement of the local people in the public subscription for the building of The Oratory and in provision of the materials for its decoration provides an insight into the relationship between the contemplative Dominican sisters and the wider community of which they were part, and the development of its symbolism to reflect commemoration in the Irish context of the 1920s and 1930s.

The myriad and changing natures of the meaning of The Oratory includes its significance to those who are committed to its preservation today. Cochran and Beaudry (2006: 194) note that the 'study of material culture began to shift focus towards addressing the formation of relationships between people and things within specific social contexts'. The relationship between The Oratory and people today is no less significant than it was in the past, with the current relationship providing a window into current values and norms of Irish society.

Speaking to those involved in its preservation, the dominant reading is the theme of peace. When it was put to a representative of the Dun Laoghaire History Society that The Oratory was originally intended as a war memorial he demurred – 'No. It was not political. The nuns intended it as a peace memorial'. This perspective is echoed by Sister Frances Lally who emphasises the peace garden which now frames the entrance to The Oratory (Sr F. Lally, pers. comm.).

This emic view led the Parks Department in Dun Laoghaire to ignore The Oratory windows which make no reference to peace and the neo-Celtic artwork which carries no explicit peace message. The Parks Department did not reflect the interpretation of The Oratory as set out in the official European Union application, but rather framed its message as an interpretation of its contemporary significance.

The period of rediscovery and preservation of The Oratory coincided with the Northern Ireland Peace Process. After three decades of bloodshed in both parts of Ireland, but especially in the North, public consciousness emphasised the need for peace, reconciliation, and mutual respect. Of the competing messages expressed in The Oratory, the dominant reading today is the message of peace, not just imposed by the Parks Department, but reflective of the lens through which those who campaigned for its preservation view its significance.

The Oratory symbolises integration of formerly conflicted aspects of Irish history. It is a superb work of artistic merit in its own right. But it is also unique in reconciling the poppy and the harp, legitimising memorialisation of the soldiers from Kingstown who fell in the Great War, and providing a tangible manifestation of the resolution of old conflicts in Ireland today.

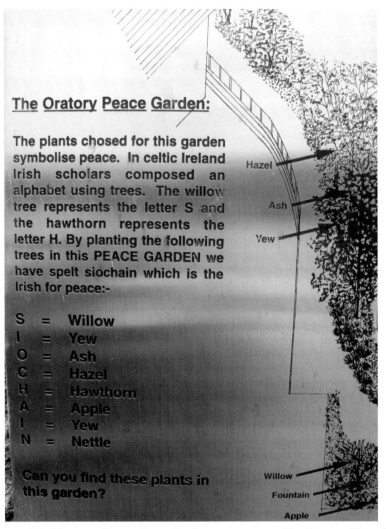

Figure 2.5: Plaque explaining Peace Garden at entrance to The Oratory. (© author)

Acknowledgements

I should like to thank Ms. Veronica Heywood, Sr Francis Lally, Mr Michael Pegum and Dr Nicholas J. Saunders, all of whom made this paper possible.

Notes

1   This view was not just in Ireland. As early as October 1917, the Bulgarian Communist leader Georgi Dmitrov wrote of 'the outrages against the Irish people who are fighting for freedom and independence' (Dmitrov 1972, 54).

2   There are exceptions such as plaques at railway stations but these are very much in the minority.

3   It is reported that it is hoped to install plaques inscribed with the names of all those from Dun Laoghaire who died in the First World War (Pegum 2010) but this has not happened at the time of writing.

4   She invented the 'Lynch Method of Celtic Art' according to a booklet published as a student guide by the Irish Dominican Sisters.

Bibliography

Published sources:

Anon. (n.d.) *Celtic Art. The Lynch Method of Celtic Illumination*. Dublin: The Irish Dominican Sisters.

Curtis, L. (1994) *The Cause of Ireland. From the United Irishmen to Partition*. Belfast: Beyond the Pale Publications.

Cochran, M.D. and Beaudry, M.C. (2006) Material culture studies and historical archaeology. In D. Hicks and M.C. Beaudry (eds), *The Cambridge Companion to Historical Archaeology*, 191–204. Cambridge: Cambridge University Press.

Davis, R. (1974) *Arthur Griffith and Non-Violent Sinn Fein*. Dublin: Anvil Books.

Dimitrov, G. (1972) *Selected Works Volume 1*. Sofia: Sofia Press.

Doerries, R.R. (2000) *Prelude to the Easter Rising: Sir Roger Casement in Imperial Germany*. London: Routledge.

Feeney, B. (2003) *Sinn Fein. A Hundred Turbulent Years*. Wisconsin: University of Wisconsin Press.

Foster, R.F. (1988) *Modern Ireland 1600–1972*. London: Penguin.

Fuller, L. (2008) Devotion to the Sacred Heart and the Irish experience. *Intercom* (May): 4–15.

Gardiner, M. (1992) *Best Remembered Poems*. New York: Dover Publications.

Gooch, J. (2000) *The Boer War: Direction, Experience and Image*. London: Frank Cass.

Horne, J. (ed.) (2008) *Our War: Ireland and the Great War*. Dublin: Royal Irish Academy.

Irish Architectural Archive. (2008) http://www.dia.ie/works/view/39298/building Accessed 5 November 2008.

Jeffrey, K. (2000) *Ireland and the Great War*. Cambridge: Cambridge University Press.

Johnson, N.C. (2003) *Ireland, the Great War and the Geography of Remembrance*. Cambridge: Cambridge University Press.

Kealy, M.M. (2007). *Dominican Education in Ireland 1820–1930*. Dublin: Irish Academic Press.

King, A. (2001) Remembering and Forgetting in the Public Memorials of the Great War. In A. Forty and S. Kuchler (eds), *The Art of Forgetting*, 147–169. New York: Berg.

Lally, F. (2008) Sacred Heart. *The Word* 57(5): 16–18.

Little, G.A. (1961) An Oratory and its Eloquent Art. *The Irish Rosary* (January–February): 21–28.

Mandle, W.F. (1983) The Gaelic Athletic Association and Popular Culture, 1884–1924. In O. MacDonagh, W.E. Mandle and P. Travers (eds), *Irish Culture and Nationalism 1750–1950*, 104–121. London: Macmillan.

McCracken, D. (2003) *Forgotten Protest: Ireland and the Anglo-Boer War*. Belfast: Ulster Historical Foundation.

Morrissey T.J. 2008. Our Founding Father: James Cullen SJ 1841–1921. *Sacred Heart Messenger* (January): 9.

O'Reilly, C. (2001) Illumination. Sister Concepta Lynch and The Oratory of the Sacred Heart. *The World of Hibernia* (Winter) 7(3): 70–79.

Pegum, M. (2010) *Irish War Memorials* http://www.irishwarmemorials.ie/html/places.php Accessed 15 September 2010.

Rainbird. P. (2003) Representing nation, dividing community: the Broken Hill War Memorial, New South Wales, Australia. *World Archaeology* 35(1): 22–34.

Rynne, E. (n.d.) *A Shrine of Celtic Art. The art of Sr. M. Concepta Lynch, O.P.* Dublin: The Irish Dominican Sisters.

Switzer, C. (2008) *Commemorating the First World War.* http://www.culturenorthernireland.org/article/148/commemorating-the-first-world-war. Accessed 9 November 2010.

Tarlow, S. (1999) *Bereavement and Commemoration: an Archaeology of Mortality.* Oxford: Blackwell.

Interviews

Ms Veronica Heywood, Dun Laoghaire Arts Centre.
Sr Frances Lally, O.P., Dominican Convent, Dun Laoghaire.

Unpublished documents

Application to the European Commission for grant aid for preservation of The Oratory under the European Architectural Award Scheme, 1995.

Letter to Veronica Heywood from Dr. Brian Kennedy, Assistant Director, National Gallery of Ireland, 1995.

3

The Bare Bones:
body parts, bones, and conflict behaviour

Susannah Callow

My aim in this paper is to demonstrate the importance of bone and body parts (as artefacts) in the rich and varied materiality of recent Western conflict, and their ability to contain and reveal complex narratives of human experiences of conflict.

Wars of the twentieth and twenty-first centuries are typically technological, high-intensity, often international in scale, and involve heavy casualties. These pressures have created man-made crucibles within which definitions of human, animal, and the value and worth of materials (including bodies), are melded and redefined. Bone and body-part artefacts can provide important insights into these changing definitions and the impact they have upon our ideas about materiality. Corporeal material culture inserts the personal and the painful into empirical, impersonal research. The artefacts are imbued with personal meanings and individual memories of the most intense and highly pressured environments that can be endured by human beings.

Here I will discuss contemporary use and perceptions of the body in conflict, explaining the reasons for studying animal and human body materiality together, and examining how the impact of technology affects the place of the body in modern conflict.

Human bodies as conflict symbols

The significance of the human body as a unique kind of conflict materiality cannot be understated. Bodies are symbiotically linked to personhood in the human psyche, and are rich sources of metaphor and symbolism in most cultures (Synnott 1993: 1). Furthermore, the body is central to human experiences of modern warfare (Cooper *et al.* 2008: 121). Thus, body parts can become a political tool, personal memento, or identifier of social status within conflicts:

> Material and human destruction...becomes a way of giving material form to discourse, and the body in pain is a vital component in battle to assert meaning and authority (*ibid.*).

Modern conflicts frequently exhibit a totality of force, and the effects of violence upon the physical body – both human and animal – can be devastating and highly visible. Human interaction within conflict is uncomfortable and difficult, and often exacerbated by witnessing the results of violence at first-hand. Bodily impacts of war are some of the most memorable and shocking aspects of conflict for soldiers and civilians alike, with dead bodies, and their parts, becoming an integral part of many conflict landscapes (Saunders 2009: 40–41).

Human bodies physically symbolise humanity. Signs of mutilation, including body parts, can evoke reciprocal, empathic pain: 'when we see or read about another's pain, we are likely to experience vicarious discomforts' (Lock *et al.* 2007: 15). Mutilation seems to evoke particular horror and pain (Fussell 1989: 271), exemplified in the use of the *idea* of mutilation to incite fear of violence and lack of mercy amongst an enemy. For example, German U-boats submarines carrying limbs and intestines and other body parts to jettison and suggest the enemy's horrific death (Fussell 1989: 272).

Conversely, mutilation can have a propaganda use, to incite anger against an enemy amongst civilians. Claims of German atrocities in Belgium at the beginning of the First World War, 'legitimised' by official British reports (Bryce 1914), focused on mutilations, e.g. stabbing babies with bayonets to create the most evocative and emotive imagery of pain and disrespect.

Moving beyond accepted moral boundaries by mutilating the human body indicates the unique pressures of conflict experience, and shows how training reinforces the need to inflict wounds. Scarry (1987) identifies wounding as the main focus of conflict behaviour. Permanent wounds such as scars or missing body parts convey messages about the success or failure of causing wounds to the 'other'– and parts removed from another person convey the military success of the individual who carries out such acts. The body has 'referential instability' in that it can represent either the victim's defeat or the enemy's victory, or another outcome (Scarry 1987: 117). Wounds obtained for 'our' side therefore take on a positive meaning.

Such physical mementoes of conflict are contained in and expressed by the human body as permanent injuries, scars, or missing body parts from dismemberment or amputation. This can convey metaphors of bravery, loss and pain beyond the battlefield and into civilian life. For example, First World War amputee veterans existed in such large numbers that their injuries and missing limbs were immediate signs of their involvement in the war (Bourke 1999: 59), and highly visible injuries often incited the most intense sympathy (MacDonald 1993: 152). Again, the referential nature of the body incites emotion on witnessing the effects of conflict.

Mutilations, and particularly the loss of limbs, are a constant theme of modern conflict. The limitations of the human body to withstand modern weaponry are a constant difficulty even in ultra-modern and highly technological forces such as the

US army in Afghanistan and Iraq. Improvised explosive devices (IEDs) are the most frequent cause of death and injury in both areas, and amputations are frequent amongst survivors. British military training now uses real amputees, with appropriate costumes and makeup, in its realistic casualty drills, to prepare soldiers for the likelihood of witnessing similar wounds in the field (MOD 2010). This underscores the often acute and traumatic psychological effects of witnessing such injuries.

Negative human body part use

The body's referential instability (Scarry 1987: 117) also shows how the enemy's body can become a symbol of victory. The failure to bury a body can be a political and sometimes religious metaphor.

In the Spanish Civil War, bodies of enemies' relatives were frequently left exposed as a symbol of humiliation and religious degradation (Beevor 2006: 99, 105). The identity of the victim was crucial in instigating such behaviour. The degradation implied in denying culturally important post-mortem rituals was a deliberate act, underlining the social power and importance of the body even after death.

In a similar way, artefacts produced from an enemy's body can symbolise narratives of dominance, power, and masculinity, conferring the power of the deceased onto the possessor, implying an increase in status through achieving a kill. The act of wounding and mutilation in itself can be an assertion of masculinity and a way to create a 'warrior persona' (Hodges 2008).

Racism is often a factor in promoting negative attitudes towards an enemy group. The physical form is a visible sign of difference, therefore bodily characteristics of individuals

Figure 3.1: US Army First World War enlistment poster. Germany is personified as a demonic ape wearing a distinguishing pickelhaube helmet. (Wikimedia Commons. Online image available at http://commons.wikimedia.org/wiki/File:%27 DestroyThisMadBrute%27-US-poster.jpg Image in public domain, out of copyright)

and groups are often the focus of racist thinking, and the body itself becomes a battleground. Use and abuse of body parts is often at the centre of conflicts where racist thoughts exist, particularly where acting on such thoughts is officially sanctioned or supported, creating a 'culture of cruelty' (Waller 2002: 229).

Dehumanisation, a concept often associated with racism, and often emerging within such cultures of cruelty, is closely linked to the creation of such artefacts from human body parts. Dehumanisation is a psychological term describing a process of denying the humanity or human characteristics of an individual or an 'outgroup' (Haslam 2006). The concept often appears in conflict contexts as a way of dealing with killing. 'Human status has often been in practice a matter of race, nationality, gender, class, and many other factors' (Sax 2000: 19); it is a subjective and culturally defined concept, which can be manipulated as required.

Dehumanisation can result in moral exclusion of an individual or group (Opotow 1990). Implying the inferiority of the victim and, consequently, the superiority of the perpetrator (Grossman 1995: 209–10), it 'removes normal moral restraints against aggression' (Waller 2002: 245).

This removal of restraint against violence finds physical form not only in mass killings but also in the production of body-part artefacts. Normally forbidden acts, such as bodily mutilation, can be enjoyed, even celebrated (Wills and Steuter 2009: 38), or at the very least, carried out without moral consideration. Human body parts can be transformed into 'conflict trophies' where this concept exists. Long-standing racist attitudes towards the enemy group make this sort of behaviour more likely.

Such behaviour can occur in a number of ways; comparison to animals is one method of dehumanisation which displays how human status can be blurred, and also how animals are often considered a sign (in the sense of a metaphor) of inferiority or lack of humanity. Discourses of hunting, pest control, and extermination can be closely connected to individual acts of bodily violence in conflicts and genocide (Waller 2002: 246–247; Livingstone-Smith 2007: 183). For example, Harrison (2006) suggests that American traditions of hunting and racism were connected to their collecting of Japanese body parts in the Pacific during the Second World War, and also, subsequently, in Vietnam. The Japanese enemy in the Second World War was repeatedly demonised, demeaned, and dehumanised by American propaganda at home and within the armed forces.

Where enemies are conceived of as animals to be hunted, taking their body parts becomes 'of no greater moral consequence than taking the head of a bear to mount over the fireplace' (Bryant 1979: 197). Thus, human leg bones could be carved into paper knives (Lindbergh 1970: 906) with reasonable moral impunity, and teeth and skulls collected as common souvenirs.

Instances of trophy taking and display have also been linked to hunting metaphors amongst American soldiers in Iraq (Wills and Steuter 2009: 88–89). Even in the First World War, popular discourse compared German soldiers to pigs (Hodges 2008: 129), and propaganda images frequently depicted the enemy as monstrous apes (Figure 3.1).

Heroic status was associated with obtaining such a trophy in the Pacific and in Vietnam, as the Japanese and Vietnamese soldiers were perceived as dangerous warriors, albeit subhuman (Weingartner 1992). Trophies implied dominance, masculinity and virility through making a kill, and invoked a warrior status. They also symbolised individual survival and dominance over death itself (Blackmore 2005: 28). Thus, a masculine 'hunter spirit', along with racism and dehumanisation formed the human body into a method of self-expression, conveying messages of victory to the enemy.

Civilian outgroups can also be subject to dehumanisation and their bodies transformed into material culture. For example, a vital part of the spectacle of lynching in the southern United States was the crowd witnessing a death. Taking, and often selling, the body parts allowed every member of the audience to participate in the activity, and conferred the status of belonging to the 'correct' dominant group (Young 2005). Here, extreme racism and pervasive beliefs in the inhumanity of the black community contributed to the body becoming a commodity. As a further example, during the recent Sierra Leone conflict, then Liberian president Charles Taylor is said to have told his soldiers that their enemies were 'no longer human beings' (McGreal 2008), so they could be cannibalised and mutilated with no moral consequence.

In extreme examples of dehumanisation, the body of a victim 'possesses no meaning. It is waste, and its removal is a matter of sanitation' (Waller 2002: 245). These examples depend on inherent, historical racism, and official support for the process. Taking the victims of the Holocaust as an example, the application of this concept can be clearly seen. Linguistically, Jews and other victimised groups were dehumanised to an extreme degree. In Nazi rhetoric, especially speeches at rallies, Jews in particular were compared to disease or parasites (Sax 2000) and to a variety of animals with negative connotations such as rats.

In practical application, words used to describe concentration camp victims homogenised them as a 'load', or as 'merchandise'; their eating habits were referenced using the German verb *fressen,* which usually referred to feeding animals (Waller 2002: 246). Victims lost possession and control of their social identity, and crucially, of their bodies (Oliver 2011: 91), that were tattooed with numbers, like cattle. They were herded and kept in cramped huts. Victims' bodies were subjected to experiments, like laboratory animals. At the last, the disposal of corpses in their thousands was clinical and abbatoir-like (Patterson 2002).

The by-products of the concentration camp killing process were also obtained: ashes from the crematoria were used as 'fill' for swamps, insulation, and fertiliser, and were spread on roads and footpaths (Levi 1989: 100). Skeletons and 'death masks' of camp victims were reportedly sold for profit (Baumslag 2005: 69–70). Human skin was said to be used to produce leather, and hair was a valuable commodity (Roberts 2008: 107–8). Reports of human-fat soap are persistent, if difficult to verify. In other words, human remains

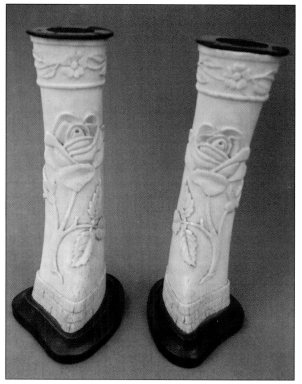

had become commoditised and objectified by conflict within a distinctively Nazi ideological framework.

Victims' bodies were not considered worthless, therefore, in a monetary sense, but in a moral sense. The bodies were viewed as raw material by-products of a necessary process. Those who were not killed were used as workers and their lives held value only whilst they could still contribute. The pseudo-science of Nazi eugenics implied that the body itself was at the root of the evil and inferiority of the Jewish race, implying connections between race, criminology, and physical infirmity. The body was therefore central to Nazi categorisation of negative outgroups, and their methods of destroying their bodies exemplified these attitudes.

Figure 3.2: Pair of carved bone vases with wooden bases, produced by civilian internees held in Knockaloe Internment Camp, Isle of Man, during the First World War. The reverse of both vases hold inscriptions, one reads Knockaloe and the other Isle of Man. (© Author)

In keeping with the zoomorphic metaphors mentioned above, but this time in a positive sense (for Nazi ideology), the German Aryan race was compared to a wolf, predator, or noble dog, virile and loyal. Dogs were generally favoured by the Nazis, especially the German Shepherd (Sax 2000: 84), and were often treated better than human groups who were considered inferior. Dogs used by the SS to guard the camp at Dachau were given individual kennels and a large exercise yard (Sax 2000: 87), in stark contrast to the conditions which the camps' prisoners endured. However, dogs belonging to Jewish people were categorised along with their human owners as undesirable, and were often killed (*ibid.*: 22). This illustrates the selective blurring of the lines between human and animal in Nazi ideology (Arluke *et al.* 1996: 133).

A further contrast in treatment exemplifies this concept's selectivity. Whilst the Nazis supported animal rights programmes and were opposed to vivisection (Arluke *et al.* 1996: 133–135), and even organised a zoo within the concentration camp at Buchenwald (Roberts 2008: 108–109), they concurrently experimented on humans and used their bodies as raw material for by-products. The Buchenwald zoo animals were given quality food including meat, and were cared for by the prisoners who were themselves suffering starvation (*ibid.*).

Two categories of body-part artefact created by dehumanisation are therefore evident. The mostly civilian victims of the Holocaust were not perceived as a worthy, combatant enemy, in the same way as American soldiers viewed their Japanese opponents in the Pacific. Holocaust body-part artefacts are a result of officially sanctioned racism, dehumanising discourse and propaganda, and the emotionless use of the by-products of killing. By contrast, the artefacts from the Pacific theatre symbolise the warrior status of the enemy, and the achievement of a kill. This underlines the variability and complexity of these concepts, and that bodies can represent a spectrum of emotions and connections.

The term depersonalisation' may be more appropriate than 'dehumanisation' in some contexts, where the victim is still considered 'human', but less so than the perpetrator. The victim may be considered inferior, but their body is perceived as worthy of mistreatment, as a visible sign of anger, and a metaphor of hatred, dominance and power. As torture converts internally-felt pain into visible signs on the victim's body, and is converted into a demonstration of power (Scarry 1987: 27), so too is mutilation symbolic of dominance and the assertion of supremacy.

Body part trophies can be a reminder of the identity of the victim as an enemy - a vanquished *human* enemy (Lang 2010). Thus, Japanese skulls are worthy souvenirs not because of their medical or economic value, as in Nazi examples, but because of the victim's identity as worthy enemy fighters, who were excluded from moral consideration because of racial traits and political affiliation. The central importance of the human body as an arena for contestation is complex, and debates run deep, but the material remains of such activities provide an enduring physical legacy.

Human uses of animals

The uses of human bodies in conflict are connected to uses of animal body parts, and an integrative approach is consequently important for a thorough understanding of the place of both in the material culture of conflict. Humans and animals have been linked in conflict for millennia, not least through the creation and use of their respective body-part artefacts. These can provide insights into broader concepts of humans, animals, enemies, and friends.

Attitudes to human body parts have been shown to be subjective and fluctuating; human status itself is revealed a relative concept. Ideas about animals and the use of animal bodies are equally variable. In conflict situations, the boundaries between humans and animals may become even more unstable. Variations and contrasts in human and animal part use and abuse reveal the flexibility and subjectivity of our conceptual classifications of being.

Uses of animals vary according to a particular conflict, its terrain and climate, and the relative availability of other material resources. Broadly speaking, however, animal treatment in recent modern conflicts has reinforced and maintained a nineteenth century doctrine of human superiority. Bones from meat supplies or deceased war animals were recycled into artefacts forming souvenirs amongst prisoners of war, civilian internees, and combatants in many conflicts – perhaps most notably during the First World War (Figure 3.2). These artefacts were often personal mementoes; others were a means to avoid boredom, still others were sold for financial gain. The underlying message in terms of the centrality of the *body* is that animal bones were valued for their material utility, not the identity or species of the animal from which they were obtained.

Many animals have played a supporting role in recent conflicts alongside humans, for example in transport, rescuing, messengers, and mascots. Some animals have been celebrated for the human-like characteristics, such as 'heroism', projected onto them. The way these animals were commemorated after death is very different to the commemoration of humans. Sometimes, animal bodies were preserved by taxidermy and displayed in museums along with descriptions of their wartime achievements, such as the First World War messenger pigeon *Cher Ami*, said to be responsible for saving the lives of an entire American battalion (Mays 1987). Such commemorations are infrequent, and focus on the few animals whose actions are perceived to elevate their status nearer to humans.

Other war animals, however, were killed or abandoned when necessary. After the First World War, millions of former war horses were butchered or rendered (Singleton 1993: 201). Thousands of dogs that served with the American army in Vietnam were left behind when the United States forces left (Burnham 2008: 244). More recently, an American army dog which served in Afghanistan and assisted with bomb disposal, found that its critical life-saving military role became invisible and worthless when back home in the US, and led to it being accidentally euthanised (Cavendish 2010).

This dichotomy of value is further exemplified by a case from the Spanish Civil War, when live turkeys were used as 'flapping parachutes' to carry airlifted fragile supplies safely to nationalists under siege in a remote monastery. The turkeys were equally valuable for the nationalists because 'they could also be eaten by the defenders' (Beevor 2006: 138).

Such examples demonstrate the inherent divisions between humans and animals in modern Western conflicts. Although animal support is crucial even in the twenty-first century, animals' bodies are considered disposable once they are no longer required. Their lack of essential humanity denies animal bodies the same status and treatment as humans. This subjective, ingroup-outgroup thinking is conceptually the same as the thought processes applied to human bodies in the previous section.

Bodies and technology

It is instructive to consider the interaction of a third category of object – the man-made – alongside the bodies of animals and humans. The positioning of natural, organic bodies amongst increasingly industrialised and heavily technological methods of conflict reveals an insightful contrast.

The increasing industrialisation of warfare in the twentieth century has transformed conflict materiality. Military technology, including weaponry, armour, and medicine, has developed rapidly throughout the twentieth and twenty-first centuries. Technology has not only changed how wars are prosecuted, but also how war has affected human and animal bodies.

The impact of modern warfare on bodies is more devastating than in earlier conflicts. Injuries in modern conflict are often more severe and harder to treat, despite constantly improving medical care. The fragility of the organic body is a unifying aspect of conflict experience, which connects man with animal in an unalterable sense. This frailty can be counterbalanced to some extent, using technology to hide the scars of violence, such as prosthetic limbs; and also by protecting the body, using items such as gas masks (Figure 3.3) or body armour. Increasingly, however, improving or replacing the form of the body itself is the focus of research into new conflict technologies.

Robots/humans/animals

During the twentieth century, conflicts have demanded less from individuals in terms of responsibility, and more from society in terms of human casualties (Coker 2008: 145). To counteract this, recent technological developments have created a third category of 'being' – the robot machine (Sheehan *et al.* 1991). Bomb disposal robots used in Iraq protected human lives and prevented many deaths from explosions, and are now often requested by soldiers

Figure 3.3: Gas masks for man and horse, demonstrated by an American soldier and his horse, c. 1918. (US National Archives: http://arcweb. archives.gov/arc/action/ ExternalIdSearch?id=516 483&jScript=true. Image in public domain, out of copyright)

(Weiner 2005). This is restructuring injury patterns and the bodily consequences of conflict.

Robotics can safeguard the fragility of the human body by replacing it entirely with more durable materials. Unlike humans, robots can repeatedly be repaired, broken parts replaced and then redeployed. Injured human bodies can be patched up with robotic prostheses that can, for example, restore function to paralysed legs (Rabinovitch 2008). Other robotic devices, such as the 'exoskeleton robotic suit' (Anon. 2010), are designed to assist with carrying heavy loads by incorporating the human body, but improving or extending its physical performance.

The implications of such developments for future studies of conflict materiality are currently unknown. Perhaps robot body parts will become legitimate trophies of war. Human bodies may become absent from conflicts, and those which remain may incorporate robotics to replace lost parts or to improve performance. This complicates issues concerning the morality of warfare, and may even move the focus of conflict away from wounding the human body. The relative value of organic body parts in the material culture of future conflicts is called into question. Perhaps taking possession of enemy robots as trophies will become a mark of military success, returning to a much more traditional souvenir of conflict, the weapon (Cornish 2009).

The place of animal bodies in conflict is also challenged by new technology. Interactions between humans and robots reveal that robots may be taking over not just the functional roles of animals, as with the quadrupedal *BigDog* robot, which acts like a pack mule to carry heavy loads (Hambling 2006), but also their roles as companions.

Small bomb-disposal robots are often anthropomorphised by being given individual names (Robson 2007) – such as *Scooby-Doo* whose 'death' was mourned by the men it worked with. The robot (assigned a male gender) was said to be considered one of the 'team' (Rothstein 2006). The attribution of a personality to a robot challenges the place of animals as human companions in conflict, and shows the subjectivity of definitions of 'being', that any creature or creation can be perceived to have positive or negative traits.

Frequently, 'biologically inspired approaches' (Hambling 2008) in military technological research incorporate ideas from the animal world, such as the 'cyborg penguin' underwater stealth suit currently being developed (*ibid.*). There is an inherent irony in simultaneously negating the value of the natural body in warfare, and using biological features as the inspiration for future conflict research, again indicating the subjectivity and fluctuations of conflict attitudes to bodies.

These examples illustrate that the physical body is not considered suitable for the military demands of the twenty-first century, and that attempts are being made to overcome its fragility. This suggests that the consequences of conflict violence on living bodies (animal and human) are becoming unacceptable in a modern technological age, where news and images of every loss can be instantly transmitted. Yet the body is still central to military research. Inspirations from both animal and human bodily forms are being used to inspire robot designs. These developments are beginning to reconfigure concepts of the body. The materiality of the body has not disappeared from conflict, but it remains, as always, subject to the increasing pressures of modern warfare and developments in technology.

Conclusions

Bones and body parts, and their varying social and cultural valuations and treatments, are of central importance to the interdisciplinary approach adopted by modern conflict archaeology. As evocative and volatile material culture, artefacts made from them convey complex messages about the conflict experience.

Human- and animal-bone artefacts represent the unique pressures of modern conflict, embodying the will to survive. Animal bones represent survival of boredom and lack of resources for self-expression. Human bodies symbolise defeating death, and convey messages of power, hatred and dominance over an enemy. Thus, individuals reconstruct their own identity, and find ways to cope with conflict by reconfiguring body parts.

Divides between humans widen during conflict, often amplifying 'residual' racism dormant in everyday society (Saminaden *et al.* 2010). Similarly, gaps in perception of the moral status of animals expand through necessity. The complexities of defining moral status in conflict, and the diverse meanings of material culture objects, are exemplified through studying artefacts made from animal as well as human body parts.

The bodies of animals and humans are both shattered and re-made by modern industrialised warfare. Technology is now creating new categories of being, which are reconfiguring definitions of human, animal, and machine, adding another dimension to the body-part materiality of conflict. The use of technology to protect, enhance and replace the bodies of humans and animals in conflict begins to confuse definitions of body and being.

Contemporary fears about blurring the boundaries between man and animal, as evident in current debates about the ethics of creating human-animal biological hybrids (Morriss 1997), highlight the difficulties faced when dealing with and categorising personhood, identity, and humanity outside of conflict. The unique pressures of modern conflict greatly exacerbate these complications, and this is manifested within corporeal material culture. It is important to study the variety and significance of bone and body parts in order to understand human and animal bodies as a unique kind of conflict materiality.

Bibliography

Anon. (2010). *Raytheon unveils lighter, faster, stronger second generation exoskeleton robotic suit*. PR Newswire: http://multivu.prnewswire.com/mnr/raytheon/46273/ Accessed 30 October 2010.

Arluke, A. and Sanders, C.R. (eds). (1996) *Regarding Animals*. Philadelphia: Temple University Press.

Axe, D. and Olexa, S. (2008) *War Bots: How US War Robots are Transforming War in Iraq, Afghanistan, and the Future*. Michigan: Nimble Books LLC.

Baumslag, N. (2005) *Murderous Medicine: Nazi Doctors, Human Experimentation, and Typhus*. Westport: Greenwood Publishing Group.

Beevor, A. (2006) *The Battle for Spain: The Spanish Civil War 1936–1939*. London: Weidenfield and Nicholson.

Blackmore, T. (2005) *War X: Human Extensions in Battlespace*. Toronto: Toronto University Press.

Bourke, J. (1999) *Dismembering the Male: Men's Bodies, Britain and the Great War*. London: Reaktion Books.

Bryant, C.D. (1979) *Khaki-Collar Crime: Deviant Behaviour in the Military Context*. New York: Macmillan.

Bryce, J. (1914) *Report of the Committee on Alleged German Outrages*. London: H.M. Stationery Office.

Burnham, J.C. (2008) *A Soldier's Best Friend: Scout Dogs and their Handlers in the Vietnam War*. New York: Sterling Publishing Company.

Cavendish, J. (2010) *Afghan war hero is put down by mistake*. http://www.independent.co.uk/news/world/asia/afghan-war-hero-is-put-down-by-mistake-2136078.html Accessed on 22 November 2010.

Coker, C. (2008) *Ethics and War in the 21st Century*. Abingdon: Routledge.

Cooper, N. and Hurcombe, N. (2008) The Body at War: Wounds, Wounding and the Wounded. *Journal of War and Culture Studies* 1(2): 119–121.

Cornish, P. (2009) 'Just a Boyish Habit'…? British and Commonwealth War Trophies in the First World War. In N.J. Saunders, and P. Cornish (eds), *Contested Objects: Material Memories of the Great War*, 11–26. Abingdon: Routledge.

Fussell, P. (1989) *Wartime: Understanding and Behavior in the Second World War*. Oxford: Oxford University Press.

Grossman, D. (1995) *On Killing: the Psychological Cost of Learning to Kill in War and Society*. Boston: Little, Brown and Company.

Hambling, D. (2006). *Robotic 'pack mule' displays stunning reflexes*. http://www.newscientist.com/article/dn8802-robotic-pack-mule-displays-stunning-reflexes.html Accessed 17 November 2010.

Hambling, D. (2008). *Attack of the Super-Strength Cyborg Penguins*. http://www.wired.com/dangerroom/2008/09/attack-of-the-u/ Accessed 25 September 2010.

Harrison, S. (2006) Skull Trophies of the Pacific War: Transgressive Objects of Remembrance. *Journal of the Royal Anthropological Institute* 12: 817–836.

Haslam, N. (2006) Dehumanisation: An Integrative Review. *Personality and Social Psychology Review* 10(3): 252–264

Hodges, P. (2008) 'They don't like it up 'em!': Bayonet fetishization in the British Army during the First World War. *Journal of War and Culture Studies* 1(2): 123–138.

Lang, J. (2010) Questioning Dehumanisation. *Holocaust and Genocide Studies*, 24(2): 225–246.

Levi, P. (1989) *The Drowned and the Saved*. London: Abacus.

Lindbergh, C.A. (1970) *The Wartime Journals of Charles A. Lindbergh*. New York: Harcourt, Brace, Jovanovich.

Livingstone- Smith, D. (2007) *The Most Dangerous Animal: Human Nature and the Origins of War*. New York: St Martin's Griffin.

Lock, M. and Farquhar, J. (2007) *Beyond the Body Proper: The Anthropology of Material Life*. Durham (NC): Duke University Press.

MacDonald, L. (1993) *The Roses of No Man's Land* (2nd ed.). London: Penguin.

Mays, T.M. (1987) A Signal Company for the Birds. *Army Communicator* 12: 26–30.

McGreal, C. (2008) Charles Taylor told soldiers to eat their enemies, court hears. *The Guardian*. http://www.guardian.co.uk/world/2008/mar/14/liberia Accessed 2 November 2010.

MOD. (2010). *Realistic casualty drills prepare helicopter force for Afghanistan*. http://www.mod.uk/DefenceInternet/DefenceNews/TrainingAndAdventure/Realistic CasualtyDrillsPrepareHelicopterForceForAfghanistan.htm Accessed 15 November 2010.

Morriss, P. (1997) Blurred Boundaries. *Inquiry: An Interdisiplinary Journal of Philosophy* 40(3): 259–90.

Oliver, S. (2011) Dehumanisation: Perceiving the Body as (In)Human. In P. Kaufmann, H. Kuch, C. Neuhauser and E. Webster (eds), *Humiliation, Degradation, Dehumanisation: Human Dignity Violated* 24, 85–97. New York.

Opotow, S. (1990) Moral Exclusion and Injustice: An Introduction. *Journal of Social Issues* 46(1): 1–20.

Patterson, C. (2002). *Eternal Treblinka*. New York: Lantern Books.

Rabinovitch, A. (2008) *Human exoskeleton suit helps paralyzed people walk*. http://www.reuters.com/article/idUSLP27939120080825 Accessed 10 November 2010.

Roberts, M.S. (2008) *The Mark of the Beast: Animality and Human Oppression*. West Lafayette (IN): Purdue University Press.

Robson, S. (2007) *Hohenfels teaching soldiers how to use downrange robots*. http://web.archive.org/web/20070910111222/http:/www.stripes.com/article.asp?section=104&article=55755&archive=true Accessed 15 November 2010.

Rothstein, J. (2006) *Soldiers Bond with Battlefield Robots*. http://www.msnbc.msn.com/id/12939612 Accessed 1 November 2010.

Saminaden, A., Loughnan, S. and Haslam, N. (2010) Afterimages of Savages: Implicit Associations Between 'Primitives', Animals and Children. *British Journal of Psychology* 49: 91–105.

Saunders, N.J. (2009) People in Objects: Individuality and the Quotidian in the Material Culture of War. In C.L. White (ed.), *The Materiality of Individuality: Archaeological Studies of Individual Lives,* 37–55. London: Springer.

Sax, B. (2000) *Animals in the Third Reich: Pets, Scapegoats and the Holocaust*. New York: Continuum Publishing.

Scarry, E. (1987) *The Body in Pain: The Making and Unmaking of the World*. Oxford: Oxford University Press.

Sheehan, J.J. and Sosna, M. (eds). (1991) *The Boundaries of Humanity: Humans, Animals, Machines*. Los Angeles: University of California Press.

Singleton, J. (1993) Britain's Military Use of Horses, 1914–1918. *Past and Present* 139: 178–203.

Synnott, A. (1993) *The Body Social: Symbolism, Self and Society*. London: Routledge.

Thomas, K. (1983) *Man and the Natural World. Changing Attitudes in England 1500–1800*. London: Penguin.

Waller, J. (2002) *Becoming Evil: How Ordinary People Commit Genocide and Mass Killing.* Oxford: Oxford University Press.

Weiner, T. (2005) A New Model Army Soldier Rolls Closer to the Battlefield. *New York Times.* http://www.nytimes.com/2005/02/16/technology/16robots.html Accessed 1 November 2010.

Weingartner, J. (1992) Trophies of War: US Troops and the Mutilation of Japanese War Dead, 1941–1945. *Pacific Historical Review,* 61(1): 53–67.

Wills, D., and Steuter, E. (2009) The Soldier as Hunter: Pursuit, Prey and Display in the War on Terror. *Journal of War and Culture Studies* 2(2): 195–210.

Woods, D.D., Tittle, J., Feil, M. and Roesler, A. (2004) Envisioning Human-Robot Coordination in Future Operations. *IEEE Transactions on Systems, Man, and Cybernetics* 34(2): 210–218.

Young, H. (2005) The Black Body as Souvenir in American Lynching. *Theatre Journal* 57(4): 639–657.

4

The Diary of an American 'Doughboy': interpreting a textual artefact of the First World War

Margaret N. Bagwell

Introduction: text and archaeology

The relationship between text and archaeology, epitomised in the discipline of Historical Archaeology, has long been contentious. Regarded often as the 'handmaiden of history', archaeology's objects have been seen as mere illustrations to history's texts. Lawrence Duggan (1989) sums up this debate, 'words ... will always remain our most precise ... mode of communication. Pictures cannot "speak" clearly, only words can' (quoted in Moreland 2001: 12). Nevertheless, the work of Deetz (1996), Buchli (2002), and Appadurai (2008), has seen objects, things, and material culture being re-evaluated and recognised for their ability to reveal historical subtexts lost from the formal linguistic record. Yet, this reclaiming of material culture has not healed the 'fragmentation' of archaeology's relationship with the written word. Text, set aside by the discipline as a non-object, remains largely unexplored for its role as material culture.

Language, and its material trace, the written word, are 'held to be the primary distinguishing feature of humanity' (Tilley 1991: 16). As such, it is an archaeologist's responsibility to elevate words beyond their use within the discipline of history as evidence, and open the discussion of interpreting texts contextually as artifacts in their own right (Moreland 2001).

Etymology has already demonstrated the extent to which the formation of words can expound our understanding of history. As with archaeologists, etymologists uncover the subsequent strata of the word in question to reveal its origins and the changes enacted upon it by a changing world (Trench 2004: 48). Words put together in bodies of text are also of human creation. As repositories of culture, texts speak plainly, but are not without their subtext. In an essay exploring the methods of material analysis, Ian Hodder argues for the interpretation of documents to understand when, with what intent, and for whom they are written. '"What people say" is often very different from "what people do"' (Hodder 1998: 113). Further, the interpretations of texts, he argues, must include their ongoing reinterpretation by the reader. Texts as objects with metastatic meaning have biographies – 'social lives' that change with each re-reading.

As with other objects, historical circumstances can add new interpretive dimensions to texts. A crucifix made from spent cartridges in a First World War trench, or graffiti carved into the trunk of a birch tree on the Defense Estates of Salisbury Plain in southern Britain (see Summerfield, this volume), are not simply what they appear: a sign of religious devotion or an absentminded act of rebellion (Saunders 2003a: 12–13). As with a piece of trench art (*ibid.*) in wartime, text exists as an individual material memory of war. Similarly, text, and the process of writing are given added meaning when the horrific landscape of industrial war, the war of *matériel*, is considered (Bourke 1999: 10). Here, I will explore the interpretation of text by archaeology in the context of war – looking at text not for its accurate historical data, but as a means of exploring an ordinary life in extraordinary times. This study takes the diary of a regular soldier in the United States army during the First World War as the object and context of 'excavation' respectively.

Words of a great-grandfather

The small diary of Morris Denton Key of Adrian, Georgia, in the United States, was recently discovered in the process of moving my paternal grandparents from their family home to a retirement apartment complex – a family 'excavation' comparable in some ways to Christine Finn's recent artistic excavation of her parents' home (Finn 2007)[1]. Morris Key was my great-grandfather, a man whom I never had the privilege to know, but who I had heard referred to in conversations with family as 'Pa Key'. The inherently personal approach of this essay within the field of modern conflict archaeology is not uncommon. Various studies have been conducted, either implicitly or explicitly with the aim of connecting with the experiences of relatives in the past (Brown and Osgood 2009). Most notably, John Schofield (2009) recently undertook a similar excavation of his grandfather's war diary for an essay exploring commemoration and memory within the experience of war (and see Leonard, this volume). With this excavation, I too attempt to discover the character of a man who I know only from photographs (Figure 4.1).

It is worth mentioning that these investigations of hitherto unpublished war diaries supplement those that were published (privately and commercially) during the 1920s and 1930s. In recent years, more diaries have been discovered and commercially published, partly as a response to a burgeoning interest in the First World War itself spurred by the approaching centenary of 2014 (e.g. Smith 2009; Martin 2009).

Born on 5 April 1891, the son of a farmer, Morris Key, apart from his brief 'excursion' with the U.S. Army in France, lived his life in a 30 mile (*c.* 50 km) radius of the place of his birth. He was not a learned man though he was able to the read and write. He

Figure 4.1: Morris Denton Key and Bertha Leila Flanders, during the 1940s. (© author)

often described his education as 'four years between plows' (B. Key, pers. comm.). His 1918 draft card reveals that he worked as a farm labourer during early adulthood. Morris Key married Bertha Leila Flanders in 1915, as reports of the 'European disturbance' were appearing on national news reports in the United States (Womack 2008). My great-grandfather, along with all Georgian males of fighting age, enlisted in response to President Wilson's approval of the Selective Draft Act on 5 June 1917. About a year later, he entered service at Camp Gordon, northwest of Atlanta, Georgia. An excerpt from his diary describing that day indicates the extent of Morris' inexperience.

> Experience as a soilder [soldier]:
> On June the 27th 1918 went to camp arrived at Camp Gordon about 530 PM went throu [through] receiving [receiving] station got down to Barrack about dark stood around untill [until] I was worrryed [worried] finally got a blanket and a cot went to sleep after a long time got up got a little breakfast went back up to my bunk they blowed the whistle. (M.D. Key n.d.)

With the sound of that first whistle, Morris Key began his year of service with the United States infantry. As Morris never attained a rank higher than private, little official information, apart from his draft card has been found. Until the discovery of his diary, reconstructing his contribution to the war had been left to the oral histories that have been passed down through the family. For a war which left so many men mentally changed and reticent, my great-grandfather was surprisingly open about sharing his experiences.

His son, Billy Key, relates, 'he came back singing the songs he learned in France: "Over There, Over There", "K-K-K-Katie", and "Its a long way to Tipperary"' (B. Key, pers. comm.). Morris also told his family that he was charged with the task of guarding German prisoners of war, several miles away from the front, but still within range to hear the sound of fighting. This experience was later confirmed by the receipt of several letters from Germany in the years following the war. The themes of lifelong camaraderie with his wartime companions extended also to the relationships he formed with other regulars with whom he was billeted.

As distant as his duties kept him from extreme danger, Morris's narratives to his family were not without their notes of solemnity. Images of 'dead soldiers stacked up like cord wood' were also part of his memory of the Western Front (B. Key, pers. comm.). And he also always believed that he had breathed toxic gas that later caused heart problems, several times even attempting to apply for a Veteran's pension.

After serving almost a year abroad, he returned to Adrian, Georgia, where he spent the rest of his life as husband to Bertha, father to Woodruff, Jack, Billy, Marjorie, and Bertha Nell (my grandmother), and as owner of the Key Cafe where he sold hamburgers for 5 cents. He died on 5 October 1952, a grandfather and great-grandfather in memory only for most of his offspring. A life of just 61 years, he is remembered as a good, honest man.

Diary-as-object: 'The Things They Carried'

In war, the objects carried by a soldier take on a unique significance. A backpack is filled with essential kit, but it is also contains objects of exclusively personal value (O'Brien 1998: 13–16). The archaeological excavation of First World War remains reinforces this trend. A recent excavation of the 1917 Messines battlefield at Ploegsteert in Belgium, revealed an Australian regular soldier carrying regulation munitions, medical kit, and water bottle, along with wallet, toothbrush, a souvenir German helmet, and a piece of trench art: a bullet strung as a necklace (Brown and Osgood 2009). The inclusion of personal items in the process of charging into battle underscores their value.

Furthermore, the horrific physicality of the terrain of industrial warfare in the First World War is totally alien – physically distant from the known landscape for some soldiers, and experientially unlike any other event (see Winterton, this volume). Within such an environment, carrying personal objects must be connected with attempts by regular soldiers to establish some semblance of normality. For archaeologists, these items attach an individual story to the remains that can lead to the identification and repatriation of one of 'the missing' (Saunders 2007: 178).

In this tradition, Morris Key carried a soft-bound notebook measuring approximately 9 cm in width, 15 cm in length, and 1 cm thick (Figure 4.2). This he used as a diary, marking the days he lived apart from his home. Formally untitled, 'Morris Key', handwritten in ink, is barely visible on the back cover. A possible price of '0.40' (40 cents) is written in a different hand inside. The interior pages, marked by a grid pattern, are double the size of the cover, folded in half, and held together in the center by rusting metal staples. Half to two-thirds of the pages have no text. What text is written is almost

Figure 4.2: Morris Denton Key's diary. (© author)

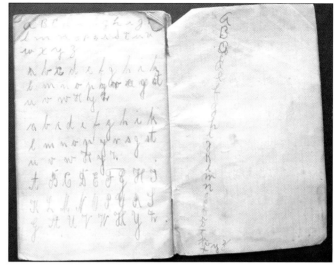

Figure 4.3: Detail of diary pages: practicing penmanship, and collecting addresses. (© author)

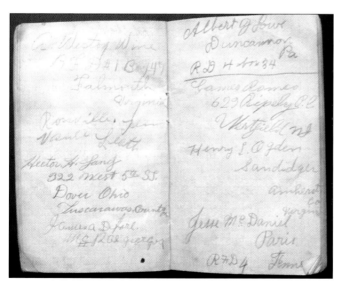

Figure 4.4: Detail of diary pages: practicing penmanship, and collecting addresses. (© author)

exclusively in lead pencil by the same hand. The physical distress of this object's life in conflict, and then years of being discarded in a drawer are evident in the diary's 'aura' (Danet 1997). The light brown cover and darker brown spine are notably worn, slightly torn, and marked by creases that one might imagine would have resulted from being held tightly in a palm or stuffed into a pocket. It smells of slow decay.

The diary as an object of conflict establishes an individual narrative of being in a place (Danet 1997; Casella and Fowler 2004; Schofield 2009; Leonard this volume). Though one can never fully appreciate the experiences of the individual who created it, object analysis can allow some conclusions to be drawn. As Saunders has observed in relation to First World War trench art:

> 'if we accept that an individual's social being is determined by their relationship to the objects that represent them ... then we may also consider that objects make people as much as people make objects.' (2002: 176)

After being acquired by Morris Key on 16 December 1918, the notebook was transformed by its use into a diary. Because we have no indication of what else of personal value he might have carried in his pack, we might also assume that the diary established some connection for Morris with his humanity.

Not unlike a small piece of ordnance 'artistically' worked and reworked by the Australian soldier described above, Morris' diary provided him with some form of entertainment during periods of rest, perhaps somewhere to write when waiting to send or receive another letter from home. Ernst Jünger wrote of similar experiences in *Storm of Steel*, his famous memoir of life in the German army: 'And so our days passed in strenuous monotony ... then I would take my notebook out of my map pocket, and jot down the salient events of the day' (Jünger 2004: 51). Several pages with repetitions of the alphabet show that Morris also passed the time practicing his penmanship (Figure 4.3), and other pages contain the names and addresses of the men in his company, another pastime activity (Figure 4.4).

> [A fellow] ask me to put my name and adress [address] in his letter book. I ask him for his he wrote W J Kissock so that was when I met Bill. Toney Dukes, Lanrom & several others was with us in the Barn. (M.D. Key n.d.)

Further evidence suggests the diary was a container of more than just memory. It was found holding several letters written during and after Morris's time in France, a newspaper clipping, and a torn piece of paper on which he had written a note (Figure 4.5). If we consider a diary's primary objective as a repository for personal memory, its seemingly nonchalant dual purpose of carrying other textual memories adds an ironic dimension to the diary's biography.

Following the linear projection of the diary's object biography, its rediscovery by my family in November 2008 establishes the diary's continued utility. This sole piece of material culture identifies Morris Key, the deceased patriarch, as a young man from Georgia transported to France. It is a physical collection of memory that formulates identity and now serves in its own way as a 'site of mourning' (Winter 1995; and see Eavenson, this volume).

Thematic analysis

With the addition of its inscribed notes, the value of Morris Key's small notebook extends beyond its utility. Providing a traditional, written record of the life of a regular

American soldier in the Great War of 1914–1918, Morris's words illuminate and reinforce thematic elements of the Great War: its foreignness, the bonds of military camaraderie, and spirituality.

'Rain' and 'Sick'

Though Morris Key never explicitly expresses the discomfort he feels travelling so far from home into a world that defies belief, words, like 'rain' or 'sick' indicate that his encounter with conflict was not without its hardships. Further, because he lacked the extensive vocabulary of a formal education, these seemingly neutral words might be read with a deeper meaning. This supposition of intent may seem slightly faulty when considered in conjunction with my personal connection with these words, but words written in the midst of conflict can often be imbued with additional meaning. Many of the entries in the diary, especially those written of France, consist simply of a weather report, 'rain', 'rain and cold', or 'rain and wind'. His fixation with recording the weather indicates the degree to which he felt the environment was different from the one he had left behind in Georgia. Their existence as solitary entries might also be considered evidence of the monotony he must have experienced.

The diary's entries detailing sickness are perhaps more telling, and reinforce the need to read what is written for contextual information. Morris first writes of feeling sick at Camp Gordon after mistakenly leaving KP duty without permission.

> I was to [too] worried [worried] & homesick to eat finally ... I lay on my bunk almost out of my head I would read my Bible and cry oh my I was disgusted with the army. (M.D. Key n.d.)

This passage details his association between physical sickness and mental anguish. Morris mentions feeling sick several other times. At least half of these instances may be read as resulting from psychological strain (the death of two fellow infantrymen in an automobile accident, and separation from a friend he made while training), though upon arriving in France he is admitted to hospital with a severe case of influenza.

> I was not feeling well at all Mon am in fact I wasent [wasn't] able to be up went on sick list marked duty did not have to drill that afternoon lay in all Pm Had a chill and High fever. But was so worryed [worried] I would not go to the hospital until they took me and carried me. I could hardly stand up far the doctor to exame [examine] me. (M.D. Key n.d.)

'We Boys'

Juxtaposed to Morris Key's accounts of weather and illness, is the theme of camaraderie. Below is his description of Christmas 1918: note how the entry begins and ends with words of companionship.

> got all or most of the Boys name[s] the 24 and 25.. for Breakfast xmas am we had grits and Bacon dinner we had beef fried potatoe [potato] jam pickle. got a Box presents from

Figure 4.5: Letters and clippings found with the diary. (© author)

> the YMCA. tobacco, gum, candy PM went up to the Y so many frogs there you could not see any thing. Bill Sellers Dailey and me set in the corner and talked. (M.D. Key n.d.)

Bill Sellers of Ellaville, Georgia, is named in the diary several times and appears to have been one of Morris's closest friends.

> the 18th [December 1918] went to Saumw [possibly Saumur] with 450 german Prisoners. was on guard the first night ... me and Bill was togeuther [together] all the time. met Tinnel and Sellers here good fellows they are. (M.D. Key n.d.)

As previously mentioned, Morris remained in regular contact with some of these men after the war ended. Their shared experiences bound them in lifelong friendship. 'There were four men he met who he kept in touch with the rest of his life. They met in Pennsylvania and before they left made a pledge to be true to their wives' (B. Key, pers. comm.). The formation of impromptu fraternities is evident in many accounts of the First World War (e.g. Coppard 1969: 43; Jünger 2004: 66). Schofield (2009: 211) draws similar conclusions from his grandfather's words. 'It seems he was a man of great integrity ... he felt the suffering of his men personally, and grieved at the deaths that occurred'.

Like Schofield, my great-grandfather's accounts of friendship illuminate his character and inspire respect. His words also confirm the picture of Morris that my grandmother and great uncles had painted for me of their father – his kindness toward others and generosity of spirit.

'Prayer Service'

Finally, the diary also reveals my great-grandfather's strong Christian faith. While perhaps not a theme that is easily transferred to other soldiers' experiences of the First World War, the inclusion of such entries is important in illuminating his character. Along with feeling seasick as he traveled to France, Morris' most revealing description of this voyage is that of a prayer service.

> We Boys got together and had song and prayer services for several days. we would have the meeting late in the afternoon they stoped [stopped] us from singing any kind of Religious songs. But a few of us would still meet and read the scripture and talk. on the day of the 4 of sept we saw some land (M.D. Key n.d.).

Later he writes of attending church services in France at the YMCA and a Catholic church. On one page of the diary is simply written, 'Psalm 34'.

> I will extol the Lord at all times; his praise will always be on my lips. My soul will boast in the Lord; let the afflicted hear and rejoice. Glorify the Lord with me; let us exalt his name together. I sought the Lord, and he answered me; he delivered me from all my fears. Turn from evil and do good; seek peace and pursue it (Psalm 34: 1–4, 14).

While these entries indicate that Morris' faith and religious sentiment were brought with him to the battlefront, for others the brutality of war inspired spirituality anew.

As evidence, consider the numerous religious motifs embodied in trench art (Saunders 2003a: 103, 132–134; and see Becker 1998). The proximity of death reinforced an understanding of the fragility of human life and led many to embrace spirituality, or at least a religious talisman, in hopes of protection (Winter 1995: 64–6; Saunders 2003b).

Conclusion: One man's words

John Schofield writes, 'text is created as a projection of people's views about themselves, and their place in the world' (2009: 208). According to Danet (1997: 9), books carry traces of 'the history of the hands that have touched them'. The 'excavation' of my great-grandfather's diary is an exploration in the social archaeology of material culture, and reveals the depth of subtext and meaning that written records can encapsulate. Morris Denton Key was one of many when he walked onto the Western Front. His words recorded in the small notebook he carried identify him apart from his companions. As no other self-written records of my great-grandfather are known to exist, choosing to write at this time in his life becomes highly significant. The themes he highlights – fear, companionship, and spirituality – can be seen to illustrate the extent to which this war forever changed generations. His words represent his individual experience of war, and serve as a testimony to the narratives of other American 'doughboys'.

Note
1   All excerpts from Morris Key's wartime diary and letters have been reprinted as originally written, attempts to clarify spelling have been made where necessary.

Acknowledgements

This paper is dedicated to the memory of Morris Denton Key and his beloved wife, Bertha Leila Flanders. I would like to thank my Uncle Tim who entrusted me with the diary to create a transcript and record for Morris's descendants.

Bibliography

Appadurai, A. (ed.) (2008) *The Social Life of Things*. Cambridge: Cambridge University Press.
Becker, A. (1998) *War and Faith: Religious Imagination in France, 1914–1930*. Oxford: Berg.
Bourke, J. (1999) *An Intimate History of Killing: Face-to-face Combat in Twentieth Century Warfare*. London: Granta.
Brown, M. and Osgood, R. (2009) *Digging Up Plugstreet: The Western Front Unearthed*. Yeovil: Haynes Publishing.

Buchli, V. (ed.) (2007) *The Material Culture Reader.* Oxford: Berg.

Casella, E.C. and Fowler, C. (eds) (2004) *The Archaeology of Plural and Changing Identities: Beyond Identification.* New York: Springer.

Caple, C. (2006) *Objects: Reluctant Witnesses to the Past.* London: Routledge.

Coppard, G. (1969) *With a Machine Gun to Cambrai.* London: Her Majesty's Stationery Office.

Danet, B. (1997) Books, Letters, Documents: The Changing Aesthetics of Texts in Late Print Culture. *Journal of Material Culture* 2: 5–38.

Deetz, J. (1996) *In Small Things Forgotten.* New York: Anchor Books.

Denzin, N. and Lincoln, Y. (eds) (1998) *Collecting and Interpreting Qualitative Materials.* London: SAGE.

Duggan, L. (1989) Was art really the 'book of the illiterate'?. *Word and Image* 5: 227–251.

Fifteenth Census of the United States, 1930. Washington, D.C.: National Archives and Records Administration.

Finn, C. (2007) *Leave Home Stay.* Deal., Kent: *Architecture Week.* http://www.architectureweek. org.uk/event.asp?EventURN=3411&Highlight=1. Accessed 20 March 2009.

Hodder, I. (1998) The Interpretation of Documents and Material Culture. In Denzin and Lincoln (eds) 1998, 110–129.

Jünger, E. (2004) *Storm of Steel.* (translated M. Hofmann). London: Penguin.

Key, M.D. (n.d.) Wartime diary: June–December 1918. Unpublished document.

Martin, A. (ed. R. Van Emden) (2009) *Sapper Martin: The Secret Great War Diary of Jack Martin.* London: Bloomsbury.

Moreland, J. (2001) *Archaeology and Text.* London: Duckworth.

O'Brien, T. (1998) *The Things They Carried.* New York: Broadway Books.

Saunders, N.J. (2002) Bodies of Metal, Shells of Memory: 'Trench Art' and the Great War Re-cycled. In Buchli (ed.) 2002, 175–206.

Saunders, N.J. (2003a) *Trench Art: Materialities and Memories of War.* Oxford: Berg.

Saunders, N.J. (2003b) Crucifix, calvary and cross: materiality and spirituality in Great War Landscapes. *World Archaeology* 35(1): 7–21.

Saunders, N. and Cornish, P. (eds) (2009) *Contested Objects: Material Memories of the Great War.* Abingdon: Routledge.

Schofield, J. (2009) Message and materiality in Mesopotamia, 1916–17: my grandfather's diary, social commemoration and the experience of war. In Saunders and Cornish (eds) 2009, 203–219.

Shanks, M. and Tilley, C. (1987) *Social Theory and Archaeology.* Cambridge: Polity Press.

Smith, L. (2009). *Drawing Fire: The Diary of a Great War Soldier and Artist.* London: Collins.

Trench, R. (2004) *On the Study of Words.* Project Gutenberg E-book.http://www.gutenberg. org/etext/6480 Accessed 20 March 2009.

Tilley, C. (1991) *Material Culture and Text: The Art of Ambiguity.* London: Routledge.

Twelfth Census of the United States, 1900. Washington, D.C.: National Archives and Records Administration.

Winter, J. (1995) *Sites of Memory, Sites of Mourning: The Great War in European Cultural History.* Cambridge: Cambridge University Press.

Womack, T. (2008) *World War I in Georgia.* The New Georgia Encyclopedia online: Georgia Humanities Council and the University of Georgia Press. http://www.georgiaencyclopedia. org/ nge/Article.jsp?id=h-3223. Accessed 2 March 2009.

World War I Selective Service System Draft Registration Cards, 1917–1918. Washington, D.C.: National Archives and Records Administration.

5

Picturing War: an intimate memorial to a lost soldier of the First World War

Matthew Leonard

Material culture tells us much about the time and place from which it originates, and those who made it. With the last of the First World War veterans now gone, we are unable to speak to them about their wartime experiences. Perforce, we must rely on the material legacies of their war if we wish to understand the human dimensions of the world's first global industrial conflict.

Much has been written about tactics and strategy in the First World War, and revisionist arguments still rage over the competence of the generals (e.g. Clark 1991; Corrigan 2003). One consequence is that individual perspectives are often elided in favour of the larger picture afforded by military history. Still today, the war is often seen in terms of its large-scale attacks, victory, defeat, and mass casualties. But casualty lists are composed of individuals, and their stories are a vital part of the so-called Great War for Civilization. By studying their intimate and individual experiences through the material culture they produced, new insights can be gained, and added to the traditional accounts of the conflict.

Here, I explore one particularly informative kind of material culture – the personal diary of William Albert Muggeridge, a family relative, and a Rifleman in the London Irish Regiment. During the Great War, he fought on the Western Front and in the Middle East, and kept a record of his experiences. Unusually, his diary contains no words, only drawings of what he witnessed. It is thus a pictorial account of the conflict through the eyes of its author, a piece of visual material culture in the form of a personal history of the war.

The drawings are an insight into the man, the war itself, and the alien world into which William was thrust. As with all objects, the diary has a 'social life' of its own. Kept with William as a very personal item during the war, it was lost in the years after the conflict, only reappearing recently to narrate the long forgotten stories of its owner. Buried in the attic, its recent 'excavation' has provided us with all that is left of his war experience. There are no photographs of William, he did not keep a written diary (as far we know), and there are no surviving letters home to his family. The only living link to William, his sister-in-law, passed away in 2010. William's notebook is now the sole item which represents the person – a single object standing for a whole life – a step in the process of the transformation of materiality, and of the history of the Great War as it becomes part of an anthropological archaeology of modern conflict.

On 8 September 1940, a German bomb hit the Army Records Office on Arnside Street, London. The building was badly damaged, and along with it the records of the enlisted men that had fought in the First World War. Some 60% of these records were destroyed, including William's, and a large number of the rest were partially ruined by fire and water damage. What could be saved of these records is available to view on microfiche at the National Archives in Kew, in south London, but often the documents are illegible or incomplete. These materials were the only official link between the soldiers and their wartime experiences. The greatest irony of the 8 September attack was that the same nation which had failed to take the lives of these soldiers in the Great War succeeded in stealing their memory and their wartime identity some 20 years later.

Because of the Arnside Street attacks, the items of material culture that give us the greatest insights are often the diaries written and/or drawn by the soldiers themselves. In other words, and in part, the official records of soldiers' experiences have been replaced by their private and 'illegal' documents. The keeping of diaries in the trenches was strictly forbidden, and as a result relatively few of these items survive today and those that do are often anonymous. Some have appeared in print since 1918, and in recent years more have been discovered and published, such as Private Len Smith's *Drawing Fire* (Smith 2009), *Sapper Martin* (Martin 2009), and that of Lieutenant Colonel H.J.H. Davson (Schofield 2009; and see Bagwell, this volume), opening our eyes to the lives of individual soldiers on the front lines. In its own unique way, the current paper adds to this small but expanding canon of published Great War diaries.

Like many objects from the First World War, William's pocketbook is a multi-vocal piece of material culture. It doesn't just tell of the experiences of the author, but also of the manner in which the war was fought, and the sort of men that the soldiers were. Small and personal possessions become important to soldiers in all conflicts, and often give them an escape from the horrors of war, or even define their actions (O'Brien 1991). However, these objects are also transformed by the following generations of the same family, who see in the images and writings a lost connection with their ancestors, who had lived in a time of titanic struggle for life and death (Saunders and Cornish 2009: 3).

Perhaps more importantly, diaries and pocketbooks can also have another purpose: they can serve as a monument to the ordinary soldiers who fought, men quickly forgotten by a new, post-war world – old soldiers in a changing social landscape. The First World War brought with it cataclysmic changes not only in the conduct and scale of warfare but also to society at home. The previously unimaginable casualty figures meant that grieving was carried out on a national scale. Unsurprisingly after the war, this huge loss of life had to be confronted. Hundreds of cemeteries were created in France and Belgium, altering the landscape from one of conflict to one of ritual, sacrifice and remembrance (Winter 1998: 78–116). Giant structures such as the Menin Gate in Ieper (Ypres) in Belgium, and the Monument to The Missing at Thiepval on the Somme in France, were built to dominate the landscape of war. These vast structures of remembrance are inscribed with tens of thousands of names, names for which there are no known graves.

The seemingly endless parade of headstones in the war cemeteries, which themselves are memorials, along with the larger gleaming stone monuments, have focused attention on the dead and the missing. Their names live on in immaculately-kept vessels of grief. The dead were deemed to have been resurrected by their sacrifice, for their death to have transcended their lives. They contributed to what Mosse describes as the 'Cult of The Fallen Soldier' (Mosse 1990: 70–106) and helped the country to heal in the upheaval of the post-war years.

For those who wish to discover the wartime activities of the dead, it is possible to do so. Their records were not kept with those of the living, and so, ironically, they have survived. The memory of the dead lives on, whilst that of the survivors has often disappeared. So how are the 'lost' remembered? They may not have given their lives, but those lives were never the same again. These men have no memorials that are somberly marched past, no nightly ceremonies of remembrance, and no official recognition. Indeed, many returned from the war with no money, no job, and no prospects. They were folded back into society as though nothing had happened. The focus was on the dead and the wounded as the country tried to move on.

The living survivors became, in a sense, a second 'lost generation'. They had spent years fighting for their country, watching friends being mutilated and killed, and living in an environment which civilians could neither understand nor imagine. Diaries like that of William Albert Muggeridge are the 'memorial monuments' of these men. They are their 'structures of remembrance', built not from shining Portland stone, but from fragile paper and ink, and sometimes stained with the mud of the trenches and the tears of their relatives – an evocative and truly multi-sensorial kind of material culture.

William Albert Muggeridge

William Albert Muggeridge was born in 1895. He came from a skilled, working class background, and was an architect by trade. With the First World War in it's second year, he, like many others, including his brother Albert Percy, signed up to go to war. On 25 April 1915 in Chelsea, London, he joined the 18th Battalion of The London Regiment (also known as the London Irish Regiment) as a Rifleman, and was quickly sent overseas. William had no previous military experience and the family does not know why he joined up. Possibly it was what he (and many others) felt that society

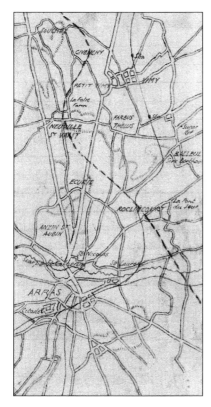

Figure 5.1: (left) Initial map in diary showing the area that William was posted to in 1915. (© author)

Figure 5.2: (above) A dugout in a trench near Arras in 1915. The drawing depicts the gas curtain that protected the inhabitants during a gas attack. (© author)

expected of them. Or maybe it was something else. The war provided a chance to throw off the shackles of a rigid class system, to go on an adventure and become a man. Whatever the reason, he enlisted, and the war consumed his life for the next three and a half years.

Images of a foreign land, 1915–1917

William's first destination was France. The records of exactly where he was sent and what he did are now lost, but from his drawings and the map in his notebook, it is clear that he was in the Arras sector of the Western Front and remained there until 1917 (Figure 5.1).

During his time in France, the London Irish Regiment was involved in the Battle of Loos in September 1915, and the subsequent actions at the Hohenzollern Redoubt in mid-October. In 1916, they were heavily involved in the Battle of The Somme, and fought also at Vimy Ridge, High Wood (which was perhaps their finest hour), and at the Butte de Warlencourt, famous for its crosses and sacred landscape throughout both World Wars. The young architect was now a soldier.

Figure 5.3: Trench 'P75' at Neuville St. Vaast, northern France, in 1916. The gas gong made from an empty shell casing can be seen hung on the trench wall. (© author)

The world that soldiers like William experienced was far removed from the one they knew before the war. It was unlike anything ever seen, a creation of the destruction caused by the mechanical and industrial weaponry of the time, and a far cry from the simulated training 'battlefields' of England. It was a landscape of terror and death, where the usual rules of life did not apply. No doubt William's ability to draw helped him to make sense of this new world, and to record what he saw. Perhaps it even helped him to survive. The dugout picture he produced (Figure 5.2) has the obligatory gas curtain for example, evidence of the lethal environment in which he now lived and worked, where even the air he breathed was a potential enemy.

In William's diary there are many sketches of trenches, such as the one at Neuville St Vaast in 1915 (Figure 5.3). It portrays a relatively clean environment, which seems strange as the area saw such vicious fighting in 1915. The French and the British occupied the region between Mont St Eloi and Neuville St Vaast in the early years of the war. In 1916, as the French were withdrawn to Verdun, the British moved up in greater numbers to take over the line. Although the drawing shows a relatively tidy looking trench, there is evidence of the new horrors of warfare.

A fired artillery shell case hangs on the wall of the trench acting as a gas gong, a warning bell to be sounded when the enemy unleashed this new and deadly weapon. It also shows how the *matériel* of this new type of war varied in nature, and how complex its social lives were. The shell that had originally been used to kill was now being used as a life saving device. These empty shell casings were often converted into trench art (Saunders 2003), then sold or given to relatives of the missing and the dead. They were then frequently used as a 'memory bridge' to aid in the grieving process (Saunders 2004:15; 2010: 55–63), further adding to the biography of the object.

It was during his time in the Neuville St Vaast region that William drew the only picture in his diary of life above ground on the Western Front (Figure 5.4). Interestingly, the title of the drawing explains that it was drawn from the German lines. Perhaps it was sketched after his unit had taken the enemy trenches. Although the front lines remained static for much of the war, this was generally due to the inability to hold

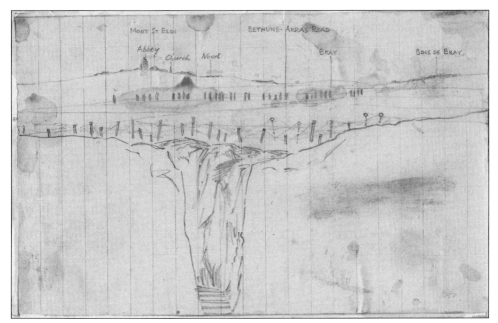

Figure 5.4: View of the Arras–Bethune road from the German lines in 1916. It is the only image from France in the diary that shows the surface rather than the subterranean landscape. (© author)

terrain as opposed to initially taking it. It is revealing that this is his only drawing of life and landscape out in the open while in France. Possibly it was one of the only times that he was able to spend time in relative safety looking above ground, in daylight. Life in the front line trenches was lived below ground, as to look out of the trench, particularly in daytime, could mean instant death from a sniper's bullet.

The defining features of the traditional landscape seem to have disappeared in the drawing, lending credence to the dissolution of form of the front lines that was experienced by the soldiers, but otherwise the drawing seems quite detailed. Trenches, barbed wire barricades, and No Mans Land can all be seen clearly, as can the remains of the abbey at Mont St Eloi. This once beautiful building was not destroyed in the war, but demolished in 1783. During the war, the Germans used it as a ranging point for their artillery, while the British observed the German lines from its towers. Accordingly it was not destroyed by either side.

This drawing, perhaps more than the others, communicates the war to the greatest effect. The paper upon which it is produced is stained with mud from the trenches: one kind of material culture of the Great War layered on another. It forms a palimpsest that communicates memory, identity, and the sensorial reality of life on the Western Front, and is thus an extremely evocative piece of First World War material culture.

At the approximate location from which this picture was drawn are the souterrain caverns of Maison Blanche. These medieval caves were appropriated by the allied

Figure 5.5: An old French Dugout in 1916. The detritus of war is clearly visible. (© author)

armies during the war, and used as a command and control station and as safe troop billets for the front line. The Maison Blanche souterrain is one example of the labyrinth of centuries-old quarries that form an underground web beneath Arras, Vimy Ridge, and the surrounding area (Grieve *et al.* 1936: 156; Saunders 2010: 127; Desfossés *et al.* 2009: 111). The walls of the caverns are covered in thousands of graffiti that range in time from the turn of the twentieth century to modern times. However, the vast majority are from the First World War. A survey of these graffiti by the Durand Group is currently underway (Dolamore *et al.* in prep.). It is possible, though there is no current evidence, that William stayed in one of these caverns when he drew his vista of the front lines.

Today, the large German cemetery at Neuville St Vaast (containing some 44,830 German graves), dominates the local landscape. The grey metal crosses stretch out as far as the eye can see. On the other side of the road, is a large French cemetery along with a smaller British one, showing the huge loss of life that occurred in the area.

There are no drawings of the horror of the trenches in William's diary, even as the war progresses through 1916. This could be due to the fact that the drawings were intended to be shown to family members, and he wanted to spare them the terrible images of modern war. Or perhaps the horror was simply too awful to draw, and his diary was a method of disguising the things he witnessed. Whatever the reason, the trenches drawn in 1916 seem to be more haphazard in nature and certainly darker than those he produced in 1915.

The limited view of landscape visible above the trench walls is shown in Figure 5.5. Above the dug-out, the earth has clearly been repeatedly churned and there is evidence of the detritus of war surrounding the entrance. It shows how men would live below

Figure 5.6: An officer's dugout at Arras, seen as a 'home from home'. (© author)

Figure 5.6: An officer's dugout at Arras, seen as a 'home from home'. (© author)

ground like animals, hiding from the artillery barrages as best they could in a troglodyte world (Fussell 2000: 36).

A contrasting image is shown in the sketch of a dugout which seems almost comfortable and homely, but certainly not the kind of living space afforded to an ordinary soldier (Figure 5.6). It shows how quickly men adapted to this new environment, and perhaps how envious the enlisted men were of the officer's accommodation! These drawings are observations of what William experienced – images of his new world, and an insight into the living conditions endured on the front lines.

The section of William's diary which covers his time in France shows a life lived beneath the surface of the ground, and in the mud and shellfire of the Western Front. His drawings describe the new world that had been created through the destruction that was wrought on the traditional, rural landscape of Northern France. Dugouts gave some protection from the ceaseless artillery fire, while gas curtains and gas warning gongs helped protect against the new weapons of mass destruction.

For a man trained as an architect, and familiar with drawing things that possessed the orderliness of form and structure, it must have been professionally as well as personally disorienting to be in a world with few reference points to normality. Perhaps this is why he drew the things he did. The neat sides of the 'P 75 Trench', or the interiors of dugouts, provided some sense of the normal, of things that could be explained and understood. His one drawing of life above ground details the things he couldn't usually see: a landscape scarred with trenches, barbed wire, and the detritus of war, covering a new landscape which was consuming the missing and the dead.

Figure 5.7: A detailed vista of the city of Jerusalem. The architect in William clearly marvels at the beauty of the city, especially after the confines of the trenches of the Western Front. (© author)

1917, a long way from home

At some point in 1917, William was transferred from the Western Front to the Middle East. The sketches of what he saw there are more numerous and varied than those from France. Indeed, his drawings of Jerusalem are exceptional, particularly the panoramas of the city (Figure 5.7). Ninety percent of a soldier's time is boredom, and being surrounded by such ancient splendours must have been a relief to William, filling his time with drawing rather than thoughts of the next attack or the ever-present risk of death by shellfire that characterised life on the Western Front. Released from the confines of the trenches, William experienced a new lease of life, and his artistic work became more detailed.

   To a young man from London, it must have been a revelation to have been posted to the Middle East, to a place that he had heard so much about, but almost certainly only ever dreamt of seeing at first hand. As an architect, he would have been fascinated by what he witnessed – a world so different to the one he knew in England, and to the one he had experienced in France. The architecture and culture, the expressions of religion, and the magnificent scenery would have been overwhelming. His notebook is packed with drawings inspired by what he was now seeing. The holy places seem to have been a major attraction: sketches of 'Abram's Oak' in Hebron appear more than once along with a section on the *Via Dolorosa* (Figure 5.8).

It is easy to understand how the impact of being in the Holy Land could have rekindled William's own faith. Although he was still in a conflict landscape, its effect was ameliorated by the many other cultural, religious and social features that surrounded him. It was war, but, like his first days in France, it was also new kind of conflict. The fighting in the Middle East could be every bit as deadly as on the Western Front, but the muddy hell of France (Leonard 2010 n.d.) had been replaced with the intense heat, abrasive conditions, and violence of the desert (Schofield 2009: 203–219). However, little appears in William's diary to hint at his fighting experiences in this theatre of the war.

The drawings of the *Via Dolorosa*

Figure 5.8: The Via Dolorosa in Jerusalem. Several drawings of this appear in William's diary. (© author)

(e.g. Figure 5.8) are the first dated images from the Middle East. They appear impressively accurate, and it is clear that, in a sense, the architect in William was competing with the soldier in him. As a religious man, the *Via Dolorosa* would have held special significance for him, especially after having witnessed the horrors of modern warfare. There are, perhaps, parallels between Christ walking to his death, loaded down with the wooden cross (i.e. the means of his own sacrifice), and the soldiers forced to go 'over the top' and walk slowly to their moment of 'resurrection', loaded down with their own heavy packs. The connections with sacrifice and suffering, religion and modern conflict, God and man, are all visible in these drawings. Such images tell us of the landscapes in which William fought, but also reveal the man himself – his beliefs, thoughts, and feelings.

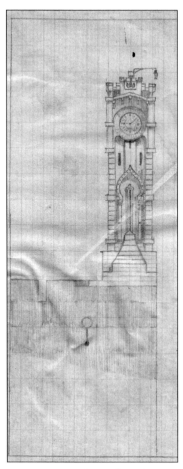

Figure 5.9: The Jaffa Clock in Jerusalem, built by the Ottomans in 1908 and destroyed by the British in 1918. William's drawing shows where he was and when, without the need for official records. (© author)

Material culture as evidence

Although we are unable to ascertain from the official records that William ever went to the Middle East, his (illegally kept) private illustrated diary stands in for his now destroyed official and legal war record. The images in his diary could only have been drawn by someone who was actually there – and thus they are a unique statement of presence.

Perhaps the most insightful images are his drawings of the Jaffa Gate clock tower at Jerusalem. He made several detailed recordings of this structure, which gives us direct evidence not only that he was there, but also precisely when (Figure 5.9). The tower was built by the Ottomans in 1908, but was destroyed by the British in 1918. They considered that it represented the wrong type of history, and that the symbols of the old Ottoman Empire should be replaced.

Although the tower was later rebuilt, it was markedly different in design to the one of 1908–1918. In William's drawing, the pinnacle on top of the tower is bent over, possibly from shellfire. It shares similarities with the famous Madonna and child statue that hung precariously from the Basilica of Notre-Dame de Brebières at Albert on the Somme. William, like every other soldier, would have known that famous French landmark. Rumours were rife that when the statue fell from the Basilica, the war would end and ironically that is what happened in 1918. Whether this connection was made we cannot know, but it is clearly the original Jaffa Gate tower which William drew, and so he must have sketched it before it was destroyed in 1918, indicating that he was there prior to that date.

One of the First World War's most renowned artworks is James McBey's painting of the British General Allenby entering Jerusalem on foot, in December 1917. The clock tower is clearly visible in McBey's painting, and it is possible that William witnessed this moment, standing in the crowd that lined the famous city walls. William's drawing of the tower highlights the importance of material culture. By studying what he drew, we are able to place him in the city without the need for his official war record. The object is able to tell the story of a soldier's war when all other records have disappeared.

Figure 5.10: Britannia on her knees – an evocative image for Britain in the Great War. (© author)

Figure 5.11: 'Salute Death'. (© author)

How will it end?

The last third of William's diary contains general imagery from the conflict which is not location-specific. It is decidedly darker than the rest of his portfolio, and gives an insight into what the years of war were doing to the man. It seems to tell of his thought processes, what he felt, what he sensed. Counter-intuitively, perhaps, sight was the least of the senses used by the soldiers to experience the war in the trenches, particularly on the Western Front (Gygi 2004: 75; see also Das 2005). During the day, the men rested, not daring to look over the trench parapet for fear of the sniper's bullet. Trench warfare was a nighttime world, and it was not long before sight was relegated, and other senses took precedence.

Figure 5.12: 'Death Is A Matter of Time?' (© author)

Touch, smell, and hearing quickly became far more important to survival than seeing. During a battle, little was visible through the smoke, gas masks, and tangible fear. Elements of this can be seen in William's drawings of his time in France. They are almost all subterranean – picturing dugouts and trenches. There was little else to look at. His imagery from the Middle East, by contrast, is not concerned with battle or trench life. Death had long surrounded William, and towards the end of his diary it becomes more evident in his drawings (and so, presumably, his thoughts), as do 'visual questions' as to when the war will end and how?

The first drawing in a sequence concerning death and loss is of Britannia on her knees (Figures 5.10 and 5.11). It was often said at the time that soldiers wondered if the war would ever end. Britain seemed to be on its knees, casualty figures were becoming unsustainable, and the German U-Boat campaign caused extreme shortages on the home front. The war was slowly killing Britain and this is perfectly captured by Williams's image of a humbled Britannia.

This is followed by several different images of a personified Death. That which shows Death saluting is particularly poignant (Figure 5.11), almost as if the artist is portraying the men as already dead, blindly accepting their fate. Interestingly, the figure of Death is saluting with his left hand. In the British army, saluting with the right hand only is permissible, and a left-handed salute is considered an insult. Perhaps this image is a direct insult to the officers who were sending men to die in their thousands, or perhaps it was meant as an insult to death itself.

Looking at these drawings one gets the feeling that death was literally seen as just a matter of time (Figure 5.12). It was everywhere, not just in the daily attrition rate, but also rotting corpses left on the barbed-wire in No Mans Land, and the bodies thrown over the parapet when burial wasn't possible. Body parts, and the dead in the ground, as well as the all-pervasive stench, meant that death became a constant companion to the soldiers and one that was impossible to ignore. It was felt with all the senses, and ingrained into daily life until it became the norm and accepted.

The sketches of Death holding an hourglass show that William may have thought he was already as good as dead and didn't expect to survive the war. These are not images of glory and sacrifice, but of inevitability and defeat. They are representations of what went through the mind of a soldier in this first industrial globalised war, and

Figure 5.13: Seen in Whitehall 1. (© author)

Figure 5.14: Seen in Whitehall 2. (© author)

are arguably more representative than the writings of the famous poets and authors in telling us of the common soldier's experience.

The end?

The last few drawings in William's diary might have been completed after the war. This possibility is suggested by the subject matter, and the fact that colour is used for the first time. These images portray the reality of what happened to men when they returned from war. The officers in these drawings are painted in full uniform and looking smart. The General appears to have a heavy drinker's red nose, perhaps indicating what some of the soldiers thought of their generals (Figures 5.13 and 5.14). The title of these drawings is *Seen in Whitehall*, suggesting that to the average soldier it seemed as though the officer class were able to return to some sort of normality, their life and habits virtually unaffected by the war.

The final drawings are labeled *Seen on the Strand*. They show what happened to the common soldier after the war. In 1914, when the war began, many employers

Figure 5.15: Mad Soldier. (© author)

Figure 5.16: Seen on the Strand. (© author)

promised to keep men's jobs open if they went to fight, as the general view was that the war would not last long. As the years dragged by and the conflict consumed more and more men, these promises were broken. By 1918, Britain was almost bankrupt, many pre-war businesses were ruined (though some thrived), and the jobs the men once had were now taken by women and the men who either did not fight, or who had already been sent home from the front.

Figure 5.15 shows a ragged, poor and mad man, destroyed by the war but still alive: one of the many 'Lost' that society failed to deal with. Often, former soldiers were reduced to selling their medals in order to survive (Figure 5.16), exchanging the objects that attested their participation in the war, their hard-won wartime 'identity', and sometimes also their valour, usually for a handful of small change (see Richardson 2009). These men were destined to fade back into the fabric of everyday post-war life. They have no memorials, grandiose cemeteries, or flamboyant parades. Their records and thereby their memory and wartime identity were stolen from them by a bomb some 20 years later – the Germans managing finally to 'kill' them in the next war.

Conclusion

William's notebook is a startling piece of material culture from the First World War. It is unique in its portrayal of a new and terrible kind conflict, and the effect it had on the men that endured it. With no words, the diary is a distinctive kind of visual material culture which allows for a nuanced investigation into the mind of its creator. It reflects the varied physical settings in which the conflict occurred, and also hints at the structure of his everyday life. The relationship between place, memory, religion, life, death, and material culture are left in his sketches for posterity – an embodiment of the notion that a picture is worth a thousand words.

This kind of material culture object sits alongside the official war diaries, or often takes their place entirely, and thus provides a very personal experience of the First World War which complements but also contrasts with the educated writings or 'high art' of the conflict. Diaries allow participation in the soldiers' war and aid in its understanding; they are a uniquely informative resource which demands recognition alongside the more traditional material used by military historians.

The drawings in William's diary describe his war, what he thought and saw and felt. It is an object which defines his identity as an individual. Perhaps more importantly, such uniquely personal items of material culture stand as a monument to the Lost, to the men who faded back into society and whose memories were gradually eroded by the lack of official records (and by another World War): something which they had all but given their lives to ensure would never happen again.

Bibliography

Clark, A. (1991) *The Donkeys. A History of the British Expeditionary Force in 1915*. London: Pimlico.

Corrigan, G. (2003). Mud, Blood and Poppycock. London: Cassell.

Das, S. (2005) *Touch and Intimacy in First World War Literature*. New York: Cambridge University Press.

Desfossés Y., Jacques, A. and Prilaux, G. (2009) *Great War Archaeology*. Rennes. Editions Quest-France.

Fussell, P. (2000) *The Great War and Modern Memory*. Oxford: Oxford University Press.

Grieve, W.G. and Newman, B. (1936) Tunnellers; *The Story of the Tunnelling Companies, Royal Engineers, During the Great War*. London: Herbert Jenkins.

Gygi, F. (2004) Shattered Experiences – Recycled relics. Strategies of representation and the legacy of the Great War. In Saunders (ed.) 2004, 72–89.

Leonard, M. (n.d) Muddy Hell: The realities of the Western Front conflict landscape during the Great War. Paper presented at the session '20th and 21st Century Conflict: Contested Legacies', at the Thirty-Second Annual Conference of the Theoretical Archaeology Group (TAG), University of Bristol, 17–19 December 2010.

Martin, A. (ed. R. Van Emden) (2009) *Sapper Martin: The Secret Great War Diary of Jack Martin*. London: Bloomsbury.

Mosse, G.L. (1990) *Fallen Soldiers, Reshaping the Memory of the World Wars*. Oxford: Oxford University Press.

O'Brien, T. (1991) *The Things They Carried*. London: Flamingo.

Richardson, M. (2009) Medals, memory and meaning: symbolism and cultural significance of Great War medals. In Saunders and Cornish (eds) 2009, 104–118.

Saunders, N.J. (2003) *Trench Art: Materialities and Memories of War*. Oxford: Berg.

Saunders, N.J. (ed.) (2004) *Matters of Conflict. Material Culture, Memory and the First World War*. Abingdon: Routledge.

Saunders, N.J. (2010) *Killing Time: Archaeology and the First World War*. (2nd edn). Stroud: History Press.

Saunders, N.J. and Cornish, P. (2009) Introduction. In Saunders and Cornish (eds) 2009, 1–10.

Saunders, N.J. and P. Cornish (eds.) (2009) *Contested Objects: Material Memories of the Great War*. Abingdon: Routledge.

Schofield, J. (2009). Message and Materiality in Mesopotamia, 1916–1917: My grandfather's diary, social commemoration and the experience of war. In Saunders and Cornish (eds) 2009, 203–219.

Smith, L. (2009). *Drawing Fire: The Diary of a Great War Soldier and Artist*. London: Collins.

Winter J. (1998). *Sites of Memory, Sites of Mourning: The Great War in European Cultural History*. Cambridge: Cambridge University Press/Canto.

6

The Battlefield in Miniature, or the multi-locational town of Messines

Martin Brown

Two scale models of the Belgian town of Messines and the ridge on which it sits were created by military modellers toward the end of the Great War of 1914–18. The first was built at Petit Pont in Belgium prior to the Battle of Messines in June 1917, but a second, more detailed and durable model, was constructed in early 1918 at an Army camp in Staffordshire, in northern England.

Modelling terrain

Terrain models built in the theatre of war and associated with military operations have an immediate and didactic use; they allow officers to pick out salient features and landmarks, to demonstrate movement and to identify objectives. Today, they can be created using Geographic Information Systems (GIS) to drape layers of data, including aerial photographs or LiDAR[1] data, over base mapping, including contours that can provide 3D renderings (e.g. Stal *et al.* 2010). However, when and where computers have not been available, the simplest and most effective way to depict terrain in three dimensions is by means of the model.

The origin of such models is unknown, but examples that predate the Great War include miniature representations of French fortifications created in the seventeenth century and associated with Vauban, the master of fortification (1633–1707). Some of these models are displayed today in the *Hotel Des Invalides* military museum in Paris (Vauban.asso.fr). These models, created in an age before contour maps, allow an overview of the landscape which renders accessible terrain which geography and enemy troops might otherwise deny. Indeed, such models permit a view impossible before the aeroplane, and, as Susan Stewart has observed, the model, or miniature, offers a complete contrast to the partial view that one might have in the city (Stewart 1993: 2).

Views could often be even more limited in the trenches of the Western Front, where to raise one's head above the parapet was to invite sudden death. Even attempts to use mechanical aids could end in disaster, as O.G.S. Crawford – the pioneer of aerial photography in archaeology – discovered during his service in the Royal Engineers (Hauser 2008: 32). By contrast, the terrain model allows an expansive view, in contrast to the space confined by the mud or chalk walls of the trench. Such models allow the viewer to experience the birds-eye or aviators-eye view.

Consequently, many examples of terrain models were made during the Great War. They came in many materials, including modelling-clay and wood, and some survive today in the Imperial War Museum (Paul Cornish, pers. comm.). The models were produced in a variety of scales, up to tens of metres square, depicting whole sectors of battlefield. These examples included the Messines model, and another created before the Battle of Cambrai (Peter Simkins, pers. comm.). Both models date to 1917.

Even today, impromptu models made from immediately-available materials can be used for military briefings, where computer technology or suitable data are unavailable. They may also be used to illustrate tactical points for the public: archaeologist Stuart Ainsworth built a model of Second World War German flak positions for a *Time Team* television programme exploring 'occupation archaeology' on Jersey (*Time Team* 2011). In summer 2010, the author watched a re-enactment group recreating 1940 Home Guard training in urban warfare, employing a model based on that used by Tom Wintringham at Osterley Park, and shown in the illustrated weekly magazine *Picture Post* (Wintringham 1940: 295).

The original Home Guard model is a generic depiction of an English village, but it shares with the Vauban models a didactic purpose which goes beyond the immediate tactical and operational considerations of their makers – the primary function of the Petit Pont and Cambrai examples. As with the *Time Team* model, they are intended to instruct the viewer in the military occupation and exploitation of ground, and while the *Time Team* model was made for entertainment, it too demonstrated this in a form which would have been familiar to the soldiers stationed on Jersey during its occupation.

Both models of Messines considered here embody the didactic nature of these manifestations of *matériel* culture. However, the meanings of both models are mutable and manifold, as is the value placed upon them over time. Although both depict the same piece of Belgium, and are products of the 1917 Battle of Messines, there are marked differences between them.

The Battle of Messines

The Belgian town of Messines is situated on the crest of the low ridge that bears its name, overlooking land to the south and west. In 1914, it was a market centre dominated by its sixteenth-century abbey church and the Royal Institute – an eighteenth-century orphanage which had become a well-regarded school (Chielens *et al.* 2006: 202–203). The location of the town and the ridge were both strategically important in 1914. As the British Expeditionary Force (BEF) withdrew from battles at Mons and Le Cateau, the town was defended in the face of the German advance before it was finally lost on 31 October 1914 (Oldham 1998: 15–18).

The British withdrawal from the ridge left the Germans in possession of a deep curving salient running from Ploegsteert in the south, to St Eloi east of the city of Ypres, before turning north, giving the Germans total control of the ridges from which they could overlook and dominate the Allies (Keegan 1998: 142–146). The ridge afforded the Germans a strong defensive position and provided a good vantage point for observation into the British Sector around Ypres.

Ypres itself sat at the centre of a British occupied salient in the battlefield, and the ridge overlooked the southern part of that salient. Any attempt to enlarge the salient would have required the capture of the ridge as a precursor to a wider offensive in front, and to the north of Ypres.

The Battle of Messines was fought between the 7 and 14 June 1917, under the command of General Plumer, Commander of the British Second Army. Plumer's mixed forces of British and Imperial troops, included II Anzac (Australian and New Zealand Army Corps). It was II Anzac which was tasked with operating in the southern sector of the front, from Factory Farm (Ploegsteert) to Messines itself. The battle included the assault and capture of the village which was to be the responsibility of the New Zealand Division. The Division included 3rd Battalion New Zealand Rifle Brigade (Passingham 2004: 186).

The assault began with the detonation of 19 large mines that were placed to breach the German line and shatter the morale of its defenders (Barton *et al.* 2004: 184–195). This worked so well that in some parts of the line there were reports of attackers moving forward relatively unopposed. The New Zealanders scaled the front face of the ridge, fighting through trench lines as they did so, before engaging in close-quarter urban warfare of a character more consistent with the Second World War and modern operations, than the Great War trenches of Flanders.

Although shaken by the artillery barrage and nearby mine explosions, the German defenders of the town managed to recover, and sought to prevent the capture of Messines, resulting in a hard-fought action. During the course of the attack a number of machine guns were captured and prisoners taken, including the German Garrison Commander and his staff. An indication of the severity of the fighting is witnessed by the number of commendations for the Victoria Cross, as well as the numerous other decorations won by those involved. One such commendation went to Lance Corporal Frickleton of the Rifle Brigade, who won the Victoria Cross for silencing a machine gun that was causing heavy casualties (www.NZhistory.net). Through the town, the fighting was sharp and victory swift – apparently as much the result of good briefing and training of troops as of the psychological effect of mines and barrage (Passingham 2004: 105).

The Messines model at Petit Pont

Prior to the battle, a model of the Messines battlefield was built at Petit Pont, near Ploegsteert in Belgium. It was used to brief troops, showing them the lines of German defences and the buildings that had been reinforced as strong-points. It appears in a number of photographs and film images taken by official photographers (e.g. AWM E00632). Many troops visited the model during preparations for the attack, and film shows Australian and British troops studying the model (*ibid.*) – and it is likely that troops attacking in the sector depicted were all given an opportunity to study the model.

The principal function of the model was instructional, showing the men their theatre of operations, but it also served as a propaganda tool and a space in which propaganda is also performance, both of which would serve to boost morale. Photographs in the Australian War Memorial (AWM E00631) show Captain Albert Jacka of 14 Battalion, First Australian Division at Petit Pont (www.AWM.gov.au). He is studying trench maps and the model.

Jacka was already a household name in Australia, having won the Victoria Cross at Gallipoli (www.Anzacsite.au). The message inherent in the images of the model, and of Jacka's presence, seems clear: despite the setbacks of Gallipoli, Arras, and the Somme, this attack would be different. The messages for viewers appear to be that the men were well prepared, having been briefed on the task ahead of them and that they included, and were led, by heroes like Jacka who knew how to win.

Currently, it is difficult to say more about the Petit Pont model. Historical records relating to its construction have not been found, and the artefact itself is not thought to survive, although its location has been identified. The model was intended for a single use: once the battle was over its instructional value ceased, so it was not designed to be permanent. In addition, it is difficult to see detail in the images because they were carefully framed and presented in order to deny intelligence to the enemy. Had too much of the terrain been visible, then the point of attack would have been obvious, while uniform and equipment details would have indicated the forces involved to an enemy intelligence officer. As a result, it is difficult to identify features on the terrain model and attempts to adduce scale have so far proved fruitless.

Belgium in Staffordshire

After the battle, a second model was created, this time in England! Unlike the Petit Pont

Figure 6.1: The Messines terrain model at Brocton Camp, Staffordshire, England, in 1918. (© J. Whitehouse)

example, it appears, from its component parts, to have been made with permanence in mind.

Between September 1917 and May 1919, the New Zealand Rifle Brigade (NZRB) was based at Brocton Camp, one of two major Army training camps on Cannock Chase, in Staffordshire (Whitehouse and Whitehouse 1996: 26), and it was here that the second, semi-permanent model of the Messines battlefield was created.

Two camps – Brocton and Rugeley – were constructed in late 1914 at Cannock Chase (*ibid.*: 3). They were part of an expansion of training facilities designed to accommodate large numbers of volunteers to the British Army following the outbreak of war with Germany (Simkins 2007: 231–244). Brocton Camp could hold 40,000 men, while Rugeley could accommodate 20,000. The camps were supported by significant new infrastructure, including sewage and water systems, and had their own electricity generation. Roads and a railway spur enabled troops and supplies to be brought to what had previously been a relatively remote piece of heathland. In addition, training facilities were also created, including rifle and bombing ranges, and networks of practice trenches that replicated the field fortifications that characterised the conflict (War Office 1921).

Although initially used for training infantry units from the Northern Command, Brocton Camp was sub-divided by mid-1916 when part of it became a Prisoner of War camp (Whitehouse and Whitehouse 1996: 26). By 1917, there was spare capacity in the camp, and the NZRB were transferred there from Sling Camp on the major training area of Salisbury Plain. Sling was the principal base for other New Zealand troops in Britain (James 1987: 112).

Figure 6.2: A section of the Brocton Camp terrain model during its investigation by the author, who is seen making a plan of the visible feature. (© author)

The 5th Battalion New Zealand Rifle Brigade was based at Brocton Camp, which became the reception centre for training new drafts of men fresh from New Zealand, between September 1917 and May 1919 (Whitehouse and Whitehouse 1996: 26). During their time at Brocton, men from the Rifle Brigade are known to have created their own version of the Petit Pont model (NZEF 1918: 257). It shows the location of their significant, recent victory during the Battle of Messines in June 1917.

For the NZRB, the primary, didactic function of the model is emphasised in this account:

> 'We have practically completed a model of a sector of ground taken from a map dimensions 40 yards square – representing 2,000 yards of ground in Belgium. The scale of the plan is 1 in 50, and the altitude 1 in 25. It was built under instructions from Lieutenant-Colonel J. G. Roache, for the use of the Regimental School, to instruct officers and NCOs in Topography. It is a facsimile of the old battlefield of Messines.' (NZEF 1918: 257)

The model includes an area of some 35 × 32 m. It appears to have been constructed on a terrace which has been cut around three sides into the natural subsoil. This served to create a raised area which may have been used as a viewing platform. A ridge occupies the centre of the model on a mound representing high ground, and it was here that the town was constructed. There is also a smaller ridge running at a tangent to the main ridge along the western side of the model itself, which may represent a drainage gulley around the base of the model.

Limited excavation in 2007 demonstrated that the trenches were formed in concrete and set into a cement skim surface over the soil which had been sculpted to represent the rise of the Messines Ridge. Brick-ends and concrete were used to make model buildings, while roads were laid out in pebbles (Brown *et al.* 2008). Examination of photographs suggests that hedges and woodland were also depicted, and contour lines may have been incised in the cement surface (Staffspasttrack.org.uk). The model was

Figure 6.3: A section of the Brocton Camp terrain model following excavation and assessment in 2007. It is possible to see trenches, a road, and the railway line. These features allowed identification of the location depicted on maps and aerial photographs made during the war, and show the level of accuracy to which the makers aspired. (© author)

situated outside Battalion headquarters, and was visible from the Prisoner of War camp that shared the site (*ibid.*).

At the time of its creation in summer 1918, there was no suggestion that the war would end in November that year: German troops still occupied parts of France and Belgium, and were still offering stiff resistance to the Allies, having already forced them back in a series of Spring offensives. Indeed, the Germans had retaken Messines in April 1918 during these offensives, and it was only recaptured by the Allies at the end of September that year (Oldham 1998: 116–119). Given the expectation that the war would continue, and that the NZRB were continuing to train men at Brocton, it is reasonable to assume that the principal aim of the model was to allow training drafts to study a successful action in detail, as the quotation above suggests.

By studying the model, new recruits could be taught an understanding of the terrain, the types of defences erected, and the way in which both factors impacted on the operation, and how the problems they presented were overcome. This method still underpins military training today, and tours of historic battlefields are common, as is the study of historic actions in the classroom, where problems and solutions can be discussed (Peter Caddick-Adams, pers. comm.).

The Brocton model allowed troops to 'visit' the battlefield, which was still in the combat zone, and learn from it in safety via a three-dimensional representation. The semi-permanent form of the model suggests that its architects foresaw repeated use over some time, unlike the original at Petit Pont.

While the principal aim of the model may have been instructional, it had a complementary role contributing to the Rifle Brigade's *esprit de corps*. Whether this was a deliberate function of the model is unknown, but the importance placed on symbols and tradition by the military suggests that such value would have been exploited by trainers. Many modern Army units visit battlefields that have a historical significance for them, partly for instruction, but also because of their contribution to what the British Ministry of Defence (MOD) refers to as 'History and Honour' (www.mod.uk).

The Great War includes a number of successful operations across difficult terrain, but the capture of Messines was almost exclusively a New Zealand victory, where unit battle honours and personal decorations were won and the Germans decisively beaten. Seen in this light, the model may also be regarded as a trophy, signifying and embodying the achievement and glory of the units involved, including, or perhaps particularly, the NZRB. The particular pride felt by the Rifle Brigade reflects their crucial role in the battle and the fact that they were a newly raised formation who had no previous battle honours to proclaim their prowess, unlike older regiments.

To the men arriving at Brocton for training, the model served as inspiration and exhortation to emulate and exceed the achievements of their comrades. Those comrades included the men who had taken Messines in record time, at minimal loss, and had a Victoria Cross winner in their ranks. This use of the model as inspiration echoes the public presence of Jacka VC at Petit Pont.

These ideas of ethos and inspiration are manifested in the model, making the battlefield a sacred space where their unit had shed its blood, won honour, and gained victory. The model may also be suggested as a memorial, representing the killing space where other men from the tribe had fallen. Both Richard Holmes (Holmes 2004: 75–79) and the author (Brown in press) have discussed the implications of the military as a collection of tribes, each jealous of the others' honour and traditions. Individual unit identity and pride may be manifest in many ways, from formal memorials and artwork to graffiti (Saunders 2001: 97–98; Cockroft *et al.* 2006: 3–7, 31–34). In this context, it is possible to characterise the model as hugely meaningful. It depicts the scene of their triumph, symbolises their maturity as a fighting unit, memorialises their fallen, and in doing all these things it seeks to inspire their comrades.

That the New Zealanders themselves saw this model as something more than a teaching aid is demonstrated by the gift of the model to the town of Stafford by the departing soldiers at the end of the war (Whitehouse and Whitehouse 1996: 26). If the model had served only for instruction, its continued existence would not have concerned the men, but this act suggests that it had been imbued with pride and symbolic status over and above its functionality. This can only have come from the fact that it depicted what would have been described as 'our' victory. The creation, maintenance and continued survival of the 'Bulford Kiwi' – a chalk-cut depiction of the New Zealand national bird carved into a scarp on Salisbury Plain – may also be seen within this context of Dominion troops seeking to commemorate their contribution to the Victory of 1918 (www.news.bbc.co.uk).

The physical location of the Brocton Camp model is also significant. It was located outside Battalion headquarters but was also clearly visible from the Prisoner of War camp that occupied part of the site from 1916 onwards. The captured town occupies a high profile position outside the centre of command for the unit. The commanding officers are constantly reminded of their task in training soldiers but they have also appropriated Messines by the direct physical relationship between their administrative centre and the manifestation of the battle honour. In addition, they have created a trophy that proclaims triumphalism over the vanquished enemy by setting before his eyes a representation of the ground that he was forced to yield.

For occupants of Brocton Camp, the model remains meaningful, but the meanings are mutable and may be renegotiated by each viewer: a soldier being instructed in front of the model may view it differently to one being marched past it on the way to see the Battalion Commander as a result of an indiscretion. Similarly, the German viewers would have regarded the model with a variety of emotions that would have been affected by their experience of the war, their place of capture, and whether the identification of the actual town on which the model was based was widely known by the prisoners. If the Germans were aware that the model depicted Messines it would also have embodied NZRB triumphalism over their enemies and captives.

For both sides, how they related to the model may also have been conditioned by experience in constructing the model. For example, local folklore, as told to the author, suggests that German POWs were used to create the model. A photograph in the National Library of New Zealand seems to confirm this (Ref:1/2-013854-G. Object #76884) as it appears to show two German soldiers working on the model. Such activity would have emphasized the propaganda message of the model, for prisoners and captors alike.

Following the departure of the NZRB, the Brocton model became a curiosity, but a lack of management resulted in deterioration until 1931, when a local journalist revived interest in it (Pitman 1931: 15). Following his newspaper articles, local Boy Scouts cleaned the model, and a member of the Royal British Legion acted as an attendant, charging a small fee for a guided tour (Whitehouse and Whitehouse 1996: 21–22). The model had now passed from being a meaningful artefact for the New Zealanders to a period of forgetting and decay, before being remembered and restored by the local community.

This gave the model a new identity. It served now as a curiosity and a tourist attraction, giving local people a chance to glimpse an idea of the battlefield with its network of trenches. Some 15 years after the events it commemorated, the model could now be seen as a symbolic space where those who had served or lost loved ones on the Western Front could go to gaze on the alien world of trench warfare. Those too young to have experienced the war, but who had grown up in its shadow, could wonder at the alteration of earth represented and symbolised in this miniature, where the networks of trenches and the fortified town were rendered in three dimensions.

Thus, the Brocton model developed a new power to evoke memory and emotion, not that of Riflemen reflecting on their own experiences, but rather the wider population affected by the Great War. As Susan Stewart has observed 'The experience of the object … is saturated with meanings that will never be fully revealed' (Stewart 1993: 133). These models have enormous evocative power, whether for anyone who experienced the Front, or for those seeking to understand it. Once again, whether soldier or civilian, the model afforded an aerial perspective, albeit of a facsimile miniature, where such a bird's eye view of the original was available to a privileged few. Moreover, it could be said to afford the opportunity to visit the battlefields which was unavailable to the great majority of Britons in the inter-war years.

The model moved from being a memorial structure gifted by its creators, and symbolising the place of loss on the battlefield, to a memorial marking of their presence and absence in the landscape of Staffordshire. It then commemorated not only the NZRB, but also the Fallen, evoked in the minds of visitors to the site during the inter-war years. Today the memorial aspect of the model is unclear, but conversations with visitors suggest that in some sense the inter-war relationship is being reproduced. As awareness of the model grows it will be possible to gauge changing responses.

Modelling Armageddon

The creation of this miniaturised segment of the Western Front represents the vision of its commissioning agent and a significant input of material and human resources during a time of war. The location of the model at the heart of the NZRB part of the camp, and the scale of the undertaking, underline its official status and suggest that its creation was imbued with both use and meaning. While the Brocton model may be an unusual manifestation of *matériel* culture away from the theatre of operations, and one which embodies a number of meanings, as will be seen, it is nevertheless part of a continuum of military model-making which has unknown origins, and continues today, whether in desert sand or on the computer screen.

The accuracy of both models in depicting the terrain and German defences around Messines are a testament to a number of specific circumstances of the Great War. By the time of the Messines battle, the Royal Flying Corps (RFC) had only been in existence for five years, and powered flight was not much older. In addition, photography was still a relatively new technology, and required cumbersome and heavy apparatus. Despite this, the RFC had spent much of the war engaged in reconnaissance flights, traversing and photographing trench lines, gun batteries, supply dumps, camps and the other infrastructures of war behind the battle-zone (De Meyer 2006: 143–144). Such flights might be for immediate intelligence about enemy activity, or to maintain up-to-date records of the state and position of enemy works. Along the front line, information was gathered on new construction and the strengthening of defences.

The ability to fly directly above an enemy's position and accurately record by photograph revolutionised warfare, allowing commanders access to more accurate information about their opponents positions than ever before. This information could be used for detailed planning of both defence and attack. For the former, unusual and significant enemy activity might indicate an attack, while in preparing an offensive, information on the strength and location of successive lines of opposing trenches and the strong-points within them were issues to be factored into any operations. It also allowed the artillery to plot the coordinates of their fire and to assess the impact of a barrage subsequent to action.

Yet it was not the photos alone that allowed the transfer of information – it was the maps created from them by men of the Royal Engineers who overlaid military information onto existing surveys and who undertook new mapping where necessary and feasible (Chasseaud 1991: 7). Such was the importance of these maps, constantly reviewed and revised to reflect new information from the front, that by 1918 the British Army alone had produced some 34,000 maps (*ibid.*: 11). Crucially, these maps enabled the general officer to consider large spaces at one time and enabled the officer in the line to see what lay beyond his own trenches.

The nature of trench warfare is concealment whereby the soldier remains the man in the earth to avoid the bursting shell and flying bullet. To be able to see is to be exposed, and to be exposed is to be in danger. For many, no-man's-land between the trenches and the ground beyond was never seen in daylight. For a few, there were opportunities to look 'over the top' of the trench parapet: Engineer officer and archaeologist O.G.S. Crawford used a periscope to see ground beyond the British lines and operated a camera extended above the parapet to create panoramas, until this camera itself fell victim to a German sniper looking for movement in the British trenches (Hauser 2008: 32).

Indeed, the use and development of technology associated with mapping was itself a product of the trenches that define the Great War on the Western Front in popular imagination. Had the war not settled into the stalemate of trench warfare toward the end of 1914, there would have been no impetus for such detailed survey and re-survey. Examination of British military mapping during the mobile phases at the beginning and end of the war both show the use of aerial reconnaissance for situation reporting on the location of enemy troops (De Meyer 2006: 143), and, in 1918, as a tactical tool identifying targets for almost immediate action (Chasseaud 1991: 11). The nature of the war defined its requirement of maps.

The availability of maps enabled the model makers at both Petit Pont and Brocton to accurately render the terrain of the battlefield and the town at its heart. In light of this, these tactical models are the product of cutting edge technology in 1917, including aerial reconnaissance and mapping for the guns of the Royal Artillery. The model could be said to epitomise the industrial power of the war, as much as the pulverised landscape that was its ultimate manifestation (Brown 2008: 196–200) and of which the model, as preparation for battle, was a part.

The value of the terrain model is that unlike a map, it gives a three dimensional depiction of the ground. As discussed above, this provides the soldier with an extra set of information in understanding and planning to operate on the ground. Unfortunately, models are, indeed, only a depiction of the landscape. They can never be accurate and are condemned to remain simulacra. The inherent problem with depiction of terrain was neatly summarised by Lewis Carroll in *Sylvie and Bruno Concluded* (1982 [1893]). One of the characters (Mein Herr) explains that when making accurate maps a desire for increased accuracy led to ever-larger scale maps:

> 'We very soon got to six yards to the mile. Then we tried a hundred yards to the mile. And then came the grandest idea of all! We actually made a map of the country, on the scale of a mile to the mile!' (Carroll 1982: 727)

What is true of the paper map is also true of the model. Although both the Petit Pont and the Brocton models are representations of the battlefield that include defences, field boundaries, buildings and the general sweep of the landscape – small features of terrain, such as the re-entrants in the Messines Ridge immediately south of the town, are not sufficiently large to be depicted. Nevertheless, such a feature has the potential to disrupt the sweep of an attack if men blunder into unfamiliar territory and become disorientated. Given that the Messines attack happened in the dark at 03:30 and while shells and bullets were flying, the potential for confusion, if not disaster was high. At Brocton, the contour lines appear to be rendered in the cement surface of the model but at Petit Pont this was not the case. Fortunately for the attackers, the shock and awe inspired by the mines and barrage, as well as the impetus of the attack carried the New Zealanders forward without mishap, or at least misfortune on a scale more generally associated with the Great War.

Continuing meaning

While the Brocton model may have been all-but forgotten since the Second World War, it has retained its interest for Great War historians. In recent years, local researchers have re-located and investigated the site, leading to the Birmingham Archaeology survey undertaken to provide archaeological condition data on the site and to assess its significance and archaeological potential (Brown *et al.* 2008). This has coincided with the wider growth of interest in the Great War.

Staffordshire County Council has undertaken initiatives to interpret and commemorate the conflict and its casualties, including a display in the Cannock Chase visitor centre and the rebuilding of a 1915 barrack hut. The Cannock Chase area also includes two military cemeteries, one run by the Commonwealth War Graves Commission and associated with the camps, and a second, larger, German cemetery, that is the last resting place of servicemen and internees from German forces of both world wars.

This physical and cultural-memorial environment frames the model anew. Once again, it has become not only a curiosity, as it was during the inter-war years, but also a memorial, though it now commemorates men whose military service took place almost a century ago and who are largely unknown to modern visitors. The local County Council nevertheless reports that descendants of NZRB men are regular, if not numerous, visitors. As the 2014 centenary of the Great War approaches, the local authority is considering the future of the model, both as an archaeological monument, and a significant heritage asset which embodies multiple meanings. Meanwhile, the investigation of the Petit Pont model in Belgium is planned as part of a wider archaeological project which explicitly includes remembrance within its objectives (www.Plugstreet-archaeology.com).

The terrain models of Messines have created representations of a part of the Belgian battlefields that could be used as training aids prior to military operations. However, both clearly embody mutable meanings that transcend the purely didactic: as a contemporary propaganda message, such as that created by Jacka's presence at Petit Pont, or as inspiration for a specific group, such as the NZRB recruits.

Once the models enter a wider environment and interact with groups outside their immediate military context, then meanings become more complex and mutable. These could include the relationship between the Brocton model and the German prisoners, or ongoing dialogues between the local people within narratives of remembrance, heritage protection and presentation. While the landscape of Messines may have been reduced in scale at both sites examined in this paper, the embodiment of issues relating to use, meaning and ownership of those miniature landscapes are no less significant and the narratives no less engaged.

Note

1 Light Detection and Ranging: a laser-based surveying tool.

Bibliography

Anzacsite.au: http://www.anzacsite.gov.au/5environment/vc/biography.html Accessed 16 February 2011.

AWM.gov.au: http://www.awm.gov.au/people/226.asp Accessed 2 March 2011.

Barton, P., Doyle, P. and Vandewalle J. (2004) *Beneath Flanders Fields*. Staplehurst: Spellmount.

Brown, M. (2008) A Pulverized Landscape? Landscape-scale Destruction and the Western

Front During the Great War 1914–18. In L. Rakoczy (ed.), *The Archaeology of Destruction*, 195–209. Newcastle-upon-Tyne: Cambridge Scholars.

Brown, M. (in press) Whose Heritage? Archaeology, Heritage and the Military. In P. Stone (ed.), *Cultural Heritage, Ethics and the Military*, 129–138. Woodbridge: Boydell.

Brown M., Kincey, M. and Nichol, K. (2008) *Messines Model, Cannock Chase, Staffordshire: Monument Assessment 2007*. Birmingham Archaeology Project Report 1735. University of Birmingham.

Carroll, L. (1982) [1893] *The Complete Illustrated Works*. New York: Gramercy Books.

Chasseaud, P. (1991) *Topography of Armageddon*. Lewes: Mapbooks.

Chielens, P. Dedooven, D. and Decoodt, H. (2006) *De Laatste Getuige*. Tielt: Lannoo.

Cockroft, W., Devlin, D., Schofield, J. and Thomas, R.J.C. (2006) *War Art*. York: Council for British Archaeology.

De Meyer, M. (2006) Lluchtfoto's uit de eerste wereldoorlog: vroeger en nu. In P. Chielens, D. Dendooven and H. Decoodt (eds), *De Laatste Getuige*, 143–146. Tielt: Lannoo.

Hauser, K. (2008) *Bloody Old Britain*. Cambridge: Granta.

Holmes, R. (2004) *Tommy, The British Soldier on the Western Front 1914–1918*. London: HarperCollins.

James, N.D.G. (1987) *Plain Soldiering*. Salisbury: Hobnob.

Keegan, J. (1998) *The First World War*. London: Hutchinson.

NZEF. (1918) *Chronicles of the New Zealand Expeditionary Force* 4(47), 5 July, 257.

NZhistory.net http://www.nzhistory.net.nz/media/photo/samuel-frickleton Accessed 1 March 2011.

Oldham, P. (1998) *Messines Ridge*. Barnsley: Pen and Sword.

Passingham, I. (2004) *Pillars of Fire, The Battle of the Messines Ridge June 1917*. Stroud: Sutton.

Pitman, W. (1931) A War-time village on Cannock Chase. *Express & Star*, 18 April 1931: 12.

Saunders, N.J. (2001) *Trench Art: A Brief History and Guide, 1914–1939*. Barnsley: Leo Cooper.

Schofield, J. (2004) *Modern Military Matters*. York: Council for British Archaeology.

Simkins, P. (2007) *Kitchener's Army*. Barnsley: Pen and Sword.

Staffspasttrack.org.uk http://www.staffspasttrack.org.uk/exhibit/chasecamps/archaeology.htm Accessed on 24 January 2011.

Stewart, S. (1993) *On Longing: Narratives of the Miniature, the Gigantic, the Souvenir, the Collection*. Durham (NC): Duke University Press.

Time Team. (2011) *Hitler's Island Fortress*. Videotext Communications for UK Channel 4 TV, Broadcast 27 February 2011.

Vauban.asso.fr: http://www.vauban.asso.fr/plansreliefs.htm Accessed 16 February 2011.

War Office. (1921) *Field Fortifications, All Arms*. London: HMSO.

Whitehouse, C.J. and Whitehouse, G.P. (1996) *A Town for Four Winters, Great War Camps of Cannock Chase*. Brocton: Privately published.

Wintringham, T. (1940) The Home Guard Can Fight. *Picture Post* 8, 21 September 1940: 12.

www.mod.uk http://www.mod.uk/DefenceInternet/DefenceNews/HistoryAndHonour/ accessed 24 January 2011.

www.news.bbc.co.uk http://news.bbc.co.uk/1/hi/engoland/wiltshire/6748189.stm Accessed 16 March 2011.

www.plugstreet-archaeology.com: http://www.plugstreet-archaeology.com/index.php Accessed 1 February 2011.

Remembering the 'Doughboys': American memorials of the Great War

Charles D. Eavenson II

In Europe, Canada, Australia, and New Zealand, the social and cultural role of First World War monuments has received considerable attention in recent years (e.g. Black 2004; King 1998; Winter 1995). By contrast, the commemorative materialities and sacred landscapes honouring the United States' 'Doughboys' have seen comparatively few attempts at description or analysis (see Budreau 2010; Trout 2010).

The term 'Doughboy' is the nickname given to the American infantry of the Great War. Several legends purport to explain the term, including that the appearance of dust on their brown uniforms resembled uncooked dough, or that the shape of their buttons resembled balls of dough (Hanlon 2010). The exact origin nevertheless remains unclear. The Doughboys and their uniforms (with the M1917 helmet) came to represent heroic values and patriotism for Americans during and after the war. Their appearance has been incorporated into statues and friezes across the nation, in much the same way as statues of the British Tommy represented the same ideals for Britain (Saunders 2007: 56).

Here, I adopt an anthropological approach through the multidisciplinary lens of modern conflict archaeology to investigate several of America's diverse monuments and memorials, as well as practices of commemoration, within the United States and beyond. This study reveals a broad picture of the ever changing role of memory-work, and of the diversity of commemoration, as well as raising issues that have excited controversy. I explore some of the traditional methods of commemoration that extend from the First World War back to the American Civil War, and newer forms of commemoration through 'living memorials' that served a variety of utilitarian purposes, such as a school, an auditorium, or a meeting hall (Trout 2006: 214). These latter monuments enjoyed a surge in popularity during the early twentieth century, and demonstrate the power of the war's legacy to shape social attitudes and behaviour.

In the United States, as elsewhere, there was no consensus of how the war was remembered (*ibid.*: 2). Strategies of remembrance were regionally diverse, sometimes controversial, changed through time, and continue to do so today.

Honouring Americans 'over there'

Initially, the United States government and organisations such as the 'American Legion' and the 'American Field of Honor Organization' (AFHO) promoted the idea of overseas cemeteries to honour those who had died during the war. General Pershing was one of the most vocal advocates for these foreign cemeteries (Budreau 2010: 70), and it was his conviction that America's war dead stay in Europe (Trout 2010: 17). At the same time, there was little intent to create any national memorials in the United States itself, as it was considered that overseas memorials best portrayed America's role as a world power (Budreau 2010: 102). In other words, America's war dead, and the cemeteries in which they lay, were not only a post-conflict material legacy of the war, but an emotional, patriotic, and highly-visible projection of America's international political influence.

The AFHO considered that the dead would be better honoured if they were buried where they fell in Europe. They believed that the: '… Sacred Dust of American soldiers had made the soil of the cemeteries in France forever American, a place where the Stars and Stripes would always fly' (Piehler 1995: 95). In part, the idea may have been based on tradition; following the American Civil War, sites of former battlefields were seen as fitting locations for memorials (Budreau 2010: 106). The AFHO attempted to convince American mothers to make a second sacrifice and offer their fallen sons to the greater good of the nation. Ultimately, these attempts were unsuccessful, and mothers chose to repatriate 70% of the dead back to the United States (Laquer 1996: 162).

It was decided to concentrate the American graves into eight large cemeteries (Piehler 1995: 98) overseen by the 'American Battlefield Monuments Commission' (Budreau 2010: 111). Each cemetery was intended to mirror Arlington National Cemetery in Washington D.C., as an open park space landscaped with trees and carpets of grass between each grave. The grave markers were simple, carved with a marble cross to mark Christian graves or a Star of David for Jewish ones (Piehler 1995: 102). The cemeteries would represent the entire nation (*ibid.*: 99). This was in contrast to U.S. Civil War memorials, that honoured regiments rather than larger groupings such as divisions and units.

Each of the eight cemeteries included a non-denominational chapel, making them living memorials (*ibid.*: 100). The chapel was designed in Christian style, identifying American nationalism with Christianity. It included the Christian cross which represented the soldiers' suffering, self-sacrifice and patriotism (*ibid.*: 101). Crosses have been viewed as an important and traditional part of First World War remembrance for Americans, British, French and others (Saunders 2007: 56). Crosses not only appeared in the overseas memorials, but also as public memorials in the United States.

Crosses and Doughboys

In Arlington National Cemetery, two separate crosses were erected to honour the war dead. The first is the 'Argonne Cross' constructed to honour 2100 reinterred American soldiers (AC 2010). The second was the 'Canadian Cross of Sacrifice', which was originally constructed to honour American soldiers that enlisted in the Canadian Armed Forces.

The use of crosses has been controversial. Some groups such as the *American Civil Liberties Union* (ACLU) argue that religious symbols are a violation of the 'Establishment Clause' of the First Amendment of the Constitution, '... Congress shall make no Law respecting an establishment of a religion'. Others argue that government endorsement of one group's religious symbols, at the expense of another group, lacks sensitivity to non-Christian Americans who made the ultimate sacrifice (Piehler 1995: 100). Supporters argue that the Latin cross has become more than a religious symbol, and serves now as a universal symbol of sacrifice.

These contrasting beliefs were put to the test in 2002, when Frank Buono, an employee of the National Parks Service, sued the Secretary of the Interior in order to remove the 'Mojave Memorial Cross' at Sunrise Rock (constructed in 1934). The memorial was on government-controlled public land, and Buono alleged it was in violation of the Constitution. The California courts sided with Buono (SvB) ordering the cross be removed. In the interim, it was ordered that the cross be boarded up. The case was taken to the Federal 9th Circuit Court of Appeals, who also decided it was unconstitutional. In 2009, the case came before the Supreme Court, which looked at options to save the cross (SvB).

In April 2010, the court ruled five to four in favour of saving the cross. The court decided that the Constitution does not require the removal of religious symbols from public land. Justice Kennedy, who made the decision, saw the Latin cross to be more than a symbol of religion, serving also as a symbol of 'honor and respect for heroism' and mirrored the crosses in American cemeteries in Europe (Barnes 2010). The case was sent back to lower court to reverse the decision.

Less than two weeks later, the case took a strange turn, when vandals removed the cross in retaliation for the Supreme Court's decision (Kelly 2010). The theft was criticised by both the memorial's critics and its supporters. The 'Veterans of Foreign Wars' (VFW) offered a $25,000 reward for the return of the cross. A few weeks later under mysterious circumstances, 'a cross' was returned to the location on Sunrise Rock. It was deemed a copy, and was removed the following day (RCMDCD 2010). The VFW regards the removal of the cross as dishonouring the memory of the veterans whose sacrifice it symbolises, and has vowed to see it replaced. Many worry that cases like Salazar v. Buono could affect similar First World War memorials, leading to their removal from government land. They consider that such removal would destroy the memory of those who fell.

Not all First World War memorials are religious in nature. Traditionally one of the more popular forms of secular commemoration included statues and other non-religious monuments, of which some of the most common are the 'Doughboy

Figure 7.1: The Victorious Doughboy, by Avard T. Fairbanks. (© author, 2010)

Statues'. They were inspired by statues that honoured the fallen of the Civil War (Trout 2010: 109), and regarded as the companions of statues depicting *Billy Yank* (representing Union soldiers) and *Johnny Reb* (representing Confederate troops) (Piehler 1995: 111). They were memorial sites of remembrance, but also comforting symbols of patriotism and stability in the communities where they were placed (Wingate 2005: 30).

Doughboy statues adopted heroic poses, and appeared larger than life. Many were mass-produced, costing less to make than by conventional craftsmanship methods; the best known of these was the *Spirit of the American Doughboy* by E.M. Viquesney. The Doughboy holds an outstretched bayonet, and in one hand holds a grenade high above his head. These distinctive commemorative materialities were erected near museums, on courthouse lawns, in cemeteries, town squares, and parks (Budreau 2010: 139). Visquesney's design enjoyed commercial success, and about 140 statues were erected in small towns across the country during the 1920s and 1930s (Trout 2010: 121).

Despite the mass-produced nature of many Doughboy statues (ironically replicating the mass casualties they memorialised), some were original works. *The Victorious American Doughboy* by Avard T. Fairbanks in 'Veteran Park', St Anthony, Idaho (Figure 7.1), and the *Washelli Doughboy* in Seattle, are either original works or limited editions. From the perspective of modern conflict archaeology (Saunders 2010) in particular, they are significant not only for portraying typical heroism, but for depicting a more controversial aspect of First World War battle-zone culture – the looting of trophies and souvenirs (Woolley 1987: 34). During the war 'souveneering' was a booming business at and behind the front, and practiced by all sides (Saunders 2007: 35).

The Victorious American Doughboy portrays war souvenirs in the form of two German helmets held in the soldier's left hand. These were intended to represent 'souvenirs of victory' (Woolley 1987: 34). A similar statue can be found in Quincy, Massachusetts, in front of the Adams Academy (QSM 2004). Similarly, when the *Washelli Doughboy*

Figure 7.2: The Waikiki Natatorium. (© Hawaii State Archives)

was commissioned as a Seattle First World War memorial, the sculptor Alonzo Victor Lewis chose to include a pair of German helmets, slung over the Doughboy's neck.

The initial and temporary plaster figure was controversial for several reasons. First, the statue portrayed a member of the Army, leaving Navy veterans feeling left out. Second, others complained that the presence of 'war booty' would likely promote continued hatred between Americans and Germans. Others thought the grin on its face, showed a '… crazed warrior without vestige of the heroic demeanor of an American soldier' (Fiset 2001). Demonstrating the contested nature of conflict-generated material culture in post-war times, the finished bronze statue, cast in 1928, was vandalized even before it was unveiled on Armistice Day, 1932. The two helmets had been cut off and removed, and no one came forward to '… accept praise or responsibility' (*ibid.*). In 1970, the statue was further damaged by having its bayonet removed.

While many of the statues attempted to portray Doughboys as heroic figures that defended the free world, occasionally a few glorified some of the darker aspects of the war. While these could be popular in many communities, nationally there was more interest in the construction of non-traditional living memorials.

Water and stone: living memorials and other non-traditional commemoration

The 'Waikiki Natatorium' in Honolulu, Hawaii, is a good example of a living memorial (Figure 7.2). After the First World War, the government of the territory of Hawaii discussed the creation of a memorial to honour the 101 individuals who served during the war and the additional 10,000 Hawaiian residents that contributed to the war effort. Many of the 101 had enlisted under both the American and British forces (Williams 2010).

It was to be a memorial which represented Hawaii's unique region and culture. The initial suggestions were fairly conservative; one was an honour roll, with the names of the island boys engraved into polished lava stone (Kuykendall 1928: 447). Others wanted something more sophisticated which could better perpetuate the legacy of the soldiers' faith and allegiance. Governor Charles McCarthy suggested that they should build something functional; he suggested a large auditorium to be called the 'Victory Hall' (*ibid.*: 448). However, the memorial committee decided to buy beachfront property on Waikiki – 'Irwin Beachfront' – and convert it into a public 'Memorial Park' instead (*ibid.*: 450).

The central feature of the park was to be a 'memorial natatorium', a structure containing an indoor swimming pool (however, in this case a misnomer, as the memorial is outdoors) and pavilion surrounded by the park (Kuykendall 1928: 451). The natatorium itself was designed as an Olympic sized swimming pool that was intended to be a 'swimming course of at least 100 meters in length' (*ibid.*: 452). The structure would honour the men and women who served during the Great War, and would be a '… temple of music, plaza and coliseum with swimming basin' (*ibid.*: 452).

Following a competition, a design was chosen which was praised for its '… interpretation of the spirit of Hawaii', and whose architectural design reflected '… the highly individual color and flavor of Hawaii and Honolulu' (Kuykendall 1928: 452). The ocean and salt water were incorporated into the design (Williams 2010), and it conjures images of the ancient fish ponds found throughout Hawaii. The stadium pavilion surrounding the natatorium itself looked over the swimming pool, out to sea, and towards the endless horizon. In a sense, this 'view of infinity' represented the perpetual memory of those who had fallen.

In August 1927, the natatorium was completed, and a commemoration ceremony was held. In his speech, the then Governor, W.R. Farrington, explained that the memorial would not only honour those who lost their lives, but also represent the present and future youth of the territory (Kuykendall 1928: 454). He, like many others, hoped that America's memorials would represent continued peace, and an end to all wars.

The memorial was then celebrated through a 100 m freestyle swimming exhibition by Duke Kahanamoku, the legendary Hawaiian surfer, and record-winning swimmer. The exhibition was followed by the 1927 swimming championships (Kuykendall 1928: 454). It was considered a fitting inauguration for the setting, honouring both those who had served, and those who would serve the territory.

The site proved difficult to maintain, however. As early as 1929, the *Honolulu Star-Bulletin* complained about the 'deplorable conditions' of the memorial and surrounding grounds (WWMN 2003–2010). The pool suffered from natural deposition and erosion and required constant dredging.

As time passed, control of the site changed hands between the 'City and County of Honolulu', the 'Territory of Hawaii', and back to the City and County. During the 1960s, it fell into disrepair again, before it was finally closed to the public in 1980. The structure itself had become hazardous. The bleachers and walkways of the natatorium were crumbling, and there were gaping holes in the pool deck (Williams 2010). Since the 1980s, the city has been debating the decision of closure and demolition for the site. However, various organisations including the 'Friends of the Natatorium and Historic Hawai'i Foundation' have argued for its repair.

In 2000, the city allocated US$ 11 million in funds for the renovation of the landmark. But restoration work went slowly, and by 2005 only the arch and façade of the natatorium had been repaired. At the time, the mayor of Honolulu, Mufi Hannemann, withdrew the funds, and considered moving the façade to another location. In 2009, the final decision was made to demolish the site. However, veteran groups and preservationists still continue to fight to save the site (11MEHP 2009). Currently it remains in limbo; its role as a site of memory endangered. Many consider its loss will be an insult to the memory of those it was designed and built for (Apo 2009). Once again, the power of such commemorative materialities to provoke and prolong contested views and conflicting attitudes beyond war is amply demonstrated.

The 'Maryhill Stonehenge Memorial' represents another non-traditional design – a full-scale replica of the prehistoric Neolithic and Bronze Age monument of Stonehenge on Salisbury Plain, in southern England (Figure 7.3). The memorial has the distinction of being the first recorded memorial in the United States (Becker 2006). It was designed by Sam Hill (who also designed the 'Peace Arch' in Blaine, Washington) to honour the soldiers of Klickitat County, Washington.

Hill gained inspiration for the Stonehenge Memorial while visiting Salisbury Plain in 1915, during his time delivering relief supplies to Belgium and Russia (SM 2010). While there, he toured the site with Britain's Secretary of State for War, Lord Horatio Herbert Kitchener. According to Sam Hill, he was told by Kitchener, 'Here the ancients 4,000 years ago offered bloody sacrifices to their heathen gods of war' (Becker 2006). It was erroneously believed at the time that Stonehenge had been a site for Druidic sacrificial rituals. Hill compared the Druid sacrifices to modern warfare, seeing them both as wasteful sacrifice; he hoped his structure would remind his fellow man of the folly of war.

The Stonehenge Memorial was thus intended to reflect 'images of primitive superstition, and sacrifices to appease the gods, and lamentation for cruel, needles death' (Clark 2006: 37). It is in its way an anti-war memorial that promotes peace; it not only honours those who served in the war, but was also intended to give the impression of the sorrow and hopelessness of conflict (*ibid.*: 38). By contrast, Sam Hill's other design, the Peace Arch, was painted white to symbolise purity, and reflect hope and goodwill founded upon peace. The arch was dedicated for the absence of war itself (*ibid.*: 37–38).

The memorial is a nearly-accurate, full-scale replica of Stonehenge itself, intended to reflect how the original monument would have appeared when it was first constructed in prehistory (Becker 2006). It was positioned to fit the summer solstice based on a total

Figure 7.3: The Maryhill Stonehenge Memorial. (Photo © Timothy Matthews. Used with Permission, 2010)

eclipse that occurred on 8 June 1918. At the time, the site was aligned to the astronomical horizon rather than midsummer sunrise, which resulted in its positional accuracy being 3° off from the original structure (SM 2010). Hill's Stonehenge was constructed from concrete, as the local stone was considered unsuitable. It is so accurate that some scientists have used the site to conduct acoustic studies to see how Neolithic man may have experienced sounds 5000 years ago in southern England (SCV 2009).

The memorial was dedicated on the 4 July 1918, while the war was still being fought (Becker 2006). Initially, there were six names inscribed on the monument, though seven more were added as they fell overseas. The monument was completed in 1929, and Sam Hill's ashes were entombed within it when he died in 1931 (Clark 2006: 37). In 1995, when the memorial was refurbished and rededicated, the director of the Maryhill Museum which oversees the memorial, said it was '… imperative that future generations never lose sight of the loss of life, as well as the heroism and valor, which result from war' (Becker 2006).

Monument recycling

Not all American cities commissioned new First World War memorials. The citizens of some towns chose to reuse monuments that had been dedicated to previous conflicts, such as the Civil War and the American Revolution (Budreau 2010: 138). By adding the names of the fallen to the earlier monuments, the towns were able to connect the new soldiers to the legacy of the old. This maintained tradition, and created a sense of continuity within communities.

When the *Soldier's Monument* in McElhattan, Pennsylvania, was re-dedicated to the soldiers of the First World War, it already carried the names of veterans from the American Revolution, the Civil War, and the Spanish-American War (Shoemaker 1920: 6). A few Civil War veterans attended the re-dedication ceremony as honoured guests, and the names of two fallen soldiers from earlier wars were engraved into the monument alongside those of the First World War soldiers (*ibid.*: 7).

During the commemoration speech, it was said that those who served were like the crest of a mighty wave, and veterans of earlier wars represented preceding waves (*ibid.*: 9) Each wave fades into the next. He spoke of the soldiers of the American Revolution securing the freedom which veterans of the First World War continued to secure. Finally, he warned of the dangers of war and its potential to reopen festering wounds such as those that caused divisions in the Civil War – wounds that took a long time to heal (*ibid.*: 10). By interring First World War dead within graveyards shared by veterans of earlier conflicts, the towns created a consoling interpretation of the dead, in which they became part of a long standing tradition of honour within the community (Trout 2010: 37).

In the years following the end of the First World War, memorials were sometimes updated with names from later conflicts, such as the Second World War, Korea, and Vietnam. For example, *The Guns Are Silent* in Modesto, California, was originally placed by the American Legion to be a Great War memorial. It consists of an old Japanese artillery cannon on a concrete base listing the name of the memorial. In 1991, a black granite plaque was added to the base of the cannon listing all the wars from the 1914–18 conflict to the Iraq war.

A granite monument nearby contains three spokes, each face contains the Honour Rolls for the city of Modesto. The six faces are marked with names from various wars; 'Peace' (First World War), 'Duty' (Korea and Gulf War), and 'Honor' (Vietnam). The last three, 'Freedom', 'Valor', 'and 'Country', list the fallen of the Second World War. There is, of course, a deep sense of irony in monuments designed to represent the First World War as 'the war to end all wars', having become memorials to represent all subsequent wars, and thereby monuments to the failure of the original aspiration.

In some cases, an 'all wars memorial' has been built where no memorials previously existed. Some were simple; in Ceres, California, there is the *Ceres War Memorial* in Whitmore Park. Built in 1991, it is a granite memorial consisting of four slabs containing the names of the fallen from the First World War to Iraq. The slabs encircle a flag pole holding the Stars and Stripes. So it not only honours the soldiers, but also the country they fought to protect. Some were more elaborate; the *All Wars Memorial to Colored Soldiers and Sailors* in Philadelphia (dedicated 1934) was designed to honour all African-American soldiers who died from the American Revolution to the First World War (the last war it dedicated) (Bond *et al.* 2007: 94). A figure of 'Justice' stands between statues of African-American soldiers and sailors holding a wreath.

The 'Tomb of the Unknown Soldier' is perhaps the most famous First World War monument/tomb to see an evolution to an 'all wars' memorial. It originally honoured those who had truly been lost during 'The Great War'. These were soldiers who never came back, alive or dead (*ibid.*: 106). The government had reverently selected an individual's remains from many unidentified remains of American soldiers that had fallen in France (Piehler 1996: 174). The individuals' lack of identity allowed people from all over America to identify with the anonymous soldier. Loved ones who had lost their own sons could claim him as their own (*ibid.*: 175). Following the Second World War, and each conflict up to Vietnam, additional unidentified remains have been added to the tomb in order to honour those lost in all these wars (Bond *et al.* 2007: 106).

In a sense, as the First World War was incorporated into previous wars, and into later, better-remembered wars, it lost definition and impact on America's collective memory. War memorials are a unique kind of conflict materiality, with an afterlife stretching into the future. As new names are inscribed alongside old ones, so memories can be elided or overwritten, and subsequent histories reconfigured.

Where is the National Memorial?

In Washington D.C., within the National Mall and surrounding Memorial Parks, monuments have been built to honour Americans who died during the twentieth century's many wars. There are several expansive memorials dedicated to the Second World War and the Vietnam War, and even a large memorial for the Korean War. Some honour specific battles – such as the iconic Marine Corps War Memorial (the 'Iwo Jima Memorial'). However, conspicuously absent is a memorial honouring the soldiers who gave their lives during the 'Great War for Civilization' (Trout 2010: 20).

Historically, there have several attempts to designate a national memorial for the First World War within the capital, but most failed. In 1929, there were plans to turn the First Division Monument into a true national First World War memorial. However, Major General C.P. Summerall defeated the scheme before it began. Throughout the inter-war period, the 'Tomb of the Unknown Soldier' acted as a *de facto* national monument to the Great War (Trout 2010: 21), and was the official means by which the United States collectively memorialised that conflict (Budreau 2010: 102). But the meaning changed as the Tomb incorporated 'unknown soldiers' from other conflicts.

Mostly recently, in 2008, the 'World War I Memorial Foundation' (WWIMF), Frank Buckles (the last Doughboy), and Senator Ted Poe of Texas, submitted legislation (*Frank Buckles World War I Memorial Act*) to convert the *District of Columbia War Memorial* into a national First World War Memorial to all American soldiers of the conflict (Hoecker 2008) (Figure 7.4). Originally, the memorial had been designed as a municipal memorial to honour the residents of Washington D.C. who gave their lives during the war.

Supporters believe that it would be appropriate if visitors paying their respects at the National Mall could have a place where they can honour veterans of the First World War as well (Lopez 2009). The act would also allow for repairs to the existing memorial plus expansions. In the meantime, the Department of Interior allocated US$ 7.3 million for the monument's restoration (Ruane 2009). The organisation continues to promote the creation of a national war memorial on the National Mall. Frank Buckles had hoped that a national memorial could be dedicated on the Mall, and also that he (and, by extension, all previous Doughboys) would be honoured by a State Funeral when he died (Dokoupil 2008). The process for this state ceremony would require an Act of Congress (Poe 2010).

Frank Buckles passed away in February 2011. His family, friends, and supporters petitioned for his body to lie in honour in the Capitol Rotunda (LVB 2011) – a privilege usually reserved for presidents, statesmen, and military leaders (BDRH 2011). Both House Speaker John Boehner and Senate Majority Leader, Harry Reid turned down the request; instead, both agreed to a special ceremony and viewing at Arlington's Memorial Amphitheater (BDRH 2011). Mr Buckles' daughter and other supporters made an urgent statement asking President Obama to intervene and allow Mr Buckles to lie within the Rotunda, but were turned down. Ultimately, even the state ceremony never came to pass, only the viewing in the Memorial Amphitheater Chapel, followed by private service, and then burial with full honours (BDRH 2011).

President Barack Obama and Vice President Joe Biden offered their respects, and visited the family shortly before the funeral. On 15 April 2011, Mr Buckles was buried not far from his commander, General Pershing (FVB 2011). Days earlier, the Liberty Memorial, in Kansas City, Missouri, gave a somewhat more formal public ceremony; it honoured not only Frank Buckles, but also the passing of the final generation which fought during the Great War (Campbell 2011). Buckles' final honour is to be a newly-commissioned Doughboy statue which portrays him leading Pershing's horse. It is to be placed either in Buckles' hometown of Charles Town, Missouri, or in France where he served (Belisle 2011).

Although the closing pages of the First World War's legacy in the United States turned out to be political, these events nevertheless demonstrate the volatile and contested role of commemoration in American culture. Time will tell if Mr Buckles other wish for a National World War I memorial in Washington D.C. will be realised.

Though respectful of Buckles, supporters of the Liberty Memorial (Figure 7.5) have dedicated their memorial as a National Monument. In 2006, the memorial received federal recognition as the 'National World War I Museum' (Trout 2010: 21). They introduced legislation which competed with the legislation to convert the Washington D.C. Memorial. They introduced the *National Liberty Memorial Act* in the hope of gaining federal recognition of the memorial as the national memorial for all First World War veterans (Lopez 2009).

The Liberty Memorial was originally designed to honour more than 400 citizens of Kansas City who lost their lives during the war (Trout 2010: 21). Many men, including (future president) Harry S. Truman's 35th Division, suffered 50–70% attrition rates. Many of those soldiers were from Kansas City. This loss of lives provided much of the impetus for creating such a large memorial (*ibid.*: 25). From the beginning it was a living monument, designed not only as memorial but also as a museum to '… house trophies of war …' (Donovan 2001: 20).

Figure 7.4: Frank Buckles visits the First World War Memorial in Washington D.C. (Photo Robin Hoecker. © Stars and Stripes. Used with permission, 2008, 2010)

The memorial is replete with symbolic imagery, representing the 'heroic' and the 'sacred' (Trout 2010: 22). The central feature is a 215 ft (*c.* 65.5 m) tall tower (Donovan 2001: 113) at whose summit light passes through steam to simulate an eternal flame (Schoeppner 2007). Just below the observation deck are four guardian spirits holding swords. Each represents a separate ideal; 'Honor', 'Sacrifice', 'Patriotism', and 'Courage', and they gaze down to the base of the structure below (Trout 2010: 22). Two sphinxes flank the base of the tower, with covered eyes; one faces the *Past* (too painful to see), while the other faces the unseen *Future* (Schoeppner 2007).

In 1921, when the memorial was dedicated, several Allied commanders were in attendance, including Lieutenant General Baron Jacques (Belgium); General Armando Diaz (Italy); Marshal Ferdinand Foch (France); General John J. Pershing (United States); and Admiral David Beatty (Great Britain) (Schoeppner

Figure 7.5: National World War I Museum at Liberty Memorial. (© Liberty Memorial 2006)

Figure 7.6: Allied Commanders at the Liberty Memorial's 1921 dedication. (© Liberty Memorial 1921)

2007), and so the monument was almost given official recognition on a national and international level (Figure 7.6).

Conclusion: patriotism and peace

Doughboys across the nation have been honoured in many different ways. Although there is no single collective manner in which all Americans honoured the memory of their Great War soldiers, there are common themes that appear in the various memorials, commemoration ceremonies, and cemeteries.

Many of the fallen were seen as the epitome of American patriots. The Doughboys were the ones who offered the greatest sacrifice for Western freedom. For other Americans, the First World War was seen as a continuing process of reconciliation, to heal the wounds opened during their own Civil War. The event brought citizens of the North and South together in order to fight a common enemy which threatened the world's freedom. The memorials honoured the fallen who were regarded as the embodiment of ideals of American exceptionalism and of traditions shared by those who had fought in the American Revolution. For others, the war was seen as futile waste of life. These Americans showed respect to the soldiers' memory through the promotion of eternal peace, and an end to all wars.

The purposes of First World War memorials have changed over time, as have memories. Sometimes they have been forgotten, and other times fallen into obscurity and disrepair. Other memorials have been restructured to incorporate more recent better-known wars. Occasionally organizations and individuals have fought to save neglected monuments, and to keep the soldiers' legacies alive.

Controversy surroun ds some memorials, turning them, ironically, into contested space. In some examples, religious iconography in memorials has become politically incorrect; some worry that the imagery may be viewed as offensive, and that it neglects soldiers who held different spiritual beliefs. Others view the iconography as a universal symbol of sacrifice, and its loss a dishonour to the memory of the fallen. What becomes controversial within changing political and social attitudes may even threaten the site's existence – in some cases inciting vandalism or removal of the memorial.

It is certain that the attitudes toward the sacred space of memorialisation will continue to develop as cultural and social attitudes continue to shift in the United States. Not least of these changes will be the way in which America's Great War Doughboys will be remembered.

Acknowledgements

I would like to thank Mark Levitch at the University of Pennsylvania for pointing out several important sources that were invaluable for this research. I would also like to thank Dr Nicholas Saunders at University of Bristol for making this paper possible. Last but not least, this article is dedicated to the memory of Frank Buckles, the Last of our American *Doughboys*. May he rest in eternal peace.

Bibliography

11MEHP (11 Most Endangered Historic Places.) (2009) http://www.preservationnation.org/travel-and-sites/sites/western-region/waikiki-war-memorial-natatorium.html Accessed 18 December 2010.

Apo, P. (2009). Restore the natatorium in Waikiki. http://the.honoluluadvertiser.com/article/2009/Apr/14/ op/hawaii904140311.html Accessed 25 December 2010.

AC (Arlingtoncemetery) (2010) Argonne Cross. http://www.arlingtoncemetery.mil/visitor_information/ Argonne_Cross.html Accessed 25 December 2010.

Barnes, R. (2010) Supreme Court overturns objection to cross on public land. http://www.washingtonpost.com/wp-dyn/content/article/2010/04/28/AR2010042801949.html Accessed 13 November 2010.

BDRH (Buckles Daughter Not Taking 'No' for an Answer on Rotunda Honor) http://www. aolnews.com/2011/03/05/frank-buckles-buckles-daughter-susannah-buckles-flanagan-not-tak/ Accessed 10 March 2011.

Becker, P. (2006) Altar stone of Stonehenge replica built to memorialize World War I soldiers is dedicated at Maryhill on July 4, 1918. http://www.historylink.org/index. cfm?DisplayPage=output.cfm&file_id=7809 Accessed 21 November 2010.

Belisle, R.F. (2011) Campaign launched to raise money for Buckles statue and documentary. http://articles.herald-mail.com/2011-02-26/news/28635382_1_statue-campaign-first-statue-gap-view-farm Accessed 24 March 2011.

Black, J. (2004) 'Thanks for the Memory': War memorials, spectatorship and the trajectories of commemoration 1919–2001. In N.J. Saunders (ed.), *Matters of Conflict: Material Culture, Memory and the First World War*, 134–148. Abingdon: Routledge.

Bond, L. and Fitzgerald, F.S. (2007). *The Mighty Fallen: Our Nations Greatest War Memorials.* New York: Collins.

Budreau, L.M. (2010) *Bodies of War.* New York and London: New York University Press.

Clark, R. (2006) *Sam Hill's Peace Arch: Rememberance of Dreams Past.* Bloomington (ID): AuthorHouse.

Campbell. M. (2011) Ceremony at Liberty Memorial to honor Buckles will be March 12th. http://www.kansascity.com/2011/03/03/2696829/ceremony-at-liberty-memorial-to.html# Accessed 24 March 2011.

Dokoupil, T. (2008) The War We Forgot. http://www.newsweek.com/id/109681 Accessed 28 December 2010.

Donovan, D. (2001) *Lest the Ages Forget: Kansas City's Liberty Memorial.* Kansas City: Kansas City Star Books.

Fiset, L. (2001) World War I memorial is moved to Seattle's Evergreen-Washelli Cemetery on November 11, 1998. http://www.historylink.org/index.cfm?DisplayPage=output. cfm&file_id=3294 Accessed 20 November 2010.

FVB (Final World War I veteran buried) (2011) http://www.latimes.com/news/nationworld/ nation/la-na-wwi-veteran-20110316,0,5385570.story Accessed 24 March 2011.

Hanlon, M.E. (2010) The Origins of the Doughboy. http://www.worldwar1.com/dbc/origindb. htm Accessed 29 December 2010.

Hoecker, R. (2008) Last American World War I veteran lends his voice to calls for a memorial. http://www.stripes.com/news/last-american-world-war-i-veteran-lends-his-voice-to-calls-for-a-memorial-1.82901 Accessed 23 November 2010.

Kelly, D. (2010) Mojave Desert cross, focus of long legal battle, is stolen. http://articles.latimes. com/2010/may/12/local/la-me-mojave-cross-20100512 Accessed 25 December 2010.

King, A. (1998) *Memorials of the Great War in Britain: the Symbolism and Politics of Remembrance.* Oxford: Berg.

Kuykendall, R.S. (1928) *Hawaii in the World War.* Honolulu: Historical Commission.

Laquer, T.W. (1996) Memory and Naming in the Great War. In J.R. Gillis (ed.), *Commemorations: the Politics of National Identity*, 150–167. Princeton: Princeton University Press.

Lopez, C.T. (2009) *Last U.S. WWI vet fights for national memorial.* http://www.army.mil/-news/2009/12/04/31389-last-us-wwi-vet-fights-for-national-memorial/ Accessed 29 December 2010.

LVB (Last WWI Vet Buckles Will Lie in Basement at Arlington, Not Capitol Rotunda.) (2011) http://www.aolnews.com/2011/03/11/last-world-war-i-veteran-frank-buckles-will-lie-in-basement-at-a/ Accessed 13 February 2011.

Piehler, G.K. (1995) *Remembering War: The American Way.* Washington D.C.: Smithsonian.

Piehler, G.K. (1996) The War Dead and the Gold Star: American Commemoration of the First

World War. In J.R. Gillis (ed.), *Commemorations: The Politics of National Identity*, 168–185. Princeton: Princeton University Press.

Poe, T. (2010) 'Over There': The Final Legacy. http://poe.house.gov/News/DocumentSingle. aspx? DocumentID=217638 Accessed 25 December 2010

QSM (Quincy Statues and Monuments). (2004) http://www.discoverquincy.com/statues.htm Accessed 13 March 2011.

RCMDCD (Replica Cross in Mojave Desert Comes Down.) (2010) http://abcnews.go.com/ US/wireStory?id=10702661&tqkw=&tqshow= Accessed 25 December 2010.

Ruane, M.E. (2009) *Monumental Repair Work Funded for $76.8 Million*. http://www.washingtonpost. com/wp-dyn/content/article/2009/04/22/AR2009042202958.html Accessed 28 December 2010.

SvB (Salazar v. Buono) (2010) http://www.law.cornell.edu/supct/html/08-472.ZS.html Accessed 25 December 2010.

Saunders, N.J. (2007) *Killing Time: Archaeology and the First World War*. Phoenix Mill: Sutton.

Saunders, N.J. (2010) Worlds Apart: Modern Conflict Archaeology and Battlefield Archaeology. *Arheo* 27: 45–55.

Schoeppner, K. (Director). (2007) *Liberty Memorial: Stories of the Great War Monument* [Motion Picture].

Shoemaker, H.W. (ed.) (1920) *Proceedings of Dedication Ceremonies, Placing Names of Wayne Township Soldiers of World War, 1917–1918, on Monument at McElhattan, Clinton Countay, PA*. http:// www.archive.org/download/proceedingsofded00shoe/proceedingsofded00shoe.pdf Accessed 1 June 2011.

SM (Stonehenge Memorial.) (2010) http://www.maryhillmuseum.org/stonehenge.html Accessed 21 November 2010.

SCV (Stonehenge was 'giant concert venue') (2009) http://www.telegraph.co.uk/science/ science-news/4108867/Stonehenge-was-giant-concert-venue.html Accessed 23 November 2010.

WWMN (The Waikiki War Memorial Natatorium: A Timeline of the Political Controversy.) (2003– 2010) http://www.historichawaii.org/Historic_Sites/Natatorium/Timelineofcontroversy1. html Accessed 24 December 2010.

Trout, S. (2006) Forgotten Reminders: Kansas City World War I Memorials. *Kansas History: a Journal of the Central Plains* 2: 200–215.

Trout, S. (2010). *On the Battlefield of Memory: The First World War and American Rememberance, 1919–1941*. Tuscaloosa: University of Alabama Press.

Williams, A.M. (2010) *Visit The Waikiki Natatorium While You Still Can*. http://www.808talk. com/2010/10/07/visit-the-waikiki-natatorium-while-you-still-can/ Accessed 24 November 2010.

Wingate, J. (2005) Over the Top: the Doughboy in World War I Memorials and Visual Culture. *American Art* 19 (Summer): 26–47.

Winter, J. (1995) *Sites of Memory, Sites of Mourning: The Great War in European Cultural History*. Cambridge: Cambridge University Press.

Woolley, A. T. (1987). *Art to Edify: The Work of Avard T. Fairbanks*. http://lds.org/ensign/1987/09/ art-to-edify-the-work-of-avard-t-fairbanks?lang=eng Accessed 12 May 2010.

8

'Lone and Captive Far From Home': gendered objects in Boer POW camps, Bermuda, 1901–2

Deborah A. Atwood

Objects, once made, are free to roam in time and space, and to accumulate and exhibit a variety of meanings. In times of conflict, these meanings are arguably more intense, and their investigation is necessarily an interdisciplinary endeavour. Yet, each conflict is different, and the objects that embody the individual's experience of it require a carefully calibrated response in order to capture its unique character. Here, I investigate a rich corpus of distinctive conflict-related items, whose meaning and symbolism possess trans-national significance not least because they are a legacy of a war which stands on the boundary between traditional nineteenth century conflicts and the industrialised global struggles of the twentieth century. My focus is Boer prisoner-of-war objects as gendered constructions of identity in the POW camps of Bermuda 1901–1902.

These items of material culture are complex, and subject to constant re-interpretation and appropriation. The corpus examined here includes walking sticks, letter openers, penholders, 'trick boxes', cutlery, crochet hooks, picture frames, jewellery boxes, and brooches; each exhibits iconic aspects of Boer culture, religion, and identity. The trade in militaria, and the consequent preservation of these objects in private and public (museum) collections, has created a richly varied database of good-condition artefacts amenable to an in-depth multi-disciplinary analysis; in particular, how they became infused with notions of self, nationalism, and gender.

The Boer War produced a multitude of objects and images that would later be used to unify a people into one nation, creating an image of Afrikaner national identity (Brink 1990; Grundlingh 1999; McClintock 1995: 352–389). The image of women and children suffering in the concentration camps was used as a platform upon which the notions of a 'wounded nation' could be created and identified with (De Reuck 1999: 79–81). The Women's Monument or 'Vrouemonument', unveiled in Bloemfontein on 16 December 1913, became a visible icon of the Afrikaner nation (*ibid.*: 71–72). Objects relating to the historic elements of Boer identity were also used during the twentieth century to construct an Afrikaner identity. In McClintock's examination of the use of gender in the construction of nationalism, she highlights how historic objects were utilised in the 1938 re-enactment of the Great Trek:

> 'Nine replicas of Voortrekker wagons were built – the reinvention of the archaic to sanction modernity. Each wagon was literally baptized, and named after a male Voortrekker hero. No wagon was named after an adult woman. One was, however, called generically, Vrou en Moeder [wife and mother]. The wagon, creaking across the country, symbolized women's relation the nation as indirect, mediated through her social relation to men, her national identity lying in her unpaid services and sacrifices, through husband and family, to the volk.' (McClintock 1993: 69)

* * * * *

There is a paradox at the heart of the material culture of conflict made by Boer prisoners of war in Bermuda. POW camps imprisoned only men and boys. Yet, a large percentage of the items possess a feminine quality, and are associated with women's work (crochet hooks, serviette rings, jewellery boxes, brooches). The international context is illuminating. At the end of the nineteenth century, and into the twentieth, women in North America and Europe were struggling for the right to vote, while women in South Africa were losing their freedom in concentration camps. This period also saw the beginning of industrialised consumerism, from branded products to warfare, mass produced items became central to notions of personhood and nationalism. The objects made in the Boer camps were produced on an industrial scale and were marketed as souvenirs for tourists seeking to redefine themselves within this consumer society. This new consumerism is inextricably linked to concepts of gender, nationalism and identity.

Appadurai (1986: 17) suggests that the movement of commodities is a 'shifting compromise between socially regulated paths and competitively inspired diversions'. Things move in and out of the 'state of commodity' throughout their social lives, and this fluidity is dependent upon tournaments of value and transvaluation (*ibid*.: 21–23). Within small communities or 'enclaved zones', restriction on exchange and value can create 'enclaved commodities' (*ibid*.: 25). However, these commoditites are subject to diversion, 'the calculated and interested removal of things from an enclaved zone to one where exchange is less confined and more profitable, in some short-term sense' (*ibid*.). Appadurai uses the example of the 'exotic everyday object' to describe this process, wherein an 'artifact of the other' is removed from its original cultural context and placed within the buyer's or collector's context of 'souvenir' (*ibid*.: 28).

Here, I examine how Boer prisoner of war objects portrayed Boer cultural identity at a time before there was an Afrikaner nation, as well as explore how political movements and the growing consumer culture affected the demand for these objects and the meanings that they accumulated. The changing role of objects in everyday life is tied to this period which saw women redefining their political status and role in society, and saw industry setting unprecedented levels of production, ultimately changing the way people live their lives, and define themselves, through objects.

Gender archaeology and nationalism

As the role of women in society has changed, so too has the archaeological approach to analysing objects become increasingly gendered. In the *Handbook of Gender in Archaeology*, Sarah M. Nelson (2006) describes the history, reasoning, and progress of gender archaeology over the past 40 years. Specifically, she identifies feminism and the women's movement in the 1960s and 1970s as the beginning of gender-sensitive archaeological thought. Nelson also identifies the different strands of gender archaeology (political feminism, gender theory, and historical revisionism), its different international approaches and theories, and its controversies and questions.

> 'Gender has become a growing and diversifying subject within archaeology; indeed, there is no sign that the stream of papers is even beginning to slow let alone 'run its course'. Rather, each exploration of gender brings more avenues to explore, more ways to think about the past. Each new facet of gender suggests another beyond.' (Nelson 2006: 2)

Nelson aims to show 'how far gender in archaeology has come and offers glimpses into new possibilities for future research' (*ibid.*). This paper has been influenced by the variety of ways in which gender plays an integral and insightful way of investigating the past. These varying perspectives have invited a similar investigation into a subject that has as yet received very little study – Boer prisoner-of-war art as gendered constructions of national identity and cultural and political movements. These gender approaches to material culture add significantly to the multi-disciplinary approach of modern conflict archaeology (Saunders 2010). However, it is the events of the early twentieth century that are crucial to understanding the role of objects in reconfiguring modern notions of self and nationalism.

Feminine and masculine ideals play a key role in defining national identity. The construction of gender and nationalism influence each other. Gender is used as a category in constructing and defining nationalism, which in turn is used to reinforce the masculine and feminine role within national identity (Dawson 1994). In *Soldier Heroes: British adventure, empire and the imagining of masculinities*, Graham Dawson examines the relationship between 'Britishness' (national identity) and masculine pleasure-culture (war games and adventure stories). He uses three biographical narratives; Victorian Henry Havelock, T.E. Lawrence, and an autobiography of his own childhood to explore the interrelation between public and private, the social and the psychic (Dawson 1994: 6–7). He explores 'a theorization of national identity as a fundamentally gendered construct', as well as 'how masculinities and femininities can be mobilized on behalf of the nation' (*ibid.*: 3). Dawson identifies the development and importance of social determinations upon narrative imagining, subjective composure, social recognition, public representations, and lived cultures and cultural production (within general and particular publics), and identifies feminism and feminist writing as a catalyst for his analysis.

Focusing on the Boer War itself, Elsabe Brink (1990) offers a similar examination of the use of gender in the construction of national identity. She examines the cultural and political creation of the ideal Afrikaner women or *volksmoeder*, who was a wife and mother not only to her family, but also to her nation (Brink 1990: 273). Brink discusses the theoretical and political circumstances surrounding a man-made image of the idealised woman and suggests that British colonial attitudes towards Afrikaner societal constructs and the lead up to the Anglo-Boer War influenced the nineteenth century origins of *volksmoeder*. Furthermore, she discusses the impact of the Boer War on the perception of Afrikaner women as heroic, patriotic and defiant in the face of their suffering (lost loved ones, burning of homes in the war, and incarceration in concentration camps). After the war ended, a publicly created image of the ideal Afrikaner woman is imagined – based on earlier nineteenth century and Anglo-Boer War historical dimensions. Brink states that although these cultural role models were initially created by men in the inter-war years, they were later appropriated by middle-class and working-class Afrikaner women during the 1930s and 1940s to legitimise their contested positions in an increasingly industrialised nation (Brink 1990: 291–292).

Objects provide tangible projections of these constructions of gender, identity, and nationalism:

> 'The object on its own cannot resist its appropriation, its reinterpretation ... It becomes the expression of norms, values and traditions, but through this it can also be used to resist or subvert its colonization ... The object is, therefore, social and it may produce explicit notions of significance and variance. As a consequence, objects are involved with the production of difference; they are partners to the construction of gender, as they provide forceful, partially sublimated, messages about importance, contribution, roles and effect.' (Sørensen 2000: 79)

Illustrating these insights into objects is Dawson's (1994) investigation of the evolution of toy production and its influences. He suggests that although the public adventure stories and physical appearance of the toy soldiers provided a basis or 'starting point' for his narrative imaginings, his adjustments to the characters and narratives were a means of acting out his own masculine identity.

The objects made in the prisoner-of-war camps during the Anglo-Boer War were also subject to the same reinterpretations and appropriations that Sørensen identifies (Sørensen 2000: 79). Boer prisoners, who made and bought these objects, and those that were intimately involved with the prisoners and the prison camps, applied personal meanings and experiences of war and the prison camps to these items. However, those who only knew the war through international newspaper coverage of the war also reinterpreted the objects. International press interest in the Boer War created a mass market for Boer souvenir objects, and as these objects took on the meanings, memories and experiences of the war, they also embodied the meanings and experiences of the socio-political issues that were intertwined with the Boer War public debate.

Boers and the media

> 'The camps controversy was the biggest scandal of the South African War, and newspapers on different sides of the war issue handled it very differently, reflecting not only the political differences among the [news]papers but also the changes the New Journalism was causing in the way war made news.' (Krebs 1999: 33)

Technological advances in printing and the postal system meant that news could travel faster from the front-lines to the reading public at home. Educational reform too meant that there were more readers from different classes reading newspapers, and a 'New Journalism' developed with the introduction of tabloid papers or 'halfpenny papers' (*ibid.*: 4). The wider readership of the popular press also saw an increasing variety of public opinion on the conflict. Many popular literary figures supported or criticised the war, including Rudyard Kipling, H. Rider Haggard, Olive Schreiner, and Arthur Conan Doyle (see Krebs 1999 for the impact of popular fiction and literary figures on the public opinion of empire and imperialism).

A number of authors have discussed this period as integral to understanding the development of the social movement of women's rights and peace politics as well as the role of gender, race, and class in understanding political and cultural developments (Krebs 1992; McClintock 1993; Nash 1999). The suffrage movement was underway in Britain and North America during the late nineteenth and early twentieth centuries, and the Anglo-Boer War became a platform through which issues important to the women's movement could be raised and discussed.

These events became entwined in public debate highlighting the Anglo-Boer War as a turning point in how the world viewed women and warfare, and set in motion a change in the role women played in war, and public debates on war. Consequently, the materialities of the Anglo-Boer War became associated with the suffrage movement as the conflict became another avenue through which women repositioned themselves within society.

> 'Not only do objects change through their existence, but they often have the capability of accumulating histories, so that the present significance of an object derives from persons and events to which it is connected.' (Gosden 1999: 170)

The humanitarian issue of how women and children were treated in concentration camps initiated the public debate during the conflict. As Krebs (1992: 39) states:

> 'the camps controversy took an issue about humanitarian conduct in war and framed it in terms of gender. Public debate centred on the questions of men's responsibilities toward women and women's role in war.'

Never before had the treatment of enemy civilians, especially women and children, been so publicly and enthusiastically discussed and criticised as a military strategy. This development also raised broader but equally serious concerns about the role women in Victorian society.

There were two points of view in the debate. For the Boers, Emily Hobhouse, who inspected the camps and wrote a report on the conditions (nowhere mentioning African camps), argued that the women needed protecting. The government responded by setting up the Fawcett Commission, and Millicent Fawcett went to South Africa to conduct her own investigation. Although Fawcett's portrayal of camp conditions was in line with Hobhouse's, her reasoning was different. Fawcett saw the camps as a military necessity and the inadequate and unhygienic conditions were solely the fault of the Boer women themselves. The spotlight on women during the Boer War created a gendered discourse in Britain which also raised questions about race and class (Krebs 1999; McClintock 1995). The Boer War was a turning point not only in how war was fought and discussed, but also in who was able to fight and write about it.

The increased readership of the popular press and the public commentary of the war by women raised questions about the role of British women during the war:

> 'British women's duties were at home, cried the patriotic letter-writers. Compassion is an appropriate quality in a woman, but an Englishwoman's compassion should be directed toward the widows and orphans of British soldiers, not toward the enemy. Not so, argued the letter writers in the pro-Boer press. 'An Englishwoman' proclaimed her 'heartache' and 'shame' in the 'Manchester Guardian' after the release of Hobhouse's report, and another noted that the British should 'have pity on all children, not just those in England'. Compassion was a female trait and duty, both sides agreed. But to whom should the Englishwoman be compassionate? Traditional associations with women's duties could be turned to the advantage of either side.' (Krebs 1992: 50)

We see in this discussion how nationalism was linked to gender, race and class. The letter-writers identified their role as 'British' women, and Hobhouse and Fawcett also used gender, race, and class to identify reasons behind the conditions of the camps (De Reuck 1999: 75–78; Krebs 1992: 44–51, 1999: 55–79). Hobhouse presented the Boer women as 'starving, noble mothers with their doomed children' (Krebs 1999:70), whereas, Fawcett posited that 'ignorant, selfish mothers' were to blame for the poor camp conditions (*ibid.*). Several authors have examined how these depictions of Boer women and their suffering during the war was used subsequently to create an Afrikaner national identity (De Reuck 1999: 69–74; Grundlingh 1999: 22–23, 25; McClintock 1993: 72; 1995: 377–379). De Reuck examines the use of private narratives of women's suffering in the concentration camps in the construction of a political group identity and nationhood, creating the identity of the 'wounded nation (De Reuck 1999: 79–84). Grundlingh (1999: 21–25) discusses the changing perceptions of the Boer War throughout the twentieth century and its effect on Afrikaner nationalism.

The public debate on women and children in concentration camps brought the Boer War to the attention of the entire Western World. In fact, the conflict was global as well, with volunteer New Zealanders, Australians, and Canadians joining ranks with the British, and the German, French, Dutch, and Scandinavians fighting for the Boers (Lowry 1999: 43–49). The international coverage of the Boer War and the concentration camp debate as well as the creation of Afrikaner nationalism after the conflict used war-related objects as emblems of the issues raised during the conflict itself.

> 'Objects can be understood only through looking at the cultural contexts which originally produced them and the circumstances into which they later moved. The histories of many objects are composed of shifts of context and perspective.' (Gosden 1999: 174)

Bermuda Boer POW camps and the Boer souvenir trade

> *Lone and captive far from home,*
> *On Muda's islands did I roam;*
> *Rest for my wearied limbs I sought,*
> *And peace and calm for mind distraught*
>
> *Pained by affliction's adverse act,*
> *A healing balm for both I lacked.*
> *Said I not well, "lacked" was the word?*
> *Comfort and nothing words are heard;*
> *Hence Fate, I will not bitter be,*
> *A friend, indeed, you brought to me –*
> *Long years of friendship, Lora P.!'*
> (Willie Honicke)

The title for this paper was taken from this poem, quoted in *Boer Prisoners of War in Bermuda* (Benbow 2006: 47–48). Written by prisoner Willie Honicke, the poem is a tribute to Lora Paschal, a young woman he met while incarcerated on the island, and who had showed him kindness when he was paroled. As Benbow (*ibid.*) astutely points out, Honicke's appreciation of Paschal's kindness can be read in the first letter of each line, which spells out her name.

The book describes the military background, camp layout and preparation, the arrivals and distribution of the prisoners onto the different islands, the treatment of the prisoners, daily routine, and even escape attempts. It provides an extraordinary insight into a little known chapter in Bermuda's history, which nevertheless pushed the island into the spotlight of the international debate on the war and women's rights.

The old Boer POW camp sites have been re-used over the years, and little remains visible on-site today. Nevertheless, the immense souvenir trade in Boer objects has provided the archaeological evidence needed to understand this period more fully. The demand for these materialities of war created the souvenir industry and the range of objects that survive today; the historical importance of these items to collectors and museums means that these artefacts are often in extremely good condition.

The number and variety of objects made in Bermuda are evidence both of the development of war souvenirs, and of the variety of meanings attributed to them. Demand for souvenirs increased as news of the conflict travelled across the Atlantic,

Figure 8.1: Boer prisoners of war displaying the industrial scale of souvenir carving. (© National Museum of Bermuda)

and the Boer POWs organised themselves and their carving industry accordingly (Figure 8.1).

The re-modelling (transformation) of these objects from icons of Boer identity to souvenir commodity (bought by persons culturally and spatially removed from the conflict) illustrates Appadurai's (1986: 47) argument that, 'tourist art constitutes a special commodity traffic, in which the group identities of producers are tokens for the status politics of consumers'.

Carving became a large-scale industry in all the camps. On Burt's [Island] they had an Industrial Association, formed by the ubiquitous August Schulenburg and aimed at getting the fellows to turn their hands to something useful while, at the same time, earning themselves a few pence to spend on tobacco at the canteen. Finished carvings were packed in a large box, cleared by the Camp Commandant, and sent over to Hamilton [the capital]. A percentage of the sale price was returned for distribution amongst those who had done the work (Benbow 2006: 28).

The Boer souvenir trade was so popular during the war that Fransjohan Pretorius highlights it as one of the larger turnovers in Boer objects out of the numerous camps all over the world (Pretorius 2006: 34). Pretorius also suggests that this was 'a period of sustained and spontaneous creation of folk art, one of the most productive and

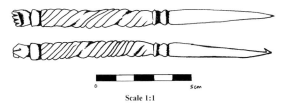

Figure 8.2: Bone crochet hook, Pelser Collection, National Museum of Bermuda. (© author)

creative times in the cultural history of the Afrikaner' (*ibid.*: 31). Pretorius's analysis of the objects and their meanings provides a valuable insight into the role that these objects played in constructing and maintaining Boer identity.

Boer POWs produced a number of varied objects including walking sticks, small boxes, knives, cutlery, serviette rings, crochet hooks, brooches, pen holders, letter openers, and picture frames. Many of these contain insightful elements of Boer identity: guerrilla warfare and resistance (clenched fists, guns, and animals fighting), religion (bibles and crosses) and life on the South African veldt (riding boots, horses, and depictions of family).

The objects that retain a feminine quality (i.e. those related to women's work in the home) can be juxtaposed with the patriarchal society of the Boers and Victorian England, and with Boer men missing their female counterparts in Bermuda's POW camps. Such items offer an insight into how they attained gendered meaning during a time when the issue of women's place in society was at the forefront of public discourse.

First, these objects were created as 'a way to pass the time' (Pretorius 2006: 33), but decisions as to what to make, and what shapes these carvings took, were more personal. They were often carved to represent those who were left behind in South Africa, and who often were subject to the British military in concentration camps.

The objects described here are part of the 'Pelser Collection' at the National Museum of Bermuda (incorporating the Bermuda Maritime Museum), and were carved by Boer prisoner Theunis Gert Pelser. He was incarcerated in Bermuda from the 13 September 1901 to the 8 October 1902, and whilst on the island, he gathered a collection of beef-bone and cedar-wood carvings. Within this collection are a number of feminine or domestic objects, serviette rings, brooches, crochet hooks, cutlery, and picture frames. The crochet hooks were made from either beef-bone or cedar and are adorned with either a clenched fist or a knot finial on one end with the hook on the other (Figure 8.2). The carving of hands in Boer souvenirs is mentioned in a 1903 *New York Times* article referring to pen holders that a prisoner had brought in to sell:

> 'On each end of the holder was a hand perfectly carved. One held a closed book. The other grasped the end of a small cannon, over which the pen was to be fitted. 'This,' said the prisoner of war 'is particularly a Boer souvenir. It typifies the common remark we used to hear when the war broke out, that we fight "with the Bible in one hand and a gun in the other"'. (Anon. 1903)

Though neither the gun nor the Bible were carved into the crochet hooks, the clenched fist is often associated with resistance movements. Its presence on an item whose function was associated with womanly pastimes emphatically places women within the sphere of conflict and resistance.

Many of the brooches in the Pelser Collection have individual women's names on them, whilst others were made specifically for the souvenir trade, and will be discussed later. The presence of so many women's names on these objects signifies the longing that prisoners felt for their homes and families.

> 'My father had to leave the two of us – mother and me – alone in the concentration camp and was sent away across the sea. In those distant foreign lands his thoughts, his whole soul, soared back to the fields of the old Transvaal, and there the most tender and sincere love lay claim to his very existence. He then made a brooch …' (Pretorius, 2006: 35)

On one brooch (Figure 8.3) are the subtle icons of Boer identity alongside the name of a loved one. Measuring 34 x 48 x 4 mm, it is made of bone and carved in a heart shape with an arrow through it. A cross (emblematic of Boer Calvinism), two palm fronds, and the name *Lettie* are carved inside the heart. The right lobe may have contained another symbol but, unfortunately, it has broken off and is missing. The heart was often used as a symbol in Boer prisoner-of-war objects, and as Pretorius (2006: 36) suggests, 'symbolised the longing for loved ones'.

Most unusual is the 'mizpah pin' (Figure 8.4), due to the fact that it is one of the few objects in the collection made from metal rather than bone or wood. Popular during the Victorian era, the mizpah brooch is a sentimental item of longing, and references a line from the book of Genesis: 'The Lord watch between me and thee, when we are absent one from another' (Genesis 31: 49).

These objects became miniature representations of the absent female Boer counterpart, as well as embodiments of Boer ideas of religion and resistance. The image of the Boer woman was used in the popular press to initiate public debate on empire, war, race and gender, and was used in the camps as a memento of home and family. Although the camps in Bermuda detained Boer men and boys, the objects also depict the detainment of Boer women and children in South Africa.

> 'The extreme behaviours provoked by war illustrate how an individual's social being is determined by their relationship to the objects that represent them – how objects become metaphors for the self, a way of knowing oneself through things both present and absent.' (Saunders 2004: 6)

These Afrikaner appropriations of the materialities of war were not the only re-interpretations of objects. Just as the international press jumped on the popularity of the Boer War in public debate, its readers created an international trade in Boer prisoner-of-war objects – what Pretorius identifies as Boer 'folk art' (Pretorius 2006: 31). The creation of these objects may have started out of the boredom of camp life but the global interest in the Boers in the popular press meant that an entire industry was created from a war of destruction. The papers at the time produced advertisements (Benbow 2006: 28) and articles (that read like advertisements) for these objects.

> 'Every souvenir store, every jewellery establishment, the drug stores, the department stores, and even the laundries and photograph galleries – in short, every place which a tourist from the United States or Canada is likely to visit – has "Boer Souvenirs"'. (Anon. 1903)

Brooches were popular in the camps and in the souvenir trade. Their popularity can be seen in their presence as explicitly-made souvenirs (Figure 8.5). The increase in American and Canadian tourists to Bermuda meant that the island had one of the largest turnovers of Boer prisoner-of-war art (Pretorius 2006: 34). These objects then found themselves and their associations transported around the Western world. Prisoners bought objects from each other, British officers purchased souvenirs as did the locals, each of whom were actively involved in the day-to-day consequences of war and the detention of prisoners on the island. The tourists, however, associated the objects with what they read, and the most printed and debated topic was women and children in concentration camps.

Commodities represent very complex social forms and distributions of knowledge. In the first place, and crudely, such knowledge can be of two sorts: the knowledge (technical, social, aesthetic, and so forth) that goes into the production of the commodity; and the knowledge that goes into approximately consuming the commodity. (Appadurai 1986: 41)

Thus, we can understand the effect of space and time on an object's associations and interpretation, and can see how the Boer prisoner-of-war art accumulated such global popularity and range of meanings:

> '[A]s commodities travel greater distances (institutional, spatial, temporal), knowledge about them tends to become partial, contradictory, and differentiated. But such differentiation may itself (through the mechanisms of tournaments of value, authentication, or frustrated desire) lead to the intensification of demand.' (Appadurai 1986: 56)

The objects created by the Boer prisoner-of-war in Bermuda had multiple associated meanings and contexts. The Boer prisoners were transported thousands of miles from their home of South Africa to the small islands of Bermuda. Once incarcerated, the prisoners began producing objects which held great personal meanings and representations and were traded between one another, the officers guarding them, and the locals sharing their country. Each of these groups added their own values to the object. However, the association of the Boer War with the women's movement in England, America and Canada put the conflict, those involved with it, and the objects associated with them, into a larger socio-political arena.

Figure 8.3: Bone brooch, Pelser Collection, National Museum of Bermuda. (© author)

Figure 8.4: Metal 'mizpah' pin, Pelser Collection, National Museum of Bermuda. (© author)

Figure 8.5: Bone 'Souvenir' brooch, Pelser Collection, National Museum of Bermuda. (© author)

Conclusions

As the role of women in society has changed so too has the way that we approach and interpret the past. Gender Archaeology developed as a response to the women's movement in the 1960s and 1970s, raising concerns over how women were depicted in the constructions of the past. This called for a more reflexive interpretation of the past, identifying various missing elements, and ushered in a multi-layered approach to archaeological interpretation. In this respect, the twentieth-century issues of the women's movement created the interpretative framework which allows for an analysis of the role of women in the nineteenth century and their changing role in warfare. This paper has identified how gender constructions play a part in determining national identity, and, conversely, how national identity reinforces concepts of gender. More specifically, I have examined how people use objects to create these constructions of gender, identity, and nationalism. As objects move through the processes of manufacture, trade, and collection, the people intimately involved with the items ascribe personal meanings to them, adding to their complexity.

The international discourse on the Boer War ushered in a new view of women in times of war. Women were now intimately involved in military conflict as collaborators, providing food and shelter to the enemy, and could be viewed as combatants. The image and treatment of women as combatants and prisoners provided a platform for the voice of women. They began to articulate public opinions for and against war, as well as on how women of a certain class and race should behave.

The Boer War – described as 'the last of the Gentlemen's Wars' (Krebs 1992: 39), was supposed to be a struggle between two white patriarchal nations. In reality, however, its imperialist motives depended greatly on constructions of gender, race, and class. Though absent from the images of the Boer War, understandings of self through gender, race, and class differences motivated and re-affirmed national identity on both sides of the conflict.

The objects made by the Boers are tangible evidence of the construction of gender in national identity and of the global impact of the Boer War. The framework conceptualised by the beginnings of gender archaeology allow for an insight into the multi-layered narratives that objects can appropriate over time and distance. At its most intimate level, objects become representations of the self for those who made them, creating images of home and family. At the other extreme, the advancement of educational reform, printing technologies, and the postal system enabled more people to read about international affairs. As the knowledge of the Anglo-Boer War spread internationally, a demand for souvenirs of the conflict increased. Now objects were being purchased and re-interpreted by people whose only involvement with the war was second hand in the international press.

The underlying cause for the international Boer War debate, and the suffering of women and children in concentration camps, raised questions about the part that women play in society and politics more generally. The women's movement was an international development, the suffrage movement was occurring in England, Canada and the United States, and the objects that tourists purchased became symbolic of changing role of women in society. The Anglo-Boer War and the portrayal of women as combatants and prisoners became a stage upon which issues of the women's movement could be popularised. The objects associated with the conflict became entwined with the larger issues of the women's movement, and as such accumulated an array of meanings beyond the personal associations of the prisoners who carved them.

Objects can attain any number of meanings and associations over time. This paper has examined how those items made by Boer prisoners-of-war detained in Bermuda not only represented the experiences and memories of war, but were also re-interpreted as symbols of gender and national identity. Yet this is only the beginning of our re-engagement with the complex array of meanings that were attributed to these fragile but subtly powerful items.

Bibliography

Alberti, B. (2004) Archaeology, Men, and Masculinities. In S.M. Nelson (ed.), *Handbook of Gender in Archaeology,* 401–434. Walnut Creek (CA): AltaMira Press.

Anon. (1903) Work of Prisoners of War. *New York Times* (25 January). <http://query.nytimes.com/gst/abstract.html?res=F40915FF34591B728DDDAC0A94D9405B838CF1D3> Accessed 1 October 2010.

Appadurai, A. (1986) Introduction: Commodities and the Politics of Value. In A. Appadurai (ed.), *The Social Life of Things: Commodities in Cultural Perspective*, 3–63. Cambridge: Cambridge University Press.

Ashmore, W. (2004) Gender and Landscapes. In S.M. Nelson (ed.), *Handbook of Gender in Archaeology,* 199–218.Walnut Creek (CA): AltaMira Press.

Brink, E. (1990) Man-made Women: Gender, Class and the Ideology of the V*olksmoeder*. In C. Walker (ed.), *Women and Gender in South Africa to 1945*, 273–292. London: James Currey; Cape Town: David Phillip Publishers.

Dawson, G. (1994) *Soldier Heroes: British Adventure, Empire and the Imagining of Masculinities.* London: Routledge.

De Reuck, J. (1999) Social Suffering and the Politics of Pain: Observations on the Concentration Camps in the Anglo-Boer War 1899–1902. *English in Africa* 26(2): 69–88.

Gosden, C. and Marshall, Y. (1999) The Cultural Biography of Objects. *World Archaeology* 31(2): 169–178.

Grundlingh, A. (1999) The Bitter Legacy of the Boer War. *History Today* (November): 21–25.

Krebs, P.M. (1992) 'The Last of the Gentlemen's Wars': Women in the Boer War Concentration Camp Controversy. *History Workshop* 33 (Spring): 38–56.

Krebs, P.M. (1999) *Gender, Race, and the Writing of Empire.* Cambridge: Cambridge University Press.

Lowry, D. (1999) When the World Loved the Boers. *History Today* (May): 43–49.

McClintock, A. (1993) Family Feuds: Gender, Nationalism and the Family. *Feminist Review* 44, 'Nationalisms and National Identities' (Summer): 61–80.

McClintock, A. (1995) *Imperial Leather: Race, Gender and Sexuality in the Colonial Contest.* London: Routledge.

Nash, D. (1999) The Boer War and its Humanitarian Critics. *History Today* (June): 42–49.

Nelson, S.M. (2006) Introduction: Archaeological Perspectives on Gender. In S.M. Nelson (ed.), *Handbook of Gender in Archaeology,* 1–27. Walnut Creek (CA): AltaMira Press.

Pretorius, F. (2006) Boer Prisoner of War Art. *History Today* (March): 31–37.

Saunders, N. (2003). *Trench Art: Materialities and Memories of War.* Oxford: Berg

Saunders, N. (2004). Material Culture and Conflict: The Great War, 1914–2003. In N.J. Saunders (ed.), *Matters of Conflict: Material Culture, Memory and the First World War,* 5–25. Abingdon: Routledge.

Saunders, N. (2010) Worlds Apart: Modern Conflict Archaeology and Battlefield Archaeology. *Arheo* 27: 45–55.

Saunders, N.J. and Cornish, P. (2009) *Contested Objects: Material Memories of the Great War.* Abingdon: Routledge.

Schofield, J. (2005) *Combat Archaeology: Material Culture and Modern Conflict.* London: Duckworth.

Sørensen, M.L.S. (2000) *Gender Archaeology.* Cambridge: Polity Press.

9

Mr Hopgood's Shed: an archaeology of Bishop's Cannings wireless station

Cassie Newland

It is a very good shed. It is made of corrugated iron (which Mr Hopgood has painted black) and is exactly 20 ft long (6 m) on each side. It has three doors and four windows. Some of the doors open. And some of them don't. Mr Hopgood doesn't mind (Figures 9.1 and 9.2). He mostly uses his shed for leaning things against. Before Mr Hopgood's shed was Mr Hopgood's, it belonged to his grandfather, Mr Hillier. Mr Hillier was the blacksmith in the village of Bishop's Cannings near Devizes in Wiltshire, southern England. He shoed horses and mended steam engines in his forge (which is where Mr Hopgood now mends cars). Mr Hillier used the shed to keep his cows in. You can still see the stalls and feed baskets that he made for them. Mr Hopgood thinks that the shed used to be part of a much longer building. He is probably right. You can see the place where Mr Hillier had to repair a large opening in one side. There are other interesting things to see inside the shed. There are wires for electric lights and slots in the roof beams to show where there was once a wall. The walls are lined with white asbestos sheets and there is a metal flu in one corner where a stove once stood.

Mr Hillier was very fond of his cows but he didn't build a stove to keep them warm! Mr Hillier's shed had a stove because it had not always been a cow shed. Mr Hopgood jokes that Mr Hillier never liked to see anything go to waste. He used to save everything. He even saved his shed. In 1929, Mr Hillier heard that the First World War Wireless Station on a nearby hill was going to be knocked down so he went up quietly before the men with the hammers arrived, put one of the sheds on a cart and brought it down to the village. He put the shed in the apple orchard behind his house for his cows to use. If you go up to the hill today, you can see the place where the shed used to stand, on a concrete base exactly 20 ft long on each side. How the shed got to be there in the first place and what it used to do up there is another story.

* * * * *

Telling the story of Mr Hopgood's shed is not as simple as it might first appear. The

Figure 9.1: (right) Mr John Hopgood, 2011 (© author).

Figure 9.2: (below) Mr Hopgood's shed, Bishop's Cannings, 2011 (© author)

shed – along with the wireless station and the wider landscape – has a complicated and condensed history which embodies the rapid and disjointed development of early military technologies. Accessing and reconstructing the chronology and purpose of the site is difficult for many reasons. Commercial secrecy shrouds technological details in a miasma of deliberately ambiguous patent specifications. The pace of technical obsolescence ensures that written specifications seldom materialise on site. Contractual u-turns and capricious government decisions are compounded by the brutal excisions of the Official Secrets Act. In use for fewer than two decades, the site was from the very beginning subject to impromptu and opportunistic reuses by a surprisingly swift succession of tenants. Here, I attempt to combine material, oral historic and documentary sources to untangle the collapsed and occluded story of the Bishop's Cannings wireless station and (by extension) Mr Hopgood's shed.

Historical background

Little mention of the Bishop's Cannings site appears in the relevant literature. Baker's (1970) *History of the Marconi Company* refers fleetingly to Bishop's Cannings as having been selected as a site for the Imperial Wireless Scheme (IWS). The IWS makes its first entrance in 1906 when wireless pioneer Guglielmo Marconi wrote a letter to the Postmaster General of the British Government (Marconi 1906). The letter, which survives in the Marconi collection, outlines a scheme to place the far flung corners of the British Empire in swift and constant communication with the Mother Country. In its initial incarnation, it was to consist of chains of high power wireless stations snaking out from the UK to the various British colonies, dominions and protectorates. Stations were to be located on British controlled territories enabling communications to be passed from one to the next in 1000 mile (1609 km) hops. The IWS was intended for government use, to complement – and to some extent to rival – existing international telegraph services (Marconi 1906).

The chain of IWS stations could be built and maintained at a fraction of the price of equivalent land and submarine telegraph lines, and, once installed, messages could be sent at less than half the cost. The proposal was received with a certain amount of incredulity by the British Colonial Office. It was, after all, just five years since Marconi's first successful transatlantic message. Wireless' best advertisement – the flagship commercial service between Poldhu, Cornwall and Glace Bay, Massachusetts – remained temperamental and functioned only intermittently (Baker 1979: 78). In light of the newness of the technology and the obvious teething problems, the IWS appeared preposterously ambitious. It was dismissed out of hand.

Two years later, undaunted, Marconi drafted a prospectus for the *The British Empire Wireless Telegraph Co. Ltd* to raise capital of £1500.00. In it he states that the company is founded 'for the purpose of establishing a telegraph service between all portions of the British Empire by means of wireless telegraphy' (Marconi 1908) and on 10 March

1910 he again wrote to the British Government to propose an Empire-wide system of wireless stations (Marconi 1910).

The new, wider-reaching system was to comprise stations at England, Alexandria, Aden, Mombassa, Natal, South Africa, Bombay, Colombo, Singapore, Hong Kong, North Australia, Sydney Australia, New Zealand, St Helena, Sierra Leone, Bathurst, British Guiana, and the West Indies (*ibid.*). A dedicated wireless evangelist, Marconi pointed out some of the many ways in which wireless could transform the administration of the empire.

The first was again cost, not only in terms of pennies per word but in terms of time saved and confusion avoided. News, which through the existing telegraph system had taken several days to reach England, could arrive in a matter of minutes. Urgent dispatches, such as orders or cancellations, could also be conveyed more speedily from Whitehall to the provinces. Economically, Marconi argued, the IWS would prove a boon to international business and would facilitate emigration by making it easier to maintain ties with far-flung family (*ibid.*).

He also pointed out that the IWS could generate not insubstantial revenue from press messages. The proposal finished with a thinly veiled warning: the IWS, if established, would set a use precedent. The British would have priority over the airwaves, cutting the German Telefunken system out of the equation. As further incentive to swift action, Marconi pointed out that the German budget released in November that same year made provision for just such a wireless scheme (*ibid.*). The argument proved persuasive.

In May 1911, the Imperial Wireless Conference was convened to give serious consideration to Marconi's proposal. The resulting memo agreed with the idea of an IWS in principle, but proposed a far more limited system (GPO 1911). It also demanded that the system should be state owned. The committee formed to consider the details was comprised of the High Commissioners for the various Dominions and Protectorates, representatives from Admiralty, the Colonial Office, War Office and the General Post Office. Crucially, it contained no engineers.

The results of their deliberations, released 15 June 1911, proposed stations to be built in Great Britain, Cyprus, Aden, Bombay, Singapore, and Western Australia. The committee demanded that sites be selected and marked out at once, two in each country, one to house the transmitting part of the circuit and one for the receiver. The Imperial Defence Committee, Admiralty, and War Office were charged with proposing suitable sites, and by late summer the selection had been made.

Bishop's Cannings was to house the receiver. The tiny Wiltshire hamlet was intended to be the hub of the British Empire's new telecommunication system. The name Bishop's Cannings was to be emblazoned on telegrams, the embodiment of cutting edge technology and world-changing endeavour. Today, few people have ever heard of Bishop's Cannings. Even fewer have any clue that the crumbling concrete bases disappearing into rabbit warrens at one time represented the future of British wireless technology. Why the site – evidently completed and operational for a time – should now be so completely absent from the historical record is a matter of interest.

The Bishops Cannings wireless station

Topographically, the land looks unpromising. The site encompasses 'Furze Knowle', a (presumably) Iron Age hillfort. Isolated and steeply sloping, it appears at first glance to present a logistical nightmare in terms of both access for station staff and the transporting of building materials. Furthermore, there is no requirement for wireless technologies to be situated on such sloping ground. In terms of wider (and largely invisible) landscape considerations the site makes more sense.

First, it lies close to the main telegraph trunk line from Porthcurno to London, which passes underground through the nearby town of Calne. Second, and more importantly, the Imperial Wireless Committee (lacking engineers but blessed with an overabundance of Captains, Majors, and Colonels) made an explicit decision to select land on the basis of defensive strategy rather than technological concerns (Brackley 1914; War Office 1914).

Bishop's Cannings sits within a vast swathe of Crown Land extending over the Wansdyke and across the plains beyond. Estates were acquired in lieu of death duties from the late 1890s in order to accumulate land in the area for military purposes (Clarke-Smith 1969: v). The site was therefore not only available at virtually no cost to the government, but was part of a wider network of military infrastructure in the area.

The first revision of the Ordnance Survey map from 1900 shows the Bishop's Cannings site under, albeit ephemeral, military use at the time. A rifle range is shown as extending into the southernmost part of the site which, along with the associated barracks, was in existence from at least 1884 (Pugh and Crittle 1956: 187). What first appears as geographical isolation should rather be seen as part of a moveable, transient or, indeed, *potential* military network.

Having selected the sites, the Imperial Wireless Committee invited the Marconi Company to tender for the building of the stations. The tender was duly submitted the summer of 1911 with a guarantee that works would be completed within three years, with the England to Bombay and England to East Africa sections completed within one year. The tender was signed in March 1912. Construction did not begin immediately, but was delayed for the best part of a year by allegations of corruption, insider dealing, and share rigging which was reported in the contemporary press as 'The Marconi Scandal'. The government select committee which investigated the affair found in favour of Marconi on 30 April 1913. Contracts were immediately drawn up between the Marconi Company and the Post Master General of the General Post Office (GPO). These were signed on 30 June, and ratified by the House of Commons on 7 August. The station building project began at once.

Copies of the telegram conversations held at the British Telecom (BT) Archives between the Marconi Company and the High Commissioners in the various countries included in the scheme show that work began immediately on the British, Egyptian, and Indian stations (various authors 1913–14). The telegrams demonstrate that ground works were certainly started at Bishop's Cannings, Leafield, Abu Zabaal (Egypt), and

Bombay. Prefabricated mast sections and material for the bases are recorded as being produced for all sites (including those at Singapore, Pretoria, and East Africa) from that point onwards.

The project continued apace. Towards the end of April 1914, the first signs that all was not well began to appear. This is evidenced by a series of increasingly urgent telegrams from the Marconi Company to the Colonial Office in London, asking (and finally begging) the government to take delivery of the completed steel mast sections and mast bases (Marconi 1914). No reply was forthcoming. The Marconi Company was left high and dry.

The reason soon became clear. On 29 July 1914, the German high power wireless station at Nauen was taken over by the military. The following day a wireless message was issued from there to the German Grand Fleet ordering them to battle stations. War was officially declared on 4 August 1914. The first British act of aggression was to cut the German deep sea telegraph cables on 5 August (Baker 1970: 159). All German war communications were forced onto the airwaves. Britain, in contrast, reaped the rewards of its strategically-planned, well defended, and extraordinarily expensive submarine cable network: the 'All-red Line'. British communications it seemed would hold.

The universal and unidirectional nature of early wireless signals meant that interception, code-making, and code-breaking became the new arena for the arms race. It seems that what was needed was not the day to day communications offered by the Imperial Wireless Scheme, but rather a wireless weapon. Baker (1970) notes that construction was pushed ahead on the British and Egyptian stations (presumably including Bishop's Cannings) while work was put on hold at all other sites (Baker 1970: 160). On 30 December 1914, the General Post Office cancelled the Imperial Wireless Scheme contract with the Marconi Company.

At that point, documentary evidence for the Bishop's Cannings site becomes scarce. Baker (1970) in his extensive documentation of the Marconi Company certainly never mentions it again. Further information about the site can still, however be pieced together from the documentary record. The name Bishop's Cannings appears on a list of long-distance wireless telegraph stations compiled by the Foreign Office shortly after the armistice in November 1918 (Foreign Office 1918). It also appears on a list of wireless sites being returned to the GPO in 1919 (War Office 1919). The existence of these documents confirms that the site was functional during the war.

The most interesting occurrence of the name, however, is on an arbitration document from the 1919 court case between the Marconi Company and the government (Marconi 1919). The name Devizes appears in connection with 'war work' undertaken, and lists a small sum as 'unpaid operator's wages'. The wage claim dates from the latter part of 1914 and the early part of 1915, and indicates that the station was at least partially operable at that time.

Knowing that the receiving function of the site had therefore been completed allows us to suggest that the running of the station was then passed to the War Office soon after the commencement of hostilities (as was the case for the GPO ship-to-shore stations). The War Office created the Wireless Signal Company as a unit in its own right on 2 January 1915. Their remit was to operate wireless sets in the field and to run the British stations. As the 1919 wage claim suggests, the Marconi Company were operating Bishop's Cannings until at least April 1915 it could be suggested that the Signals Company was not fully operational by that time. It also suggests that operators must have been housed on site and that some form of accommodation must have been provided.

That the station was built as a receiving – rather than transmitting – station is a clue to its likely war time role. Long wave receivers were frequently employed not for the reception of telegraph messages (the submarine cable system dealt with that) but as direction finding stations. Papers relating to direction finding in the First World War in the Marconi collection, Oxford (MS. Marconi 355.n.d.) suggest that the station would have been fitted with the latest, top secret 'Round' receivers (named for the Marconi engineer Captain H J Round and famously employed in the battle of Jutland), and could have been used to determine the position of enemy wireless stations and the movements of Zeppelin airships. It may also have had a role as a listening station employed to eavesdrop on enemy transmissions. The Germans, unaware of the existence of the Round receiver, and thinking their transmissions safely out of range, continued to issue orders openly and unencrypted over the airwaves (see MS.Marconi 355 for a selection of newspaper cuttings from 1920 when the existence of the Round receiver hit the popular press).

After the war, it seems likely that the station was redundant for a short time while the GPO was searching for a new role for Bishop's Cannings. Pugh and Crittle (1953) note that around 1919 the site was converted for use in long-range 'ship to shore' communication (Pugh and Crittle 1953: 187). Ship-to-shore work requires two-way communication, and would have necessitated the installation of transmitting equipment and generation plant to provide power. It is therefore likely that further buildings were erected on the site at this time.

The experimental long-wave ship-to-shore service appears to have been highly successful and was subsequently moved to a purpose-built site at Burnham-on-Sea in 1924 – the short-wave service also relocating there in 1926 (Bennett and Lea 2000). This would suggest that the site had again been used as an experimental test-bed by the GPO, this time for an embryonic short-wave service. Further physical modifications to the site would have been required at this time. In 1929, the Burnham-on-Sea station closed and its duties passed to a new station recently constructed at Portishead near Bristol. The Bishop's Canning station appears also to have been decommissioned at this time.

A brief history of the site can therefore be pieced together from extrapolation and surviving documents. From 1911 to 1929, a period of 18 years, the wireless station site at Bishop's Cannings had passed from the Marconi Company to the GPO, the War Office and Signals Corps, and back to the GPO. Built as the flagship station of the Imperial Wireless Scheme, it was probably employed as a listening station, a direction finding station, a long-range ship-to-shore station, and as a test bed for experimental wireless technologies. Four distinct phases of use had taken place on the site each requiring changes to the station's fabric and layout. This scanty history, however, tells us little about Bishop's Cannings place in wider geographical and political landscapes, how the site developed physically, or what life might have been like for those working in and around the site. With such a swift succession of occupations on site and few material traces remaining – excepting the concrete bases – how can archaeology add to understandings of the site? To begin to answer these questions we must return to Mr Hopgood's shed.

An archaeology of Mr Hopgood's shed

There appears to be little doubt that the shed was part of the station site. The footprint, 20 ft (6 m) on either side, could drop perfectly onto any one of the several 20 by 20 ft (6 × 6 m) plinths remaining on site. Its corner timbers would slot neatly into the fossilised post-holes in the bases. Even the wavy lines imprinted into the wet concrete by the corrugated iron of the walls can be clearly seen. Furthermore, it is not impossible to determine the exact location of the shed. The arrangement of doors and windows suggest that it was 'end of terrace'. The buildings were all raised above ground level and the placement of steps on the site constrains possible orientations.

Mr Hopgood's shed can confidently be said to have resided at the western end of the upper range of buildings (Figure 9.3). It would have been orientated to the small gravel track running east to west across the site, with its windows facing downhill

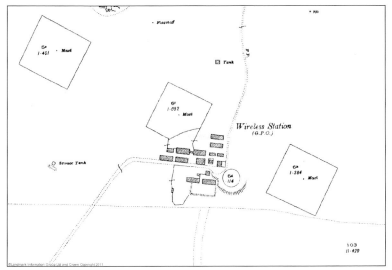

Figure 9.3: Bishop's Cannings Wireless Station as shown on 1924 OS map 1:2500

Figure 9.4: General view of the site of Bishop's Cannings, 2011. (© author)

towards the south, overlooking the main entrance. Steps would have led from a door at the back of the building towards the masts on the hill above. This would have been the only external access to the building. It would, however, have been connected to a range of interlinking, identical buildings to the east. A further range of buildings was situated downhill to the south. It is not difficult to place Mr Hopgood's shed on the site; the difficulty arises from determining its role within the site and the phase from which it dates.

Concrete bases laid down over a period of just two decades do not lend themselves to tight dating (Figure 9.4). Many of the materials remaining at the site do, however, display design features that enable them to be confidently dated to the initial Marconi build of 1913. For example, the poured concrete mast bases, 6 ft (1.83 m) square are identical to those remaining at Poldhu, Cornwall. A better-documented, if not iconic site, the Poldhu mast bases were erected *c.* 1912. That these were still in use two years later suggests that mast design was not subject to the rapid evolution of other aspects of early wireless telegraphy.

What survives at Bishop's Cannings, however, are parts of a steel mast footing and base. The 25 mm thick plates would have clamped cylindrical steel masts to a plate set into the concrete. Evidently broken beyond use at the time of demolition in 1929, the base section was discarded. The isolated and geographically inaccessible location appears to have protected it from later salvage operations. As the only known surviving example, the base section not only helps to date the site, but provides vital clues to mast construction on this and many other early wireless sites. It also provides dating evidence for many other concrete structures on site, including the associated poured concrete anchor stones and guying anchors. Mr Hopgood's shed itself, however, does not seem likely to date from the initial 1913 Marconi build.

Although the Marconi Company did employ sheds as station buildings in the early days of wireless telegraphy, they appear to have been of a particular and standardised design. Photographs of contemporary stations at Poldhu and Clifden, Ireland, show sheds of identical construction, employing timber cladding and topped by a distinctive asymmetrical roof (MSS A.5.5, MSS A.5.9 n.d.). Mr Hopgood's corrugated iron shed is distinctly different. The specifications for the IWS stations would also seem to suggest a different origin for Mr Hopgood's shed.

While prefabricated sheds were employed at Poldhu and Clifden they do not appear to have been part of the original plan for Bishop's Cannings. Surviving architect's plans instead depict rather grand, decidedly un-shed-like brick built buildings both for the station and for operators' housing. These were evidently never built. Not only would the surviving footings be insufficient to support them but moreover, the comprehensive collection of receipts from local construction firms for goods and services on site (including the erection of fences, the making of roads, the digging of pits for the anchor blocks, and the materials for the bases and stones themselves) makes no mention of building having commenced on the planned station or associated housing.

The footings surviving on site appear far more temporary in nature. The generator and transmitting room floors (identifiable by particular arrangements of mounting blocks set into the concrete) appear more similar in appearance to those already in existence at Poldhu than to that originally planned for the Bishop's Cannings station. Baker (1970: 160) mentions that basic plant rooms were hurriedly built in an attempt to complete the Egyptian stations at the outbreak of war, and it seems likely that a similarly hurried construction took place at Bishop's Cannings. One point is clear, Mr Hopgood's shed, along with the surviving concrete footings, paths, floors, and steps were not part of Marconi's original IWS design.

A closer inspection of Mr Hopgood's shed provides clues to its origins. The internal timbers bear signs of having been internally divided from front to back into two rooms. There is an integral timber floor which would have raised the building above the cold concrete of the base. It boasts opening windows, a stove and chimney, and walls insulated with asbestos sheets. It is clearly not a storage shed or a plant room, but appears intended for some form of human habitation. The existence of these (albeit scant) concessions to domestic comfort provides us with a further clue to the shed's origins, especially when these are considered in the light of the wider landscape.

Conflict landscapes

Bishop's Cannings lies within the Salisbury Plain Army Training Estate. From 1898 military camps such as Ogbourne, Chiseldon, Larkhill, Bulford, Warminster, and Tidworth were established throughout the area (Clarke-Smith 1969). Many began life as tented camps at the beginning of the First World War, providing urgently needed temporary accommodation for troops during training. The tents were gradually replaced with 'huts' by the War Office from early 1915. Some of these, such as the huts at Chiseldon Camp, are particularly well documented – indeed, a few remained standing into the 1970s (Anon. 2008).

These camp huts of the First World War – though individual details vary – display striking parallels with Mr Hopgood's shed. Contemporary photos of the camps demonstrate they were invariably framed in timber with a symmetrical, pitched, corrugated iron roof. As with Mr Hopgood's shed, they were asbestos lined, fitted with a stove, built onto a raised wooden floor, and would have afforded a similarly Spartan standard of living (*ibid.*).

They were also modular in design, allowing the square huts to be fitted together in rows on long concrete bases, an arrangement which can clearly be seen at the Bishop's Cannings site. Moreover, surviving receipts in the BT Archives from the Bishop's Cannings ground works were made out to 'Chivers of Devizes', the same firm noted by Bailey (1998) as having constructed the prefabricated huts for Chiseldon. This, coupled with a shared War Office 'landlord', suggests that Mr Hopgood's shed in fact began life as an army hut.

This probability offers a window into what life would have been like on site. Living conditions inside First World War camps are legendary and much documented in contemporary literature (e.g. Simkin 1988: 243). The huts at nearby Chiseldon Camp were described as 'notoriously cold and damp' (Anon. 2008). In the tin-roofed sheds it was impossible to stay warm, sleep properly, or dry clothing and boots (Bailey 1998). Conditions were so terrible during the first 1914–15 winter of the war (one of the wettest on record) that the huts become the focus of much complaint. The difficulties in the camps found their outlet in comedy postcards and doggerel verse.

> *There's lots of little huts, dotted here and there.*
> *For those who have to live inside, I've offered many a prayer.*
> *Inside the huts there's RATS as large as any nanny goat.*
> *Last night a soldier saw one trying on his overcoat!*
> (Anon. postcard, Chiseldon Camp, *c.* 1915)

That Mr Hopgood's shed remained in use at Bishop's Cannings until 1929 offers further insights into life on site. While the end of the war brought relief for many of the troops billeted in the Wiltshire camps, it did not bring a reprieve for those staff (now under the GPO) stationed at Bishop's Cannings.

Mr Hopgood's shed outlived the military phase and appears to have continued to provide damp and draughty accommodation for the station staff throughout the operational life of the site. Certainly the subsequent material changes made by the GPO at the time of the ship-to-shore expansion in 1924 seem not to have included any further residential provision.

This is evidenced by the one upstanding building remaining on site (now a cow shed). Constructed from brick with distinctive buttressed side walls, the building is identical to one shown in a photograph from Burnham-on-Sea taken around 1924. The materials within suggest that it probably relates to the addition of transmitting and power plant during the ship-to-shore phase rather than upgraded staff accommodation. It appears that Mr Hopgood's shed remained in use as staff accommodation until the staff were re-located to more permanent stations first at Burnham-on-Sea and then at Portishead. Far from becoming the internationally recognised centrepiece of Marconi's grand IWS plans, Bishop's Cannings wireless station was, at all times, temporary, experimental, and rather 'hush hush'.

The archaeology of a shed may sound of limited interest. But, from the inclusive perspective of modern conflict archaeology, the journey taken in the search for Mr Hopgood's shed has offered new ways of understanding the site. Not only has it allowed us to characterise the site and provide a chronology, but, by placing it within a wider conflict-related landscape, it permits wider connections to be suggested. Exploring the shed ensures that we approach the site broadly, going beyond technologically focused descriptions of historic wireless technologies to encompass economic, political, and indeed personal landscapes.

The story of Mr Hopgood's shed highlights the accidental and contingent nature of technology. The documentary record for the intended high-spec station is complete in every way. Cancellation of the project at the last minute left very little in the way of a paper trail and – on the basis of the paper record alone – it would be easy to assume that station construction went ahead as intended. It is only upon visiting the site that the ad hoc and experimental nature of building and use becomes evident.

Moreover, sheds such as Mr Hopgood's *are* interesting in their own right. Sheds often represent the physical vanguard of a site. Swiftly deployed, cheap and easily modifiable, initial shed-based layouts may become fossilised by more permanent structures in later phases of a site. The study of temporary buildings, such as the humble shed, offers archaeologists a window onto fast-moving technologies and indeed the wider world.

More importantly, the focus on Mr Hopgood's shed allows us to explore the wider military infrastructure of Salisbury Plain. Using one object as the subject and narrative of an archaeology enables us to draw in a disparate collection of artefacts, documents, people, and landscapes to create new perspectives and understandings.

Mr Hopgood's shed highlights the *ad hoc* nature of the urgent provision of military infrastructure and sets this against the long term strategic planning decisions involved in the accumulation of Crown Estate land for military purposes. It also sheds light on the economic importance of military projects to the local population in terms of contracts and employment. At the same time it reveals the human face of government by unmasking the individuals and decisions behind site selection, staffing and building construction.

Most important of all perhaps, Mr Hopgood's shed reminds archaeologists that conflict does not only take place on the battlefield – a key point re-iterated throughout this volume. The training, accommodation, factories, hospitals, roads, and, in the case of the Bishop's Cannings, wireless site *information* necessary for prosecuting war, form an ever present network without which battles would not and could not take place. Mr Hopgood's shed reminds us that modern war has unpredictable and enduring consequences, and is frequently a peace-time activity engaging thousands of hectares, objects, and lives. Archaeologists interested in conflict should endeavour to recognise and investigate this diversity of evidence.

Bibliography

Anon. Postcard. (*c.* 1915) *Chiseldon Camp.* Maybury's Picadilly (from the collection of T. Midwinter).

Anon. (2008) Chiseldon Camp. *Guide to Swindon.* http://www.swindonweb.com/?m=8&s=116&ss=763&c=2501&t=Chiseldon+Camp

Bailey, D. (1998) *The Story of Chiseldon Camp: Part 1: 1914–1922.* Salisbury: Chiseldon Local History Group.

Baker, W.J. (1970) *A History of the Marconi Company.* London: Methuen.

Bennett, L. and Lea, B. (2000) *GKA History.* British Telecommunications plc. http://www.gka.btinternet.co.uk/history.htm

Brackley. (1914) *Letter to Wireless Telegraphy Committee regarding site selection in Egypt* (8 January). POST 30/2573B. British Telecommunications plc Archives, Holborn, London.

Clarke-Smith, E. (1969) *Salisbury Plain: an Historical Introduction Covering General History to Saxon Times and Military History from the 1890s.* Salisbury: Private printing.

Foreign Office. (1918) *List of Long Distance Stations.* POST 30/2977–2979. British Telecommunications plc Archives, Holborn, London.

GPO. (1911) *Minutes of Proceedings of the Imperial Conference, 1911.* MS. Marconi 220. The Marconi Collection, Bodleian Library, Oxford.

Marconi. (1906) *Proposal to Erect an Empire-wide System of Wireless Stations.* POST 30/2977–2979. British Telecommunications plc Archives, Holborn, London.

Marconi. (1908) *Draft prospectus for the The British Empire Wireless Telegraph Co. Ltd.* POST 30/2977-2979. British Telecommunications plc Archives, Holborn, London.

Marconi. (1910). *Letter to George Preece, Post Master General proposing to establish an Empire-wide system of wireless stations.* (10 March). POST 30/2977–2979. British Telecommunications plc Archives, Holborn, London.

Marconi. (1914) *Telegrams Sent to the Colonial Office Enquiring as to the Delivery of Mast Sections for the Overseas Imperial Wireless Stations.* POST 30/2977–2979. British Telecommunications plc Archives, Holborn, London.

Marconi. (1919) *Letter to the GPO regarding expenditure incurred in War Service 1915.* POST 30/3419–20. British Telecommunications plc Archives, Holborn, London.

MS. Marconi 355 (n.d.) *Papers Relating to Direction Finding*. The Marconi Collection, Bodleian Library, Oxford.

MSS A.5.5, MSS A.5.9 (n.d.). (MSS A.5.5 (Clifden); MSS A.5.9 (Poldhu). The Marconi Collection, Bodleian Library, Oxford.

Pugh, R.B. and Crittall, E. (eds) (1953) *History of the County of Wiltshire*. Vol. 7. Oxford: Oxford University Press.

Simkin, P. (1988) *Kitchener's Army: the Raising of the New Armies*. Manchester: Manchester University Press.

Various authors. (1913) *Copies of Telegrams Concerning the Erection of the Overseas Stations of the Imperial Wireless Scheme*. POST 30/2977–2979. British Telecommunications plc Archives, Holborn, London.

Various authors. (1914–20) *Papers Relating to Direction Finding*. In MS. Marconi 355.

War Office (1914) *Letter to Clerk of Works, Leafield Suggesting Defensive Arrangements to be Made* (19 January). POST 302977–2979. British Telecommunications plc Archives, Holborn, London.

War Office (1919) *List of Stations Being Returned to the Post Office*. POST 30/2977–2979. British Telecommunications plc Archives, Holborn, London.

10

'Hitler Loves Musso', and Other Civilian Wartime Sentiments: the archaeology of Second World War air-raid shelters and their graffiti

Emily Glass

This work will refer to a program of archaeological mitigation conducted in Winchester, Hampshire, by Oxford Archaeology in 2005–2006 which was co-supervised by the author. The area of excavation was positioned to the rear of Winchester Library on Jewry Street and was to be the location of a new public Discovery Centre. The programme brief included the partial removal of two Second World War air raid shelters as well as the excavation of any earlier Roman, Saxon, and medieval remains. The air raid shelters contained numerous pieces of wartime graffiti created by local people during the conflict and, despite retrieval not being specified in the original work brief, a few decorated concrete wall panel pieces were salvaged during the shelter removal process. Previous documentation and recording of the Jewry Street air raid shelters had been undertaken by Context One Archaeological Services (Context One 1998; Marter and McConnell 1999) and Oxford Archaeology (Oxford Archaeology 2006; 2007; Underdown 2011), which have been referenced for historical information.

The story of the Jewry Street shelters and their associated graffiti is situated within the general context of modern conflict archaeology (see Schofield *et al.* 2002; Saunders 2003; 2007), and is set specifically within the parameters of Second World War conflict landscapes as contested urban civilian space. The material response to this conflict was produced on the internal walls of the air raid shelters, and can provide a unique insight into the conditions under which they were created. Moreover, this cultural biography will address the conception, career, and cultural markers within the life-history of the structures, and, more specifically, will address what happens to these defensive objects when they reach the end of their original use-life (Kopytoff 1986: 66).

Across the United Kingdom, sites of Second World War remains have an ever-increasing national degree of importance which is often coupled with a deeper level of poignancy for local people living in the vicinity. These sites of war have immense emotional and educational values which are evoked through their *matériel* culture, not only to those who were involved in Wartime Britain, but also those of present and future generations (Schofield 2002: 145). Notably here, this is evident for people whose living memory encompasses Winchester at war and a component of this can be seen within the framework of this chapter.

The archaeological and historical remains on the Jewry Street site were set within the mechanics of British statute and planning guidance operational at the time: *Planning Policy Guidance* (PPG) 15 (for Planning and the Historic Environment) and *PPG* 16 (for Planning and Archaeology). These came into force in the 1990s, and allowed for consideration to be given during the planning process for all archaeological remains, whether they had been scheduled or not.[1] This impacted wartime monuments in two ways: those visible above ground and those below ground adjacent to earlier archaeological remains. Depending on the depth of the proposed development, both extant and buried structures would need to be recorded in order to access any further below-ground archaeological remains. At that time, relatively few twentieth century wartime remains had been Scheduled, and subsequently this became the subject of two major projects on twentieth century military heritage.

In 1994, as part of a wider review of the country's archaeological resource (the *Monuments Protection Programme*), English Heritage initiated an examination of twentieth century military defence sites in Britain. This coincided with the 50th anniversary of the end of the Second World War, and was a response to increased public concern regarding the vulnerable state of defence remains (English Heritage 1998: 2). Sites dating from the First World War to the Cold War were examined and recorded in order to quantify the surviving resource (Dobinson *et al.* 1997: 289). This process was informed using a review of primary sources at the National Archives undertaken by Colin Dobinson. With regard to Second World War Civil Defence, a representative rather than exhaustive sample was examined, as structures were too numerous to be recorded accurately in this manner (Schofield 2009: 28). Subsequently, in 1995, the Council for British Archaeology (CBA) led the *Defence of Britain Project*, which undertook a nationwide survey of twentieth century military archaeological sites and defence structures in response to increased development and coastal erosion. This programme comprised a level of community involvement and relied on public interest, using numerous volunteers to collate information for the promotion of local and national understanding (Schofield 2004: 3).

Annemarie Troger stated that 'The Second World War may be defined as a war against civilian populations' (Troger 1987: 285; Archer 1997: 45). This is best reflected on the Home Front where the majority of Second World War defensive structures were built during an intense period of construction in response to the immediate threat of war. They were temporary in fabric, not intended to be permanent, and were to last only 'for the duration'. For these structures, which are often of a standardised and rushed construction, this has created a number of challenges regarding conservation for the long term survival of these monuments of war (English Heritage 1998: 2, 2007: 4, 9; Schofield 2002: 143). Both the *Defence of Britain Project*, and Dobinson's studies, ultimately led to improved statutory protection levels by the assessment and classification of known and newly identified sites. This information was then used to assist the development of conservation policies and enhance the Historic Environment Record (HER) database, and highlighted the importance and vulnerability of contemporary military remains to the archaeological sector and the general public.

Winchester Library site background

The County or City archaeologist governs working practice regarding historical structures; he or she will specify the project brief and approve the methodology for any given development application within their area. The state of Scheduling as it stood in 2006 meant that Grade II or unlisted structures involve the Local Planning Authority, whereas any at Grade II* or Grade I require an approval or consultation through English Heritage before any amendment permissions are granted. The library building (and its immediate surroundings) in Winchester, southern England, has been at Grade II* status since 1950, designated thus for its architectural and historical interest. The building was originally constructed in 1836–8 as a corn exchange and agricultural market. Later, in 1915, it was used as a public entertainment hall and became the city library in 1936 (Oxford Archaeology 2007).

In 1939, two air raid shelters, known as the 'Jewry Street shelters', were constructed adjacent to the library as part of Winchester's civil defence programme. Both were 'covered trench shelters' constructed from standard units which adhered to Government guidelines with the capacity to accommodate a total of 550 people (Figure 10.1). They were purchased from the Trussed Concrete Steel Co. Ltd in London at a cost of £1649 and assembled on site, forming a rectilinear pattern of interconnecting tunnels (Context

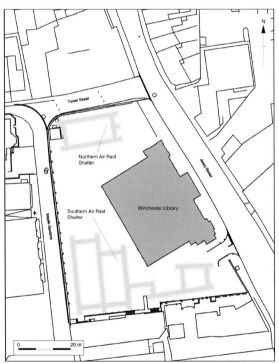

Figure 10.1: Plan of Winchester library and curtilage showing the location of the northern and southern Jewry Street air raid shelters. (© Oxford Archaeology)

One 1998: 8). The walls and roof were created from a series of narrow, pre-cast reinforced concrete panels that formed box-tunnels measuring almost 2 m square. The southern network of tunnels encompassed a more extensive and complex layout when compared to the single rectangular design of the northern shelter. Both were classed as communal and, being centrally located, could accommodate groups of people who had been in town shopping, at work, or at school. The Jewry Street shelters were one of the earliest public wartime air raid defences constructed in Winchester (Marter and McConnell 1999: 149).

During the use-life of these shelters, numerous examples of graffiti were produced by shelter occupants on the internal walls in pencil, chalk, and lipstick. These covered a range of both creative and banal themes, encapsulating a unique insight into the civilian wartime experience and the attitudes of Winchester's Home Front population. These graphic forms of dialogue also possess the potential for alternative narratives to be teased out and interpreted alongside more orthodox resources. English Heritage guidelines for the recording of military wall art define it as 'any decoration deliberately applied to, or executed on, the surface of a building or site in the context of its military use or occupation' (English Heritage 2004: 2). It goes further to suggest that there is the potential for surviving wall art to be encountered on almost any military, or former military, site from a single isolated pillbox to an entire airfield. Studies which comprise military wall art can enhance understanding by adding further layers of collective and individual character to the use-life of military sites (*ibid.*). These artistic expressions work alongside the use of words, photographs, and objects, when examining the last century of conflict, with particular significance for articulating the human response to war and conflict (Schofield 2005: 75).

The Jewry Street shelters went out of use at the end of 1944 when it was suggested by the City Engineer that they could be left *in situ* and the entrances sealed up (Marter and McConnell 1999: 158). The post-war years led to increased development

Figure 10.2: Machine excavation of the northern shelter roof (north-west corner) with Library building in background. (© Oxford Archaeology)

pressure on many military sites of this period, and several sites were destroyed or put at serious risk through neglect. Sites which have endured, such as air raid shelters, are now enveloped with new layers of cultural significance extending beyond their previous roles as research subjects for enthusiasts or as children's playgrounds (Anderton 2002: 189). Sites in Winchester were no exception to this, as noted by Marter and McConnell (1999: 158) during their research when interviewing local residents who recollected playing in air raid shelters once the war was over. Around this time, the Jewry Street shelters were cleared and blocked up, and a car park constructed overhead, with entry granted to each shelter through the roofs via manhole hatches. This access was necessary as an electric sub-station was installed and utilised part of the underground structure, and also the Fire Brigade used the spaces for drills and equipment testing (Context One 1998: 11).

In 1998, an archaeological survey was undertaken by Context One Archaeological Services for the Winchester Museums Service to appraise the condition of the shelters and the state of the graffiti. The survey noted that the tunnels were not well maintained and the pre-cast concrete was constantly damp in places, which had caused the exposed steel reinforcements to rust, and the concrete to shatter, thus accelerating corrosion. The interior tunnel corridors had been stripped of their fixtures and fittings, benches, chemical latrines and lighting, but retained 75 pieces of contemporary graffiti (Context One 1998: 4). This assessment was undertaken at a time when the only threat to the future of the shelters was of potential collapse rather than redevelopment.

In 2005, a proposal was made to expand and modernise the existing library and create a new 'Discovery Centre' for Winchester. This re-development would result in the near total loss of the northern air raid shelter and a partial loss of the southern shelter. Any remaining intact tunnels were to be backfilled. Both shelters were regarded as curtilage structures within the library II* grading. The senior archaeologists of Hampshire County Council and Winchester City Council noted that these wartime structures were of national importance, while an English Heritage review concluded that their current protection and status was sufficient (Oxford Archaeology 2006: 1). It was agreed that preservation by a newly commissioned archaeological survey and photographic record of the graffiti within the Jewry Street shelter, adhering to English Heritage guidelines, would satisfy the planning process. These shelters fell into one of the 'more significant' English Heritage categories identified for twentieth century wall art remains:

> 'Second World War, particularly where it can be attributed to a particular social group or local community perhaps identified through artistic expression in a communal air raid shelter.' (English Heritage 2004: 4)

Graffiti description

During the Oxford Archaeology recording process, a further 30 pieces of graffiti were identified, making a total of 105 for both shelters. Each example of graffiti was given a unique reference number and location point, and recorded using high-quality photographs and sketch drawings (Underdown 2011). The graffiti encompassed a mixture of cartoons, political statements, mathematics, instructions, times, dates, names, and initials. Many drawings and comments were emotive reactions to being at war: weapons, swastikas, flags, boats, and planes (Figure 10.2).

Other, more political sketches, include the figure of Hitler next to a crashed aeroplane with '*Hilter* [sic] *reviews his air force*' written alongside, and another with Hitler in a saluting pose. Two expressions refer specifically to Hitler and Mussolini stating '*hell to Hitler and Musso*' next to a drawing of the former's head, and another reads '*Hitler loves Musso*' below a speared love heart (Figure 10.3). Other sketches of male and female figures or faces were present along with depictions of Snow White and Pinocchio cartoons, which all reflect the fashion and popular culture of the period (Oxford Archaeology 2006: 7). Numerous graffiti represents times, dates, and people ranging from simple initials to a full name and address: '*Patricia Ivy Philips, 68 High Street, Winchester, done by me.*' The dates recorded in the shelter range between 1939 and 1940 and presumably coincide with air raids with three separate instances of 1.30pm documented.

The presence of children amongst the shelter occupants is not only verified by the Disney characters (Context One 1998: 11) but also by mathematical sums, a partial alphabet, games of 'noughts and crosses', smiley faces, and other more incoherent scribbles. There is also one instance of a hand drawn in chalk which Context One suggested was perhaps a reference to the 'V for Victory' campaign which ran throughout the war (1998: 19). The material form of the 'V' sign in this context has previously been examined in detail by Gillian Carr in her work on the occupation of the Channel Islands, where it was used extensively as an open form of resistance to the German forces and as a morale booster (Carr 2010: 575). The expression of this 'V for Victory' rallying emblem in the Jewry Street shelters may have provided a form of encouragement and inspiration to raise spirits during the stress of an air raid.

The *Public Shelter Rules* were posted opposite both entrances covering a long list of criteria and procedures for the shelter users to adhere to. This included no drunken people, trading, leafleting, weapons, littering, cooking or heating apparatus, bedding, or pets being allowed. It was also an offence to '*by forcible or improper means enter or seek to enter any sanitary convenience in or appurtenant to the shelter. Or knowingly intrude upon the privacy of a person using such a convenience*'. There were four instances of graffiti within the screened off latrines, one of which comprised images of military sea vessels: an aircraft carrier and a galleon, and another of division mathematics. Another shelter rule of note is that a person shall not '*wilfully make any mark on, or affix any bill, placard or advertisement to any part of the shelter.*' In the northern shelter '*Please keep Tidy*' was written in white chalk next to a latrine cubicle to re-affirm these rulings. The graffiti in the shelters is testament to the fact that rules were knowingly broken in such a manner as a way to ease boredom, be mischievous, and distract from the fear of bombers overhead.

Removal methodology

The initial groundwork for excavation entailed removing the shelter parts within the area of impact using a mechanical excavator, without causing any damage to the surrounding stratigraphy. The Project Manager, Ben Ford, designed a removal methodology using historical construction information combined with an examination of the shelter architecture exposed during a previous evaluation phase. This was tested first on the southern shelter and it was unclear how these robust blast proof structures would respond.

250mm SCALE BAR   *Photography undertaken by Oxford Archaeology (Buildings Department)*

Figure 10.3: Wartime transport graffiti: Two planes and a ship in vertical alignment pencilled graffiti. (© Oxford Archaeology)

The initial step exposed the upper thick concrete protective roof slab with a machine bucket. This was located about 50 cm above the internal roof of the shelter, with soil and rubble sandwiched between the two levels of concrete. The upper concrete roof slab was divided into short segments using a heavy-duty diamond cutter to facilitate a clean removal operation. The packing material below the roof slab was scraped away to expose individual roof panels which were loosened and lifted off by the machine (Figure 10.4). This enabled us to view the interior shelter space for the first time, noting the remains of bench fittings which ran along dimly lit tunnels of grey concrete and brown rust. The narrow concrete wall panels of the galleries had been set into a solid floor and were to be dislodged by the machine bucket to enable their efficient

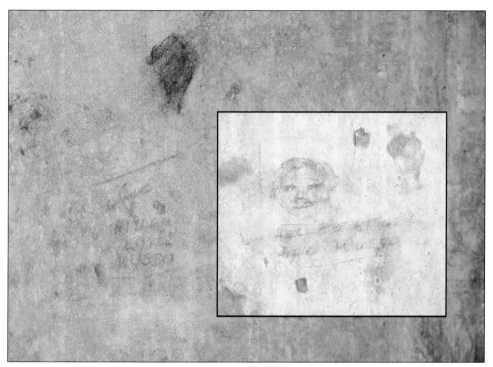

Figure 10.4: Political graffiti: 'Hitler loves Musso' and 'Hell to Hitler' pencilled graffiti. (© Oxford Archaeology)

removal. There was a possibility that these would crumble and split under pressure, and so they were removed from the tunnel base as a twisted mass of concrete and steel reinforcements. It had been agreed in advance that the shelter floor would remain in place to avoid the destabilisation of adjacent archaeological deposits.

Once the corner of the southern complex had been removed, two deep tunnel openings were exposed along the site edges leading to the rest of the shelter. In order to make these safe for the duration of the project they were blocked off using large sheets of thick plywood braced against the remaining concrete side panels. This wood was held in place with soil and the remaining trench void was part-filled with excess soil for safety. Finally, large steel plates were placed over the tarmac across the top of the tunnel opening points to spread any surface weight and prevent collapse. The northern shelter was removed using this same system, proving that the methodology was a success and the result was a neat dismantling of these 65 year old civilian defence structures.

During the removal of the north shelter the first obvious wall graffiti was encountered along the northernmost corridor, where the concentration of drawings was particularly dense. The shelter roof was removed and pencil-drawn images came to life along the walls in daylight for the first time. A final photographic record of the graffiti *in situ* was conducted and, while doing so, the possibility of saving some examples was discussed.

Retention of wall art from the air raid shelters was not a requirement of the work brief and therefore no time had been budgeted for it. Fortunately, the Project Manager was supportive, and with excitement and apprehension a recovery attempt of wartime material culture was undertaken.

The degraded condition of the wall panels meant that it was a gamble as to whether the concrete, and therefore decoration, would shatter when dislodged with the machine bucket. A few pieces were removed almost complete, whereas others crumbled and the graffiti disintegrated before our eyes. Approximately eight portions were retrieved successfully depicting themes including '*Hitler reviews his air force*', military transport, a female face, Patricia Ivy Philips' name and address and the *Public Shelter Rules*. The retained pieces consisted of faded sketches on brittle concrete which needed careful handling, but were also very heavy objects with awkward sharp metal reinforcement rods protruding from their edges. These were made manageable by removing any excess metal with a hacksaw and the pieces then stored under cover for the remainder of the project.

Public engagement

Throughout the archaeological works, the site policy regarding the general public was that of open visual access. A viewing point was positioned from the upstairs library windows and a see-through fenced barrier lined two edges of the excavation. Both areas had information boards pertaining to the archaeology, history, and future plans for the library and environs. Although this approach was beneficial for promoting understanding, and allowed people to follow the progression of the project, it also transmitted a feeling of working under constant and intense local scrutiny. Members of the public would engage with archaeologists through fences adjacent to the location of the northern shelter, meaning that the tunnels were frequently a focal point of conversation. It was relatively common that individuals would discuss the air raid shelters and recollect wartime Winchester rather than consider the earlier archaeological phases visible across the site. This perhaps demonstrated the strong level of cultural significance felt towards these evocative and symbolic structures of conflict, against a lesser affinity with the Roman or medieval town. A multi-period archaeological excavation had become a public arena for the recollection of personal memories from the Second World War.

It was Winchester within the realms of living memory that members of the public felt that they could connect and engage with. Noakes stated that 'If the Second World War can be seen as a key moment in our national identity and national history, then the Blitz is a key moment in the war' (1997: 90). The collective local and national identities associated with the experiences of being bombed or sheltering from an air raid are encounters which span temporally and spatially beyond the individual person, shelter, city, or country and can be observed as recently as 2011 within the context of recent conflict across the Middle East and North Africa, creating and adding further layers of 'key moments' within the histories of nations.

In Winchester, however, a local viewpoint regarding the Jewry Street shelter removal was published by the *Hampshire Chronicle* who covered the story alongside a photograph of the partially removed northern shelter. In the article a local history enthusiast, Adrian Jones, voiced his concerns stating:

> 'History covers all periods. I understand archaeologists are more interested in our ancient history, but this shouldn't be at the expense of our more recent past. I believe this should be saved for future generations and perhaps even opened to visitors, so please think before it's destroyed.' (Masker 2006)

Hampshire County Council responded with a re-iteration that the archaeological mitigation had been approved in advance with English Heritage plus conservation officers from both the County and City Council (*ibid.*).

It had originally been proposed to line the remaining shelters with a non-compressible material and backfill with gravels to protect the remainder of the graffiti and secure the tunnels against collapse. This was modified as a consequence of media coverage, and it was decided to spare one length of underground tunnel and install staircases at each end to allow entry. This would be accessible on special heritage open days or viewed by appointment. The consequence of the aforementioned local concern meant that the prior retention of twentieth century graffitied material culture pieces had also become a beneficial public relations manoeuvre.

An open day was hosted toward the completion of the project for members of the public to examine the archaeological remains which had been uncovered during the two month project. A variety of Roman and medieval objects were on display accompanied by the graffiti, exhibiting the full range of stratigraphic remains encountered during the dig. It was during this community engagement that Ben Ford introduced the author to Mr R.J. Ford (no relation) who, on seeing the decorated concrete panels, had confessed to being an air raid shelter graffiti artist 65 years before (Figure 10.5). One of the pieces he had drawn was actually on display, and contained pencil images of wartime transport: a vertical alignment of three types of plane and a boat (Figure 10.2). Mr Ford also agreed to be interviewed by the Oxford Archaeology Historic Building team to add a personal perspective of the civilian shelter experience.

During the war, Mr Ford worked as an ARP (Air Raid Precautions) Messenger and would regularly use the northern shelter, once the sirens had sounded. He recalled that the numbers and demographic of the shelter users would vary depending on the time of day. People using the library, out shopping, working nearby, at the cinema or out running errands, would use the shelters whenever the alarm was raised, day or night. The shelters were monitored and maintained by wardens who abided by the regulations of the shelter, but would not always strictly enforce each principle. Despite

Figure 10.5: Site open day, Mr R.J. Ford and Emily Glass examine graffiti drawn by Mr Ford in his youth. (© Ben Ford)

being against the rules, singing was frequently used to pass the time spent underground and often conflict would arise as regular users would have their own preferred seating area. The act of daubing graffiti on the shelter walls was therefore used as a way of defining internal space and granting the users some degree of control over an otherwise stressful situation.

Any anxieties amongst tunnel users were certainly not alleviated by the lack of fresh air, poorly functioning ventilation tubes, and chemical toilets situated behind curtains at the corridor ends. This unpleasant odour was worse when the tunnels were particularly crowded and claustrophobic, thus adding further emotion to the existing tensions felt inside the shelter (Oxford Archaeology 2006: 8). That some of Mr Ford's most prominent memories are related to smell is significant as this particular sense can evoke strong, often subliminal, emotional responses by association with either good or bad memories coupled with the experiences and sentiments attached to them (Classen 1994: 2). With specific reference to Wartime Britain, many of the stories submitted to the BBC's *WWII People's War* website concern memories that have become synonymous with certain smells. For example, the odours of cats, disinfectant, burning, or specific brands of cigarette have persisted in taking people's minds back to that era for their whole lives (BBC website 2011). This use of sensorial anthropology when dealing with oral history is an integral feature of interdisciplinary modern conflict archaeology, combining the essences of memory and identity with authenticity (Howes 1991; see Winterton, this volume).

Meeting Mr R.J. Ford was a particularly significant marker within the confines of the recent life-history of the Jewry Street air raid shelters. It allowed a face, voice, and personality to be assigned to this hitherto anonymous graffitied material manifestation of a past conflict. The physical expression of Mr Ford's Second World War Jewry Street shelter experience was in effect destroyed by the Winchester Library development mitigation works. However, the subsequent process of excavation, documentation, and investigation raised the profile and importance of Winchester's civilian wartime defences leaving a small proportion retained for the future.

Figure 10.6: Project Manager Ben Ford in the City Space gallery with the Jewry Street Shelter Public Shelter Rules. (© author)

Over recent years, there have been a number of archaeological excavations which have investigated the significance of Second World War air raid shelters. One of these, at Tottenham Hale in north London, has enabled air raid shelters for factory employees to be physically investigated, while highlighting their social significance through public archaeological initiatives (Harrison and Schofield 2010: 71). At Edgware Junior School, also in London, an air raid shelter was excavated below the playing field and used as a teaching resource for children to learn the principles of archaeological excavation and as a focus for social history teachings. This included the contribution of a former shelter user who provided a living memory connection to the use of the shelter with interviews and discussions for both archaeologists and pupils (Moshenska 2007). The number of investigations such as these has increased steadily over the last 10 years with the trend likely to continue through increased commercial development coupled with a higher level of community interest.

Discussion

The Jewry Street air raid shelters were frantically dug during a period of heightened emotion and uncertainty in the build-up to the outbreak of war, and under the potential threat of aerial bombardment. The main period of bombing over Britain occurred in 1940–41 and was an unprecedented experience, particularly for the majority of civilians who had not been involved in the Great War of 1914–18. The subsequent development of nuclear bombs has meant that it is unlikely that such a persistent assault could ever happen again on home soil (Calder 1992: 1). Consequently, this means that the scale of Civil Defence construction seen across Britain is unlikely to be repeated to the magnitude seen during the Second World War due to the evolution of military technology. This was best commented on by Paul Virilio in his study of Second World War concrete bunkers that constituted the German 'Atlantic Wall', overlooking the English Channel from the coast of occupied northern France and Belgium: 'The bunker is the protohistory of an age in which the power of a single weapon is so great that no distance can protect you from it any longer' (Virilio 1994: 46). This highlights both the importance and limits of this physical resource within the specific realm of Home Front defences and across the wider sphere of modern conflict archaeological studies.

The graffiti encountered within the Jewry Street shelters offers a unique insight into the conditions both above and below ground for the users of the tunnels. The majority of the sketches and scribbles appear to have been done by children as a response to being bored and scared in a confined space. Perhaps, by personalising this space, they sought to alleviate the heightened emotion experienced at the time. The instances of lipstick to create graffiti are indicative of children, perhaps infants or pre-school age, who, as such, were not carrying a pencil. The lipstick was likely to have come from the child's mother and the graffiti done by either the child or by an adult for entertainment or distraction during a raid. Of the 12 recorded instances of lipstick graffiti, only three are decipherable: as a female face, a body, and a male head with '*RA*' written below. The other nine recorded are either remnant drawings which have since deteriorated or were merely scribbles in the first place.

Stylistically, the wall art of the Jewry Street shelters is relatively rudimentary when compared with more professionally designed Second World War examples, such as those at Spring Quarry, Corsham, in Wiltshire, where, in 1943, Olga Lehmann was commissioned to paint wall murals in the underground munitions factory complex (English Heritage 2004: 114). However, there are much closer stylistic parallels, such as those in the Sutton High School air raid shelter in Plymouth investigated by Steve Johnson. This underground shelter was adorned with an assortment of pencilled images similar to those in Winchester, illustrating the ridiculing of prominent enemy figures (including Hitler and Mussolini), wartime weaponry, transport, and cartoons. These were often laced with a mocking tone (Hitler with a single testicle and a plucked German Eagle) and nationalistic elements (Churchill and V-for Victory signs) (cyber-heritage 2011).

The scale of informal graffiti in air raid shelters across Britain is unclear, but it does seem to have a presence to varying degrees wherever a shelter was used, especially by children. Even the Edgware School shelter contained two pieces of chalk graffiti on the walls, despite pupils taking their notebooks, pencils, and reading book into the shelter with them to pass the time until the all clear (Moshenska 2007: 239).

Conclusion

In November 2007, the Winchester Discovery Centre hosted a celebratory opening night. This was not only an opportunity to view the final result of the Library re-development, but also a chance to view one of the newly created exhibits within the regeneration works, the *City Space* gallery. This had been specifically designated for local artists and Winchester related exhibitions.

The first exhibit on display concentrated on the history of Jewry Street with a portion dedicated to the history and excavation of the air raid shelters. This included one of the retained concrete pieces, the *Public Shelter Rules*, exhibited on open display in a specially fitted wooden box supported with sandbags at the base (Figure 10.6). This was exhibited for only a limited period of time, and then the graffiti put back into storage with the rest of the site archive. Future plans are to put all the decorated concrete portions into the preserved segment of air raid tunnel so they can be viewed as and when this retained shelter section is accessed (Geoff Denford, pers. comm.).

It is unfortunate that current Health and Safety legislation means that confined spaces training and oxygen monitoring is required in order to visit the tunnel. It is for this reason that only a few people have actually been through the tunnel since the Discovery Centre opened and that the preservation plan was more aspirational than practical (Tracy Matthews, pers. comm.). Despite this hindrance, the graffiti and retained corridor are the only remaining parts of these civilian landscapes of conflict that survive and with which the public can physically engage. The graffiti remains one of the most intimate and suggestive expressions of material culture from the excavation. It has the potential to evoke the impact and experience of warfare on the civilian population of Winchester and enables people to bond with the past through their own or connected living memory.

Acknowledgements

The author is indebted to Ben Ford of Oxford Archaeology for information, advice and images. Appreciation also goes to Richard McConnell of Context One Archaeology Services, Geoff Denham (Principal Curator at Winchester Museums Service), Tracy Matthews (Winchester City Archaeologist) and Martin Hallum (Senior Architect, Hampshire County Council) for assistance and information. And finally to Mr R.J. Ford for his invaluable insights into the life-history of the Jewry Street air raid shelters.

Note

1   In March 2010 *PPG*16 and *PPG*15 were amalgamated and superseded by a single Historic Environment Policy: *Planning Policy Statement* 5 (*PPS*5).

Bibliography

Anderton, M. J. (2002) Social Space and Social Control: Analysing Movement and Management on Modern Military Sites. In. Schofield *et al.* (eds) 2002, 189–198.

Archer, B. (1997) 'A low-key affair': Memories of Civilian Internment in the Far East, 1942–1945. In M. Evans and K. Lunn (eds), *War and Memory in the Twentieth Century*, 45–58. Oxford: Berg.

BBC website. (2011) http://www.bbc.co.uk/ww2peopleswar/ Accessed 8 February 2011.

Calder, A. (1992) *The Myth of the Blitz*. London: Pimlico.

Carr, G. (2010) The Archaeology of Occupation and the V-sign Campaign in the Occupied British Channel Islands. *International Journal of Historical Archaeology* 14: 575–592.

Classen, C., Howes, D. and Synnott, A. (1994) *Aroma: The Cultural History of Smell*. London: Routledge.

Context One Archaeological Services (1998) *Two WWII Air Raid Shelters, Jewry Street, Winchester, Hampshire: An archaeological survey for Winchester Museum Service*. Unpublished report.

Cyber-heritage. (2011) http://www.cyber-heritage.co.uk/waiting/forstpage.htm Accessed 8 February 2011.

Dobinson, C. S., Lake, J. and Schofield, A. J. (1997) Monuments of War: Defining England's 20th century Defence Heritage. *Antiquity* 71(272): 288–299.

English Heritage (1998) *Monuments of War: The Evaluation, Recording and Management of Twentieth-Century Military Sites*. London: English Heritage.

English Heritage (2004) *Military Wall Art: Guidelines on its Significance, Conservation and Management*. London: English Heritage.

English Heritage (2007) *Military Buildings Selection Guide*. London: English Heritage.

Harrison, R. and Schofield, J. (2010) *After Modernity: Archaeological Approaches to the Contemporary Past*. Oxford: Oxford University Press.

Howes, D. (1991) Introduction: 'To Summon All the Senses'. In D. Howes (ed.), *The Varieties of Sensory Experience*, 3–21. Toronto: University of Toronto Press.

Kopytoff, I. (1986) The Cultural Biography of Things: Commoditization as Process. In A. Appadurai (ed.), *The Social Life of Things: Commodities in Cultural Perspective*, 64–91. New York: Cambridge University Press.

Marter, P. and McConnell, R. (1999) Preparations for War: World War II Civil Defence in the City of Winchester. *Hampshire Field Club Archaeological Society* 54: 146–142.

Masker, R. (2006) Bomb Shelter to be Saved. *Hampshire Chronicle* 19 January 2006: 10.

Moshenska, G. (2007) Unearthing an air-raid shelter at Edgware Junior School. *London Archaeologist* 11(9): 237–240.

Noakes, L. (1997) Making Histories: Experiencing the Blitz in London's Museums in the 1990's. In M. Evans and K. Lunn (eds), *War and Memory in the Twentieth Century*, 89–104. Oxford: Berg.

Oxford Archaeology (2006) *Two World War II Air Raid Shelters: Graffiti, Historic Building Recording*. Oxford: Oxford Archaeology, unpublished report.

Oxford Archaeology (2007) *Winchester Library, Jewry Street, Winchester: Historic Building Investigation and Recording*. Oxford: Oxford Archaeology, unpublished report.

Saunders, N. J. (2003) *Trench Art: Materialities and Memories of War.* Oxford: Berg.

Saunders, N. J. (2007) *Killing Time: Archaeology and the First World War.* Stroud: Sutton.

Schofield, J. (2002) Monuments and the Memories of War: Motivations for Preserving Military Sites in England. In Schofield *et al.* (eds) 2002, 145–158.

Schofield, J. (2004) *Modern Military Matters – Studying and Managing the Twentieth-Century Defence Heritage in Britain: A Discussion Document.* York: Council for British Archaeology.

Schofield, J. (2005) *Combat Archaeology: Material Culture and Modern Conflict.* London: Duckworth.

Schofield, J. (2009) *Aftermath: Readings in the Archaeology of Recent Conflict.* New York: Springer.

Schofield, J., Johnson, W.G. and Beck, C.M. (eds) (2002) *Matériel Culture: the Archaeology of Twentieth Century Conflict.* London: Routledge.

Underdown, S. (2011) Winchester Library, World War II Air Raid Shelters, Buildings Report: CD Part 2. In B. Ford and S. Teague (eds), *Winchester, a City in the Making.* Oxford: Oxford Archaeology Monograph 12.

Virilio, P. (2010) *Bunker Archaeology.* (transl. G. Collins). New York: Princeton Architectural Press.

11

The Many Faces of the Chaco War: indigenous modernity and conflict archaeology

Esther Breithoff

The Gran Chaco is a vast and under-populated semi-arid lowland plain in South America. It is divided between south-eastern Bolivia, northern Argentina, a small part of north-western Brazil, and north-western Paraguay along the Paraguay River (Figure 11.1). Hot and hostile, and difficult to farm, the Gran Chaco is rich and diverse in flora, fauna, and history. It is home to several of Paraguay's indigenous populations, and a haven for animals and plants, many of them unique to the area.

From 1932 to 1935 it was the setting for one of the most bloody and obscure wars of the twentieth century. Bolivia and Paraguay both claimed ownership of the *Chaco Boreal*, the region lying north of the river Pilcomayo. Whereas Bolivia based its legal rights over the region on territorial regulations dating back to the Spanish colonial rule, Paraguay believed it was entitled to the territory through its current occupation and exploitation.

Paraguay's indigenous peoples, such as the *Guarani,* lived in the Chaco, and were culturally and linguistically rooted in it (Johnson 1996). Paraguay had developed a tanning industry there, and allowed Anglican missionaries to venture into its wilderness to convert the indigenous populations. By the end of the nineteenth century, the missionaries had established a clear Paraguayan presence in the territory. The Bolivians, in contrast, had never settled nor exploited the region.

During the 1920s, the Chaco attracted international attention and fuelled tensions between Paraguay and Bolivia due to speculations concerning the presence of oil. The oil claim sparked Bolivia's interest. Both landlocked countries (Bolivia having lost its coastal province to Chile in the War of the Pacific, 1879–1883), now sought access to the Atlantic Ocean via the Paraguay River, which forms a natural border between the Chaco and eastern Paraguay.

At this time, the Paraguayan government invited Canadian and, later, Russian Mennonites to settle in the Chaco Boreal. Bolivia and Paraguay both began building *fortines* (military strongholds) that became focal points in a conflict landscape which saw

Figure 11.1: Map of Paraguay and the Gran Chaco. (© author)

the two countries' armies fighting each other with modern European and US weaponry (Hughes 2005: 416). Ironically, the Chaco proved to have no major oil resources. Although the region was eventually secured by Paraguay, victory was bittersweet. Often referred to as the most futile war of the twentieth century, the conflict between Paraguay and Bolivia cost around 100,000 lives (excluding the indigenous victims), and left the two already poor nations in an even more precarious financial condition.

The Chaco War was a tragedy for the indigenous peoples of the area, and beyond, as they were the proxies of the Hispanic elites who created and prosecuted the conflict. The Chaco itself was predominantly inhabited by native groups, and Bolivia recruited mainly indigenous people from its Altiplano highlands who had no connection with the

Chaco, and yet were expected to give their lives to defend it. Hitherto, academic research has primarily focused on the military history of the war (English 2007; Farcau 1996; Verón 2003; Zook 1960), and has only recently addressed the indigenous experience of the conflict and its consequences (Horst 2010; Richard *et al.* 2008; 2010).

The Mennonites form another group which has largely been neglected in the history of the Chaco War. They are an evangelical free church which originated in the Low Countries of northern Europe during the sixteenth century Reformation era. Persecution and restriction of religious freedom continuously forced them to emigrate, and in 1927 the first group of Mennonites arrived in the Chaco Boreal, with a second wave following in 1930, and a third in 1947.

The proximity of their villages to military strongholds meant that the Mennonites were in regular contact with soldiers. They also established relationships with indigenous communities who suddenly saw their ancestral lands transformed into fenced pastures and battlefields. It was the Mennonite and military presence in the territory that would have the greatest and most enduring impact on both the indigenous people, and the Chaco landscape.

The Mennonite introduction of agriculture and western Christian values, and the arrival of industrialised warfare with the Bolivian and Paraguayan armies, imposed themselves onto a predominantly hunter-gatherer landscape, resulting in a fusion of three completely different worlds amidst the Chaco's thorny shrubs and arid plains.

The war created a hybridisation of the Chaco which manifests itself in the landscape as well as in the material culture, language, and activities of its current inhabitants. Thus, in the middle of South America, exists a complex multifaceted battle-zone created by twentieth century technologies and politico-economic concerns, and operationalised by otherwise marginalised indigenous peoples on behalf of their respective governments' Hispanic elites. Here, as along the First World War's better-known Western Front, conflict sites constitute 'highly sensitive multilayered landscapes that require a robust, multidisciplinary approach' to their investigation (Saunders 2010: 45–46).

This paper aims to demonstrate the potential of a modern conflict archaeology approach to the Chaco War and its aftermath. The absence of an established archaeological presence in today's Paraguay means a lack of preconceived definitions of and ideas about what modern archaeology is, and its temporal remit. This situation is a double-edged sword. While it might avoid superfluous justifications of the validity of an archaeology of the recent past, it might also mean that such an inter-disciplinary endeavour carried out by foreign archaeologists might not be taken seriously.

This paper is based on initial archaeological and anthropological fieldwork conducted in the Paraguayan Chaco Boreal around the three Mennonite colonies of Fernheim, Menno, and Neuland, in 2011. It attempts to identify new landscapes and objects generated by the destructive force of modern warfare, to locate their archaeological remains, and to analyse their altered meanings in the context of material culture anthropology. In this sense, it follows Saunders' statement that 'War is the transformation of matter through the agency of destruction, and industrialized conflict creates and destroys on a larger scale than at any time in human history' (Saunders 2002: 175).

A land of conflicts

Conflict in the Chaco has many faces, and is not restricted to armed encounters between two armies. Consequently, its legacies transcend empty artillery shell cases, recorded war strategies, and memoirs written by war veterans. Besides their own internal conflicts, the Chaco's native peoples experienced violence during Paraguay's War of the Triple Alliance with Brazil and Argentina (1864–1870). One consequence of this earlier conflict was allowing foreigners to purchase land in the Chaco, a development which:

> 'forced natives into the cash economy as cheap laborers for the Argentine and British ranchers, fragmented their societies, and opened the way for British missionaries to initiate proselytism to the Enxet [indigenous people].' (Horst 2010: 288)

Before and during the Chaco War, alcohol, disease, and serious mistreatment at the hands of the Paraguayan and Bolivian military, added to the suffering of the indigenous population (*ibid.*: 288–289). According to local Mennonites, the soldiers considered indigenous people as 'creatures without a soul' that could be shot without hesitation. Nonetheless, the indigenous populations were indispensable in the conduct of the war. Both armies used indigenous people as guides in the unknown territory, and as workforces for digging trenches; many men, women, and children were murdered for fear of espionage (Horst 2010; Richard *et al.* 2008; 2010).

The indigenous people and the military also established contact with the Mennonite communities that had started to farm the barren soils of the Chaco. The Mennonite Church practices adult baptism and believes in pacifism and a 'separation from the world'. The Canadian Mennonites had escaped the standardisation process in Canada, which had put an end to privileges such as the right to run their own schools in German and teach religion in class. The Russian Mennonites, for their part, had fled persecution under the Bolshevik regime, which no longer granted them exemption from military service.

The remoteness of the Chaco Boreal, and the privileges promised to the incoming Mennonites by the Paraguayan government seemed ideal for building a new life. When a small number of Mennonites traveled to the Chaco to inspect the area they sent home a message declaring that they had found the 'promised land' (Ratzlaff 2009: 16). They had arrived during the rainy season when the Chaco was in bloom and the lagoons carried abundant water. Little did they know about the dry conditions and water shortage that would later continuously threaten their existence.

To secure their immigration to the Chaco, Paraguayan authorities guaranteed the Mennonites freedom of religion, control over their own education system, and exemption from military service. However, they were not aware of the territorial disputes between Paraguay and Bolivia. Neither did they realise that their immigration was part of Paraguay's strategic plan to reinforce its presence in the Chaco (Ratzlaff 2009: 20). The Russian Mennonites, in this instance, had fled armed violence in Russia only to move into the heart of another conflict zone.

The Paraguayan army traversed Mennonite villages and fields on a daily basis, depleted their wells, and installed themselves in their schools (Ratzlaff 2009: 43). The Canadian and Russian Mennonites established two different colonies close to one another. While they shared the same religion, they differed in many cultural aspects and attitudes. The Canadian Mennonites officially refused any involvement in the Chaco War, whereas the Russian colony of Fernheim agreed to let its members decide for themselves whether to engage in trade with the military or not (*ibid.*: 41). Life in the Chaco was hard, and the flourishing trade with the army allowed some Mennonites to improve their lives. Bernhard Penner, a Mennonite from Fernheim recalls:

> 'We Mennonites sold many things to the soldiers: eggs, watermelons, and chickens. We also traded them for flour and rice. We only traded food, never for metal or weapons. We had nothing. This was the first time since our arrival in the Chaco that we were able to make a little bit of money.' (Bernhard Penner, pers. comm. 2011)

The military also provided the Mennonites with medical treatment (Ratzlaff 2009: 43). In a twist of irony, industrial war, which at its very essence symbolizes large-scale destruction and death, allowed the Mennonite colonies to survive.

Despite the destructive power of modern warfare, it was not enemy bullets, grenades, and bombs that posed the biggest threat to the soldiers. Often described as a 'Green Hell', the Chaco with its thorny plants, mosquitoes, and incredible heat made life in the trenches a nightmare. Thirst was every man's biggest enemy, and the lack of water and disease the cause of countless casualties (Farcau 1996: 230). Soldiers went mad with thirst, hallucinated, and even committed suicide (*ibid.*: 215). At least in the oral tradition, the battle of *Boquerón* was mainly about control over a small lagoon alongside the military stronghold (Heinz Wiebe, pers. comm. 2011). Water had to be carried into the territory where the soldiers were stationed – the Paraguayan army benefiting from the comparative proximity of Asunción, and the Mennonite wells. Thousands of soldiers nevertheless died of thirst, heat, and exhaustion in the Chaco bush, their graves unknown to this day, and thereby constituting another (albeit unheralded) twentieth century conflict landscape of 'the missing' (Breithoff, in prep.).

Archaeological remains in the landscape

When asked about the Chaco today, Paraguayans often claim that it is 'beautiful but too hot' and that 'there is nothing to see'. The problem however, is not the lack of visual attractions, but their inaccessibility. The landscape of the Chaco Boreal is dotted with historical sites that date back to the 1932–5 war, but accessing them is difficult and potentially hazardous. The region has virtually no tourist infrastructure. The *Ruta Transchaco*, the motorway connecting Asunción to the Bolivian border via the Chaco, is the only paved road in the region. The various indigenous and Mennonite villages are linked by dusty roads that run a high risk of flooding, and often become impassable during the rainy season. Its isolated location, harsh environment, and extreme climatic conditions have prevented the Chaco from becoming an easy tourist destination, though this in turn has, on occasion, helped preserve parts of its conflict landscape.

Conflict sites in the vicinity of the Mennonite colonies differ significantly in their conservation and preservation. *Fortín Toledo* and *Fortín Isla Po'i* serve as two examples of sites suffering neglect. Although both have undergone some restoration by the Paraguayan government and military in the past, they are now in a state of disintegration (ABC Digital 2008). By contrast, *Fortín Boquerón* is probably the most famous and best conserved battlefield site in the region, and quite possibly in the whole of the Chaco; it attracts considerable attention from Paraguayan officials and the national media.

Even though *Fortín Toledo* and *Fortín Isla Po'i* are Chaco War conflict-related sites, not all such fortified locations saw military action, or, if they did, it was not always of the same kind. While *Fortín Toledo* is a stronghold which did become a formal battle-site, *Fortín Isla Po'i* did not see ground fighting, but was subjected to aerial bombardment, perhaps because it contained the headquarters of Marshal José Félix Estigarribia Insaurralde, the Paraguayan commander-in-chief, a military hospital, and soldiers' barracks.

Some of *Fortín Isla Po'i's* original structures have survived, and were partially restored by the Paraguayan authorities in 1993, and again in 2006 (ABC Digital 2007; 2008). Unfortunately, the site has not received much attention since that time, and its physical remains are slowly disintegrating. *Fortín Isla Po'i* has considerable archaeological potential, but due to space restrictions, I will focus here on *Fortín Toledo* and especially *Fortín Boquerón* as examples of surviving archaeological features in the Chaco.

Fortín Toledo witnessed an armed confrontation between the two enemy armies which lasted 16 days, and claimed around 1000 soldiers in February–March 1933. It was built and occupied by the Paraguayan army in 1927 to mark the western boundaries with Mennonite-owned land, and only briefly seized by the Bolivians in 1932 before it was re-captured by Paraguayan forces (Farcau 1996: 107). The military historian Bruce Farcau gives a visual description of the physical presence and strategic position of this military stronghold in the Chaco landscape during Paraguayan occupation:

'Toledo was poorly sited for defense, as the heavy woods that dominated the area made it difficult to clear fields of fire for more than fifty meters in any direction. Estigarribia had ordered the *fortín* held primarily because of its position at a vital crossroads and also because of the morale factor of preventing the impression that a Bolivian offensive was actually gaining momentum. The defenders lacked the tools necessary to establish an interconnected line of trenches, so they organized a system of company-sized strong points about a hundred meters apart with interlocking fields of fire to cover the gaps. The strong points were composed of shallow trenches, deep enough to shelter a kneeling rifleman, with separate bunkers with overhead protection for refuge during artillery bombardment. The Paraguayan defenses bulges southward, forming a rough semicircle around Toledo itself, and then extended eastward along the northern edge of a broad, grassy meadow.' (Farcau 1996:107)

Today the site of *Fortín Toledo* emits an air of abandonment and oblivion. A small rusty sign announces that the site can be entered through a little wooden gate. Just behind the gate stands a lone information board concisely recalling the events of 1933 in Spanish. Behind the information board a narrow path leads into the bush and to the surviving war structures.

With the exception of one bunker which has been restored, all the others have collapsed, and are gradually being reclaimed by nature. Hans Fast, a Mennonite tourist guide, explains that in the language of the indigenous *Guaraní* people, *tuca* means bunker. The word derives from the *tuca tuca*, a subterranean rodent which, like the soldiers, hides underground.

The outlines of trenches are still visible, yet they are often hard to discern by the untrained eye. Soil erosion and neglect have reduced them to small ditches crossing the landscape. Like the crumpled bunkers, they are overgrown with thorny shrubs, and inhabited by stinging insects. Just as in the First World War, it is difficult to imagine the multi-sensory-experience of trench life here in the Gran Chaco.

The insect-infested trenches, the din of artillery bombardment, the cries of the wounded, the lack of water, and the smell of rotting bodies offered a 1930's South American parallel to the Western Front of 1914–18 (Eksteins 1990: 146, 150–1; Howes 1991: 3–5; Farcau 1996: 230; Saunders 2003: 128–129; Winterton this volume). The horrors of European industrialised warfare were visited on armies composed of non-literate indigenous Amerindian peoples. Here, modernity forcefully subverted and reconfigured native moral and natural philosophies.

And, just as with so many other twentieth century conflicts around the world, evocative layers of memory are being added to the conflict landscape (Breithoff in prep.). In the Chaco, the elements are unforgiving. The extreme climatic conditions make preservation in the sandy landscape difficult. Over the years, flooding has caused trenches and bunkers to fill with mud, which hardens during the dry season, and becomes overgrown with vegetation (Figure 11.2).

In contrast to *Fortín Toledo* is *Fortín Boquerón*, situated south-east of the Mennonite town of Neuland. From 7 to 29 September 1932, the Bolivian and Paraguayan armies fought a bloody battle here which left more than 7000 casualties, and marked the official outbreak of the war.

'Boqueron comprised a handful of adobe huts located in the heart of an *isla* of heavy woods surrounded by open grassland with a few gnarled trees. The *fortin* was constructed in the shape of a blunt arrowhead pointing southwest toward the Bolivian outpost of Yucra, and with its forked tail aligned roughly north and east, measuring approximately five hundred meters in length. The place was fortified by Jordan and Santanella with a line of trenches reinforced with barbed wire entanglements and clusters of sharpened stakes around the perimeter. Lanes had been cut through the surrounding bush to the north and northeast to provide interlocking fields of fire for automatic weapons. Machine guns had been set up in platforms in the trees to give them improved observation, and *chapapas* [bunkers reinforced with earthworks and quebracho log walls] housed key strongpoints. The jugular of the *fortin* was the well left by the Paraguayans and two others dug by the Bolivians, as there was no other source of water for miles in any direction … The heart of the *fortin* was composed of the few Paraguayan *pahuichis* [mud and thatch huts], which had been turned into officers' quarters, aid stations, and supply bunkers.' (Farcau 1996: 46)

Unlike *Fortín Toledo*, *Fortín Boquerón* has undergone major conservation efforts, and attracts a number of both national and international tourists. Some of the stronghold's original features, such as the military bread oven and the commander's hut, have been rebuilt. Others, such as a bunker, have been restored. An old Ford 4 automobile, which was used to transport water, is also on display. Alongside, is a small museum which houses weapons and other military equipment. The walls are covered with black and white photographs and information about the battle of *Boquerón* and the war in general.

Outside the museum, wooden signposts marking places of interest have been erected along a trail which takes the visitor around the site. The path runs along and cuts though the surviving trench system which, like the trenches at *Fortín Toledo*, have been reduced to shallow ditches, overgrown with thorny bush.

At a considerable distance from each other lie two cemeteries, one for Paraguayan soldiers the other for their Bolivians counterparts. Local people claim that both cemeteries are in fact mass graves containing an unknown number of nameless dead. Rows of a symbolic number of white crosses commemorate the bodies that have been robbed of their identity – present, but 'missing', liminal entities who are truly betwixt-and-between (Turner 1995: 95).

Closer inspection reveals that the Paraguayan crosses are slightly more elaborate than the Bolivian ones. By creating two separate cemeteries and a clear distinction in the commemorative crosses, Paraguay is conveying a poignant political message: even in death Bolivian soldiers remain enemies.

Over the years, *Fortín Boquerón* has received considerable attention from the Paraguayan authorities, the military, and the national media. The government declared 29 September a national holiday, marking the Paraguayan victory at the battle of Boquerón. The military stronghold which had once been a place of violence and death, has turned into a site of commemoration and national pride, where ceremonies are carried out and families have picnics. Various memorials have been erected around the site's central space, with the majority commemorating the brave and proud Paraguayan soldier, almost completely eliding the Bolivian victims.

Figure 11.2: Restored bunker at Fortín Toledo. (© author)

Figure 11.3: Ayoreo belt with rattles made of recycled war metal. (© author)

Indigenous and Mennonite trench art

When the military left in 1934, the area was littered with rotting bodies and all kinds of war *matériel*. Although most of this has now been cleared, the indigenous people and the Mennonites occasionally discover bullets, rusty weapons and truck parts in the bush. According to local oral tradition, the old battlefield sites are haunted by souls and the noise of gunshots, truck engines, and the screams of those who perished.

Figure 11.4: Left: Mennonite ploughs made of metal debris and oil canisters from the Chaco War. Right: Bell made from the rim of a Chaco War military vehicle wheel in a Mennonite village. (both © author)

The war might be long over, but it has left a lasting imprint on the Chaco landscape created by 'the bones and material remains that impregnate the Paraguayan bush with living echoes of the Chaco War' and in which 'memory seems to be eternally inscribed in space, erasing historical time and making old battles linger indefinitely' (Gordillo 2004: 241).

More prosaic, but equally significant, the weaponry, shells, trucks, and other military equipment left behind has proved a readily available source of metal, which had not previously existed for the inhabitants of the Chaco. At the end of the war, the indigenous people and the Mennonites began collecting the scattered objects, and recycling them primarily for practical use.

The concept of trench art, especially in the context of the First World War, has been explored and defined by Saunders as:

> 'any item made by soldiers, prisoners of war and civilians, from war *matériel* directly, or any other material, as long as it and they are associated temporally and/or spatially with armed conflict or its consequences.' (Saunders 2003: 11)

Objects have their own form of 'communicative agency' (Tilley 2002:25) and people's interaction with them can alter the message they convey.

After the war, the indigenous people began to complement traditional resources such as wood and natural fibre with industrially produced metal and wire, creating objects that merged two entirely different worlds. They shaped items such as metal knives into arrowheads, which they attached to a wooden cane with a piece of telephone wire. They also used war debris in the manufacturing of jewellery and certain music instruments and ritual artefacts in an astonishing display of recycled hybrid material culture (see Coote *et al.* 2000).

Verena Regehr, a local ethnologist of Swiss origin, possesses an extensive private collection of indigenous trench art. One of her more intriguing objects is a type of belt made of natural fibre from which hang two rattles made of metal from the war (Figure 11.3). *Ayoreo* indigenous men traditionally wore belts with attached wooden rattles during festivities, and for signaling their peaceful intent upon approaching another community.

However, by substituting the wooden rattles with metal ones made from war debris, the *Ayoreo* bestowed the belt with a new and rather paradoxical meaning. Ironically, an object originally made and worn to express peace and celebration was generated from material produced and employed to kill people – an indigenous South American variation of the widespread trench art philosophy of 'swords into ploughshares' (and see below). To what extent, if any, the indigenous people were aware of this underlying irony remains debatable.

When asking Verena's partner, Marco Moreno, an old man of the *Nivaclé* indigenous people who was a child at the time of the war, why the members of his community started using metal instead of wood to make weapons and instruments, he replied that metal was easier to work with than wood and that metal rattles were louder.

The Mennonites also gathered war *matériel* abandoned in the bush, and crafted it into predominantly utilitarian trench art objects, such as household items including pots, strainers, mugs, and a soap-cutting machine, which were often made from melted-down empty shell cases. Many such items were handed down through the generations, and were often lost or discarded along the way. Others have survived and remain in private homes or in the colonies' respective small museums. The metal war debris and the objects made out of it have been, and some continue to be, an integral part of Mennonite every-day life; its war provenance is often ignored and overlooked or simply just forgotten.

The second type of Mennonite trench art relates to agriculture. The abundance of metal discarded by the military allowed the Mennonites to produce farming equipment such as cow bells, watering cans, shovels, and ploughs. When asked why the pacifist Mennonites did not refuse the use of military equipment, members of the colonies repeatedly replied that they did as the Bible says, and literally 'beat their swords into ploughshares' (Isaiah 2: 4).

In their struggle to survive in the harsh conditions of the Chaco, the Mennonites transformed matter associated with death and devastation into objects that cultivate the land and promote growth. The provenance of the material and the circumstances under which, where, and by whom it was turned into a new artifacts, grants the latter a biography, a 'social life' which influences people's personal and cultural identities (Appadurai 1986; Miller 2005; Tilley 2002) and creates new associations and meanings that often go unnoticed by the people that handle the objects.

Some Mennonite villages still preserve the old village bell which used to be struck to announce school and mass. At the end of the war, the military left numerous military vehicles behind to rot in the bush. The meager resources of the Chaco forced its inhabitants to become inventive. The military trucks were thus a welcome source of metal for the Mennonites, who turned the wheel rims into bells, fusing the two opposing worlds of armed conflict and belief in pacifism (Figure 11.4).

Towards an anthropological archeology of the Chaco War

Today, Chaco War sites are being reclaimed by nature. New trees have replaced their broken predecessors, and dense bush has overgrown trenches and human bones. Although there remains a (Paraguayan) military presence in the Chaco Boreal, it no longer dominates the landscape. The war sites now form scars in a landscape composed of a curious mixture of wilderness and industrial and urban development.

Mennonite ploughs made of war debris have long since been substituted by modern machinery. Large-scale crop production, such as peanut and raw cotton, and extensive cattle farming, now dominate large parts of the landscape and economy. Although untouched territory still exists in the Gran Chaco, the Boreal has to a great extent been 'colonised'. The Mennonite colonies have developed into a network of multi-cultural and small modern towns and villages, where Mennonites, indigenous people, and Latino-Paraguayans live in a symbiotic relationship, linked to the rest of the country by the *Ruta Transchaco* highway.

Numerous oral histories recounting the indigenous peoples' experiences with the military from the time of the war have survived. Many of them can be found in the archives of the *Mennoblatt*, the newspaper of the Fernheim colony, which has been published since 1930, and which now offers invaluable insights into the conflict's archaeological record. Other histories have been collected together in books, and many more are stored as memories in the hearts and minds of the war veterans and the few surviving old people (Mennonite and indigenous), who were children during the war years.

The Chaco War and the effects it had on people, objects, and landscape is complex, and transcends the introductory nature of this paper (Breithoff in prep.). The war stretched far beyond the Mennonite colonies, and many sites still wait to be explored. The many faces of the Chaco are the multi-vocal layers of a uniquely contested landscape that is unstable and continuously re-inventing itself through human interaction (Bender 1993; Saunders 2003; Tilley 1994). The versatility of those groups and their actions in shaping the Chaco landscape, and the different conflicts arising from them, require a muscular and multidisciplinary approach. Modern conflict archaeology allows an unrestricted unfolding of the Chaco's archaeological and anthropological potential, opening a door to unlimited possibilities and interpretations of the Chaco War and its aftermath.

Bibliography

ABC Digital. (2006) Empezó restauración del fortín Isla Po'i, en Presidente Hayes, Jueves, 08 de Junio de 2006. http://archivo.abc.com.py/2006-06-08/articulos/257366/empezo-restauracion-del-fortin-isla-poi-en-presidente-hayes. Accessed 10 April 2011.

ABC Digital (2008) Fortín Isla'Poi se encuentra en ruinas, Domingo, 15 de Junio 2008. http://archivo.abc.com.py/2008-06-15/articulos/424216/fortin-isla-poi-se-encuentra-en-ruinas. Accessed 10 April 2011.

Appadurai, A. (ed.) (1986) *The Social Life of Things*. Cambridge: Cambridge University Press.

Barbosa P., Capdevila, L., Combès, I. and Richard, N. (2010) *Les hommes transparents: Indiens et militaires dans la guerre du Chaco (1932–1935)*. Rennes: Presses Universitaires de Rennes.

Bender, B. (ed.) (1993) *Landscape: Politics and Perspectives*. Oxford: Berg.

Breithoff, E. (In prep.) Between Disintegration and Commemoration: The Conflict Landscape of the Chaco War.

Coote, J., Morton, C. and Nicholson, J. (eds). (2000) *Transformations: the Art of Recycling*. Oxford: Pitt Rivers Museum.

Eksteins, M. (1990) *The Rites of Spring: The Great War and the Birth of the Modern Age*. New York: Anchor/Doubleday.

English, A.J. (2007) *The Green Hell: A Concise History of the Chaco War between Bolivia and Paraguay 1932–35*. Staplehurst: Spellmount.

Farcau, B. (1996) *The Chaco War: Bolivia and Paraguay, 1932–1935*. New York: Praeger.

Gordillo, G.R. (2004) *Landscapes of Devils: Tensions of Place and Memory in the Argentinean Chaco*. Durham (NC): Duke University Press.

Horst, R.H. (2010) Crossfire, Cactus, and Racial Constructions: the Chaco War and Indigenous People in Paraguay. In N. Foote and R.H. Horst (eds), *Military Struggle and Identity Formation in Latin America*, 286–306. Gainesville (FL): University Press of Florida.

Howes, D. (1991) Introdution: 'To Summon All the Senses'. In D. Howes (ed.), *The Varieties of Sensory Experiences*, 3–21. Toronto: University of Toronto Press.

Hughes, M. (2005) Logistics and the Chaco War: Bolivia versus Paraguay, 1932–1935. *Journal of Military History* 69(2): 411–437.

Johnson, R.C. (1996) The Gran Chaco War: Fighting for Mirages in the Foothills of the Andes. http://worldatwar.net/chandelle/v1/v1n3/chaco.html. Accessed 3 March 2011.

Miller, D. (ed.) (2005) *Materiality*. Durham (NC): Duke University Press.

Ratzlaff, G. (2009) *Zwischen den Fronten: Mennoniten und andere evangelische Christen im Chacokrieg 1932–1935*. Asunción: Editora Liticolor s.r.l.

Richard, N. (ed.) (2008) *Mala Guerra: los indígenas en la guerra del Chaco (1932–35)*. Asunción: CoLibris – Museo del Barro – ServiLibro.

Saunders, N.J. (2003) *Trench Art: Materialities and Memories of War*. Oxford: Berg.

Saunders, N.J. (2004) *Matters of Conflict: Material Culture, Memory and the First World War*. Abingdon: Routledge.

Saunders, N.J. (2010) Worlds Apart: Modern Conflict Archaeology and Battlefield Archaeology. *Arheo* 27: 45–55.

Tilley, C. (1994) *A Phenomenology of Landscape: Places, Paths and Monuments*. Oxford: Berg.

Tilley, C. (2002) Introduction: Metaphor, Materiality and Interpretation. In V. Buchli (ed.), *The Material Culture Reader*, 23–26. Oxford: Berg.

Turner, V. (1995) *The Ritual Process. Structure and Anti-Structure*. New York: Aldine de Gruyter.

Verón, L. (2010) *La Guerra del Chaco, 1932–1935*. Asunción: El Lector.

Zook, D.H. (1960) *The Conduct of the Chaco War*. New Haven (CT): Bookman Associates.

12

Trees as a Living Museum: arborglyphs and conflict on Salisbury Plain

Chantel Summerfield

Landscape has long been of central interest to archaeologists and anthropologists, as one way of explaining how humans have shaped their world in distinctive ways, and whose consequent patterns of behaviour are visible in the material record. Recently, this interest has been particularly marked in the formation of new landscapes that have resulted from the twentieth century's many industrialised conflicts (e.g. Saunders 2001; 2010a).

The last century witnessed wars that were unprecedented by virtue of their industrialised intensity and global scale. Men who had rarely ventured out of their villages or towns, were sent across the world in order to fight for King, Country, and Nation. Despite an expanding literature on the general experiences of individual men (e.g. Macdonald 1993; Arthur 2003; Martin 2009; and see Bagwell and Leonard, both this volume), often little is known about the materialities of their personal lives, motivations, beliefs, and loves. With the passing of time it has become evident that while these men have been remembered and honoured as a collective group in annual remembrance ceremonies, many have also disappeared from view – their remains scattered over foreign battlefields, and their memory equally lost. Yet, sometimes, unique insights appear from unexpected quarters.

In the research outlined here, tree graffiti, known as 'arborglyphs', are investigated from a multi-disciplinary perspective, and recognised as being a way of preserving the memory of men who died during the First and Second World Wars. The uniqueness of conflict-related arborglyphs lies in the fact that they are 'living memorials' whose creation is part of the ongoing transformation of conflict landscapes.

The arborglyphs studied here are located in two woodland areas: 'Half Moon Copse' and 'Polo Wood' on the Salisbury Plain Training Area (SPTA) in southern England. Nearly 250 trees were recorded at these locations in an attempt to situate individuals within a landscape of industrialised war (Dicker 2009), and to explore their experiences, identities, and fates.

What are arborglyphs?

Arborglyphs can be considered a sub-division of the well-studied subject of culturally modified trees (CMTs). However, the term 'arborglyph' refers specifically to trees that have been altered by humans, whereas CMT more generally encompasses trees that have been altered by any living creature and by any means. For example, in the United States, claw and teeth marks from brown bears and beavers contribute to the creation of many CMTs (Beesley and Claytor 1978: 3).

Arborglyphs are a way in which a person can record their thoughts, feelings, and even sexual fantasies (Mallea-Olaetxe 1991: 4) in an animate 'object' which may potentially outlive their human agent. The most enduring (i.e. still legible) arborglyphs created on the SPTA were made using the so-called 'scratch' technique. First defined by Andrew Guillford (2007), this method allows arborglyphs to survive through time by virtue of the shallow/thin incisions made into the bark using a knife or bayonet. Over time, the indentation will heal itself, leaving a dark legible scar that contrasts with the pale bark of the tree.

In the past, no military arborglyphs created during the twentieth century have been investigated as an integral part of the archaeological record; this study therefore occupies a distinctive location on the boundary between archaeology and material culture anthropology, and is thus an example of the inter-disciplinary approach of modern conflict archaeology (Saunders 2010b). The information obtained from the description and analysis of these arborglyphs contributes to our understanding of the personal lives of soldiers during the twentieth century, and, importantly, illustrates the interaction between humans and nature in times of conflict.

Why study arborglyphs?

Arborglyphs made during war hold unique and insightful information regarding the lives of the soldiers who carved them. The recording and analysis of arborglyphs on the SPTA can shed light on soldier's thoughts and feelings whilst training, and, significantly, before they experienced front line action.

The twentieth century marked a period of historic change, as, for the first time, total war engulfed whole populations around the world. The material residue left behind by the First and Second World Wars is vast and international, from the shell damaged landscapes of the Western Front, to the German batteries on the Normandy coast line, and vast amounts of weaponry, uniforms, memorabilia, and trench art now found in homes and museums around the world. However, unlike the study of these kinds of material culture, different problems arise when recording arborglyphs due to the delicate nature of trees as living raw material – and attitudes to which have shifted markedly during recent decades. For example, beech trees are well known for having a short lifespan (approximately 300 years), when compared with other species of trees (Muir 2005: 41). Within their lifetime, they are constantly at risk of being destroyed through the threat of insects, fire, logging, or construction activities. This inevitably means that, unless the information is recorded, beech tree arborglyphs could potentially be lost forever (Beesley and Claytor 1978: 3). In other words, arborglyphs as a material trace of war, form a constantly diminishing resource due to natural as well as cultural forces.

Furthermore, the majority of arborglyphs discussed here were created over 60 years ago. Those carvers who were adventurous in what they produced tried to include more information than simply a name and a date. Unfortunately, and ironically, this over ambitious desire to carve large amounts of information onto trees has often resulted in the loss of that information over time, when the carver did not employ the scratch technique. Instead, soldiers often preferred to gouge the information out of the bark, which destroyed the carving over time as the girth of the tree increased, or the tree began to heal itself; the consequence of these natural processes were that arborglyphs became increasingly illegible. This fact may be one of the main reasons that such carvings have been overlooked or discounted as a useful way in which to study and explore the individuals and groups involved.

Arborglyph recording

Arborglyphs at the two sites studied here were recorded using a combination of survey techniques so that all potential information could be fully explored. Initial GPS locations were recorded for all trees so that each tree could be relocated. Digital photographs were taken of each arborglyph and notes made of the information displayed on the trees. Amongst the categories of information that were recorded were the girths of trees and the height of arborglyphs from the ground – in an attempt to create a detailed catalogue of marked trees for future study.

Salisbury Plain Training Area (SPTA)

The arborglyphs at the heart of this study are located on Salisbury Plain in Wiltshire, in southern England. The SPTA is the largest army training estate in the United Kingdom, covering over 39,000 hectares of land which approximately equates to the size of the Isle of Wight (McOmish *et al.* 2002: viii).

At present, the SPTA can be considered a multi-dimensional (and partly fossilised) landscape which includes medieval towns, Bronze Age round barrows, and medieval field systems, that have been serendipitously protected by the military. Despite this generic landscape protection, none of the trees is currently individually protected, as they are not accepted as traditional forms of monuments, even though they bear witness to the presence and emotional state of individual soldiers, and to the period of time which they trained for war, before travelling to a battle zone. In this sense, the SPTA can be examined as a facsimile of a war landscape in that it possessed all the attributes of a battlefield except the danger of being killed (though woundings and rare fatalities did occur).

As already stated, almost 250 trees with arborglyphs were recorded at the SPTA locations known as Polo Wood and Half Moon Copse. These are within a few kilometres of each other, yet exhibit different characteristics through their arborglyphs. While the study of military arborglyphs offers new ways to understand soldiers' emotions before conflict, these carvings cannot be seen as a direct reflection of a soldier's behaviour, but rather a transformation of that behaviour (Hodder and Hutson 2003: 7).

The SPTA has been under military control since 1897, when the Ministry of Defence (MOD) first acquired the land for training purposes. The area is still used for training, and the fieldwork upon which this paper is based has shown that many new arborglyphs are being created, often within sight of the historical examples. Perhaps such activity is seen by new recruits as a ritual/tradition which should be continued. While these newer/younger arborglyphs were recorded as part of this study, this paper deals only with those created during the First and Second World Wars.

Once arborglyphs are created they can be thought of as delicate items of archaeology, always evolving from the time of their creation, often morphing into shapes and images that are far removed from what the carver initially created. This is attributed to the fact that arborglyphs exist on living natural entities, and thus with the growth of the tree the carving will become distorted and perhaps lost over time. At Half Moon Copse and Polo Wood, many arborglyphs have already been lost, and only scarring on the oldest trees can be seen. The carving of arborglyphs transforms the tree into an irreplaceable cultural artefact which should be treated and recorded as any other kind of monument. In fact, its very fragility, combined with the generally predictable and circumscribed lifespan of the tree into which it has been carved, arguably makes a case for special consideration as a unique kind of war heritage.

Landscape

Until recently, many assessments of landscapes associated with military activity have erroneously regarded them as 'inert' – empty backdrops to military action (see Saunders 2001 for a contrary view). A more modern interpretation is that the landscape was a crucial part of each war, affecting the outcomes of battles, but also being adapted by the soldiers who then left behind them remnants of an artificially created world (N. Saunders, pers. comm. 2008). The SPTA – and other training areas – acted as unique landscapes – transition zones between the comforts of men's home lives and the horrors of war that would soon confront them. This is reflected in the conflicting archaeological landscapes that the SPTA contains, such as the practice trenches dug to simulate those of the Western Front (McOmish *et al.* 2002: 139), as well as structures for training soldiers in the urban warfare of more recent conflicts such as Iraq and Afghanistan.

At first glance, the trees that have grown at Half Moon Copse and Polo Wood give the impression of a pristine natural landscape, untouched by human hand. However, many beech trees were planted during the eighteenth and nineteenth centuries as an aid to the increasingly popular 'culture of hunting'. When the military took control, these trees were retained to act as cover for army manoeuvres. Human intervention on the SPTA can still be observed in the way that roads have been laid through and around these arboreal areas, as well as in areas where trees were felled to create a managed landscape required by the army. The arborglyphs, therefore, can be considered an addition to the overall appearance of the landscape which has been moulded during the past two centuries by human hands.

The SPTA is made up of expanses of 'wild' landscape that are characteristic of the chalk geology in the area. Long uninterrupted vistas are common in the area, and are only broken by the copses that have been planted in the recent past. This is especially true of the land surrounding Half Moon Copse, where it overlooks the artillery training field, offering clear views of the surrounding area, and which partly explains its use

Figure 12.1: Arborglyph of a 1940s-style pin-up carved at Polo Wood (SPTA) with the associated words Sept 12th 1944. (© Author)

Figure 12.2: Image of a suspected 'failed' arborglyph of a woman at Polo Wood, SPTA. (© Author)

as outposts for soldiers. Perhaps this may explain why the most detailed arborglyphs were recorded at this site; if soldiers were posted at these locations for long periods it is arguably more likely that they would have both the time and motivation to create more complex arborglyphs.

Gender

The arborglyphs of the SPTA owe their survival to the fact that they occur on land privately owned by the MOD, which protects them, and safeguards their authenticity. Those dating to the First and Second World Wars were carved exclusively by men, as at this time frontline warfare was a male preserve (Goldstein 2001: 213). However, a small proportion of women's names were recorded at these two sites, possibly carved by soldiers in remembrance of loved ones at home, or to immortalise sweethearts that they had met before or during the war. It may even be that trees were assigned a gender by some soldiers. While trees carved with women's names might simply indicate an absent loved one, those carved with men's own names might serve to 'claim' the 'female' tree as a symbol of a wife or sweetheart, as well as obviously being a statement of presence on the plain.

Identity

Arborglyphs are about communication. The most common theme of tree carvings in general, as well as the SPTA's conflict-related examples in particular, are names, initials, and nicknames. At Half Moon Copse and Polo Wood, a large number of trees are inscribed with the carver's name, the names of loved ones, and, mostly, with initials. The inscribing of one's name into a tree is a symbolic act on the carver's behalf, and will mean something different for each carver. To cut one's own name on a tree can be interpreted in several ways, not least as an act of possession. It is this tree that the carver feels connected to, and which possesses the right qualities to be engraved. Second, the carver may deliberately choose a tree which holds significance to him in ways that could not be understood by a civilian. Finally, the tree may represent a place where the soldier spent his final time, before being sent off to war.

Graphic imagery is common on the beeches of the SPTA, where most trees have at least one 'picture'. The most favoured are a 'cross' and the 'love heart'. It is generally assumed that these images were chosen due to the ease of their execution. However, there is probably also an association between image and emotion. The heart, albeit a symbolic image which is easy to produce, may also be construed as a shape of peace, the love of another (even if their name is not present), or simply as an image reminding the soldier of happier times. The cross is also easy to carve for those with no real artistic ability. Nevertheless it may be viewed also as an expression of religious belief.

Hitherto, it has been assumed that each arborglyph was created by a different individual. This may not be the case, as many carvings may belong to one soldier. The practice of inscribing a cross into a tree may be how an individual announces who he is, and what his beliefs are. Another possible explanation for the predominance cross-shaped arborglyphs could be that the design is a way for a soldier to find a certain spot in the woods of the SPTA; a place where the soldier feels at peace with himself away from the reminders of war associated with the camp.

On several occasions more complex arborglyphs portrayed humour and lust. One such arborglyph was recorded at Polo Wood. It is an intricately carved image of a woman with the associated words: *Sept 12th 1944* (Figure 12.1). The woman was carved in the style of a 1940's pin-up girl with characteristically American attributes. In addition to this image (perhaps of sexual longing), another arborglyph was recorded on a nearby tree which appeared to have similar attributes to the 1940's pin-up, but for which some unknown reason was adapted into a love heart (Figure 12.2). Perhaps it was created by a soldier who wished to imitate the pin-up girl, but did not have the artistic skill to achieve it.

Memorialisation

It is commonly believed that many arborglyphs were created out of boredom and loneliness – representing a time when a soldier would have a few spare moments and was able to use a pen knife or a bayonet to execute a tree carving. While this is a fair initial assessment of these graffiti, many SPTA arborglyphs are relatively large, and would have taken a considerable amount of time to complete. This suggests that there may often be hidden and underlying meanings to these carving activities.

When looking at a military landscape, it is important to consider the nature of memory and the rituals of remembrance (Black 2004: 134) that are undertaken by the people associated with that time and place. Many soldiers who joined or were conscripted into the army were 'lost' during the war: in many cases, all the men of a single family were wiped out and that family ceased to exist, their names inscribed on an official stone memorial, but in reality engulfed by the mass of other men's names that surround them. Arborglyphs can sometimes be the only enduring visible link to these men as individuals. The act of carving a name into a tree prevails as a form of memorial to that person, whether that was its original intention or not. Any form of mark that is left on a tree whether legible or not will remain, until the death of the tree, a connection to the soldier who carved it.

It can be argued that not all names that were carved were made by the named soldiers themselves, as is often the case with First World War souvenirs and trench art more generally. Indeed, it has been speculated that the names were carved by fellow soldiers who wanted to remember them after their departure from the SPTA, or perhaps even to memorialise those men who had already died in action. The creation of arborglyphs as 'grave markers' for the dead were unlike traditional grave sites however, as there were no physical remains to be buried. Yet, and equally unusually, these markers which remember the physical presence of the deceased will only disappear if the tree is felled or heals itself through continued bark growth.

Arborglyphs may also have been created by soldiers wishing to mark their travels. Many soldiers had never left the village or town of their birth, and travelling from America, Australia, Canada and even other parts of England to the SPTA could have had a significant emotional and psychological impact. The carving of place names, and/or personal names and dates could perhaps have been intended by the soldier who wished to be show where he had been in his life – a form of souvenir which, once made, cannot be taken away from that place. In this way, the tree acknowledges the soldier's existence and the presence on the SPTA at a particular point in his life.

In times of war, soldiers are taken to an unfamiliar landscape in which they must survive. Soldiers always try to improve their situation, and perhaps the creation of arborglyphs may be considered one way of doing this. Carving on a tree might bring familiarity into a place that they do not know, thereby, perhaps, creating an emotional landscape that they can live and work within. Furthermore, the addition of place names to an arborglyph seems to be a symbol of pride for the soldier who created it; many appear to have been carved on trees that are in sight of other place names, a way for a soldier to show where they have come from, and where (they would like to think) they will be going back to.

It also became apparent during fieldwork that the SPTA arborglyphs were created by soldiers of various nationalities. It was insightful too that once a soldier had carved his name or a place-name on a tree (rather than just his initials), the surrounding trees would also succumb to this activity, often made by people of the same nationality. Perhaps the practice of carving arborglyphs acted as a way of linking them together in a foreign land – in other words tree-carving became a way creating and maintaining a social bond and a common identity within and through the transformation of a facsimile conflict landscape.

Many of the soldiers who were sent to the SPTA for several weeks/months may have come to think of the beech trees as 'friends'. Every day visiting the same spot and sitting next to the carved beech tree perhaps psychologically made the tree in some way a compatriot, or a symbol of the memory of a loved one. This idea is perhaps more likely when the presence of nearby fox-holes indicate that soldiers remained in one area for a long period of time, allowing them time to become familiar with their surroundings and emotionally attached to them.

The First and Second World Wars are often the conflicts that have received most study and analysis, and research itself is an act of memorialisation. Sometimes, it is the researchers' opinions that teach us most about these events. Memories of those who took part in these conflicts are easily forgotten or re-moulded into something that is believed to be true, but in itself is a facsimile of the truth accepted to create a glossed view of the period. Nevertheless, using material created during these periods has the potential to enrich our knowledge of those who lived during these times, creating a complex and more satisfying analysis of the relationship between human memory and material culture. These varied aspects of conflict materiality are often the last connection that the world has with individual soldiers, who themselves wished to be remembered.

Identification

Several trees that were recorded at Half Moon Copse were identified as being created by Commonwealth troops from Australia and from the United States. From some of these carvings a number of soldiers were identified as the makers. The identification of the arborglyph creators relied on the individual carving an image in such a way that it remained legible for a long time, and, of course, on the amount of information each carving contained. Also important was the soldier's country of origin, as many identification papers of British soldiers from the First World War were destroyed during the Blitz in London during the Second World War. Furthermore, privacy policies prevent access to many soldiers' papers from the Second World War, which hampers the process of identification. Nevertheless, some soldiers were identified, and several are described below.

Horace Pearce
At Half Moon Copse, a tree inscribed with the words *H. Pearce, A.I.F, Sept 22, 18* was recorded. H. Pearce was identified as being Horace Pearce, service number 3862; he was born in 1894 and was from North Richmond, Australia, the son of Arthur and Emma Jane Pearce. He joined the army at the age of 22 on 11 October 1915 with a height of 5ft 7¾ in. In May 1916, after serving in France, Horace Pearce was transferred to England. Interestingly, while in England he went 'absent without leave' (AWOL) and was punished with 96 hours detention, and forfeited five days pay. He became ill with the mumps, but proceeded overseas to France in February 1917. On 18 October 1917, he was put on a charge for 'W.O.A.S without reasonable excuse allowing to escape a person committed to his charge whom it was his duty to keep' (Australian National Archives 1915: 5). This event was followed by further disciplinary action while in Belgium. He then fought in France and was killed in action on 5 June 1918, and was buried at Fanvillars on the Somme in France (Figure 12.3). Three of Horace Pearce's cousins were also killed in action. No living relatives have been found at present.

Clyde Henry Walker
Also at Half Moon Copse was a tree was inscribed: *C.H. Walker, Australia* (Figure 12.4). From the Australian National archives only three results were present for a

Figure 12.3: Just visible on the left of the photograph is the wooden grave marker for Horace Pearce. (©Australian National Archives)

C.H. Walker, and it quickly became apparent that this carving related to a Mr Clyde Henry Walker, the son of a Mr Henry Clyde Walker (Australian National Archives 1916). Clyde Walker was born on the 20 August 1898, and came from Essendon, Victoria, where he was a clerk before the outbreak of the First World War. In 1916, he joined the army in the 37th Battalion, at which time he was 5 ft 3 in tall, and unmarried. From his records, it can be established that he trained partially in Australia at the A.I.F's Signal School, from where he journeyed to France, later to be awarded the Military Medal, and promoted to Lance Sergeant.

Clyde Walker then travelled to England, where he trained first at Dunstable and then on the SPTA; on the 19 June 1918, he carved the arborglyph that has been used to trace his wartime life. On 11 September 1918, he was discharged from the A.I.F and was awarded a cadetship at the Cadet College, Quetta, joining the Indian Army. At this point he was also awarded the Victory Medal and the British Cross Medal. It appears that Clyde Henry Walker remained in the army and that he fought also in the Second World War. He died on the 5 May 1962. He had been married to Carmen Hardy Carmichael and had two sons called Kenneth Carmichael Walker (1944–) and Ian Carmichael Walker (1947–).

Frank Fearing

A Second World War arborglyph, also at Half Moon Copse, recorded: *F. Fearing, Hudson, Mass, US, 6-4-44* – with a related love heart inscribed *Helen* (Figure 12.5). Archive research showed that F. Fearing was Francis 'Frank' Fearing, who was born in October 1917 in Hudson, Massachusetts. He joined the army at the beginning of the Second World War (Figure 12.6), and participated in many battles, including the D-Day landings. Frank trained on the SPTA where he carved his arborglyph. His daughter, Mrs Barbara Fearing, remembers her father telling her about the carvings in later life (Barbara Fearing pers. comm. 19 September 2009).

On Frank's military papers, it states that he was unmarried when entering the army, but the woman's name he carved on his arborglyph (and associated with a love heart) is now known to be that of his wife.

Due to restrictions on marriage during the Second World War, Frank and Helen Fearing had secretly married on the 26 April 1941, when Frank was home on leave from the army. Few people attended the 'secret wedding' – only the priest and a few friends. It was not until after the war that Frank and his wife had wedding photographs taken, faking them at Frank's brother's wedding. Frank died in 2001, but kept in contact with many of his friends from the army.

Conclusions

In the past, arborglyphs have received little attention for the cultural information that they hold, being regarded, erroneously, as insignificant and unimportant, sometimes even by those who created them. However, research on the SPTA arborglyphs refutes this view, and demonstrates that this unique transformation of the natural world by military hands can provide valuable (sometimes unique) insights into the lives of individuals within the industrialised wars of the twentieth century.

The arborglyphs of the SPTA have shown how soldiers adopted a tradition of carving messages into trees from the moment the land was acquired by the government in 1897 to the present day. The arborglyphs record a variety of information including names, dates, places and even sexual fantasies in order to communicate with the world. By studying two woodland areas on the SPTA a difference in land use and arborglyph style has been established. It is apparent that more personal names and place names were carved by soldiers from visiting nations on the trees during the major conflicts of the twentieth century at both locations. But the iconography changes from Polo Wood to Half Moon Copse, as less detailed pictures are recorded at the latter, yet more military insignia are located there – a reasonable explanation for this may be that soldiers copied one another in what they carved at each location.

The tree carvings located on the SPTA act as silent witnesses to bygone years of two global wars that the majority of people now alive have not experienced. Arborglyphs are a unique and uniquely informative kind of conflict materiality that are, variously, part memorial, souvenir, statement of presence, love letter, and trench art. They are inscribed into a living entity whose continued life (i.e. growth) subsequent to the carving episode simultaneously preserves and distorts (and ultimately destroys) their original designs and legibility. The continued use of the study area for military training means that there is little doubt that the creation of arborglyphs of a military nature will continue, and that, in part, the SPTA can be regarded as a symbolic landscape of remembrance encapsulating the memories and desires of those who trained there (Saunders 2001: 46).

Figure 12.4: Arborglyph found at Half Moon Copse inscribed C.H. Walker, Australia. (© Author)

Figure 12.5: Arborglyph inscribed F. Fearing, Hudson, Mass, US. 64-44, with associated love heart and the name Helen. (© Author)

Figure 12.6: Photograph of Frank Fearing during his time in the military. (© B. Fearing)

Acknowledgements

I would like to thank Professor G. Astill at The University of Reading, who acted as undergraduate dissertation supervisor for the birth of this work. Also, the immense help that Richard Osgood, Martin Brown, Nicholas Saunders, Elizabeth Hertogs, Anna Powell, and Barbara Fearing gave in order to help develop the work. I would also like to acknowledge the financial support of the AHRC.

Bibliography

Australian National Archives, 1915. Horace Pearce service records. http://naa12.naa.gov.au/scripts/Imagine.asp Accessed 2 February 2009.

Australian National Archives. 1916. Clyde Henry Walker service records. http://naa12.naa.gov.au/scripts/Imagine.asp Accessed 16 April 2009.

Australian War Memorial Collection Record: J00035. n.d. http://cas.awm.gov.au/photograph/J00035 Accessed 9 February 2009.

Arthur, M. (2003) *Forgotten Voices of the Great War*. London: Ebury.

Beesley, D. and Claytor, M. (1978) 'Adios California' – Basque Tree Art of the Northern Sierra Nevada. *Centre for Basque Studies Newsletter* 19: 3–6.

Black, J. (2004) Thanks for the Memory: War Memorials, Spectatorship and the Trajectories of Commemoration 1919–2001. In N.J. Saunders (ed.), *Matters of Conflict: Material Culture, Memory and the First World War*, 134– 148. Abingdon: Routledge.

Dicker, K. (2009) Family Trees. *Estatement Magazine* (Summer) 67: 19–20.

Goldstein, J. (2001) *War and Gender: How Gender Shapes the War System and Vice Versa*. Cambridge: Cambridge University Press.

Gulliford, A. (2007) Reading the Trees: Colorado's Endangered Arborglyphs and Aspen Art. *Colorado Heritage Magazine*, (Autumn).

Hodder, I. and Hutson, S. (2003) *Reading the Past, Current Approaches to Interpretation in Archaeology*. Cambridge: Cambridge University Press.

Macdonald, L. (1993) *They Called it Passchendaele*. London: Penguin.

Mallea-Olaetxe, J. (1991) Basque Aspen Carvings. *Centre for Basque Studies Newsletter* 43: 3–6.

Martin, A. (ed. R. Van Emden) (2009). *Sapper Martin: The Secret Great War Diary of Jack Martin*. London: Bloomsbury.

McOmish, D., Field, D. and Brown, G. (2002) *The Field Archaeology of the Salisbury Plain Training Area*. Swindon: English Heritage.

Muir, R. (2005). *Ancient Trees Living Landscapes*. NPI Media Group.

Saunders, N.J. (2001). Matter and Memory in the Landscapes of Conflict: the Western Front 1914–1919. In B. Bender and M. Winer (eds), *Contested Landscapes: Movement, Exile and Peace*, 37–54. Oxford: Berg.

Saunders, N.J. (2010a). *Killing Time: Archaeology and the First World War*. (2nd edn) Stroud: History Press.

Saunders, N.J. (2010b) Worlds Apart: Modern Conflict Archaeology and Battlefield Archaeology. *Arheo* 27: 45–55.

13

Hadrian and the Hejaz Railway: linear features in conflict landscapes

John B. Winterburn

This paper explores the Hejaz Railway in southern Jordan, conceptualised as a large scale linear monument and principal component of a First World War conflict landscape. The term 'Macro-Linear Feature' (MLF) is used to describe large scale linear features that exceed 50 km in length to differentiate them from shorter linear boundaries, ditches, field and territorial boundaries more familiar to landscape archaeologists in Britain (McOmish *et al.* 2002: 56, 112) and in Jordan (Barker *et al.* 2007: 146–160). Using examples of other MLFs, in particular Hadrian's Wall, I aim to synthesise new meanings and narratives for the Hejaz Railway landscape based on linearity, power, control, and gender.

This approach illustrates a new discourse for a categorisation of conflict landscapes which originates from an analysis of linear features which extends the principles of 'degrees of freedom' to encompass all conflict spaces. This is further developed into a hierarchy of conflict spaces.

Hadrian's Wall, in northern Britain, and the Hejaz Railway in southern Jordan were built 1800 years and 4000 km apart; both are macro-linear features within multi-faceted conflict landscapes. Retreating from an examination of the self-evident aspects of both structures enables the inter-disciplinary exploration of these features using a modern conflict archaeology approach. The First World War conflict landscapes of southern Jordan incorporated and were partly defined by the Hejaz Railway (Saunders and Faulkner 2010). The railway was completed in 1908 – its construction and history are well documented (Nicholson 2005; Ochsenwald 1980; Tourett 1976), and it has been studied also from an architectural perspective (Fahmy 2001). The railway – as technology that 'transformed the physical and cultural landscapes of a traditional desert routeway' – is described by Shqiarat *et al.* (2011), and as a 'Linear Heritage Attraction' (Orbasli and Woodward 2008: 159). Western travellers in the early twentieth century, shortly after it was inaugurated, described the railway in terms of its geography and the journey as a travelogue (Maunsell 1908).

Figure 13.1: The route of the Hejaz Railway. (© author)

The Hejaz Railway

The Hejaz Railway extended 1302 km from the city of Damascus, in modern Syria, to Madinah in present-day Saudi Arabia. It was a single track, narrow gauge railway whose purpose was to take travellers on the Hajj pilgrimage to the holy city of Mecca. Local opposition from Bedouin tribes who made a living from transporting pilgrims ensured it never reached its final destination. The railway reduced a typical 40 day journey by camel caravan to just four days (Shqiarat *et al.* 2011) (Figure 13.1).

In the mid-nineteenth century, the Ottoman Empire was in decline. Described by Tsar Nicholas as 'the sick man of Europe' (Finkel 2005: 459), the empire was defaulting on its debt repayments and losing territory. Following Greek independence in 1832, the empire was forced to withdraw from the Balkans, control over north Africa had been lost, and Egypt was taken by the British in 1882 (Mansfield 2003: 114). The empire's problems lay in its inability to keep pace with the rapid industrial and military expansion taking place in Europe and its inability to repay it debts.

On 2 May 1900, the Ottoman Sultan Abdülhamit II issued an imperial order for the construction of a Holy Railway. It was intended to strengthen his claim to be Caliph of the World's Muslims, and was the single physical embodiment of a Pan-Islamic movement which sought to bring all Muslims under one Islamic state or Caliphate (Ochsenwald 1980: 23). He called on all Muslims for support and financial backing, and a military engineer was despatched to survey the route (Nicholson 2005: 14).

Initial survey work was undertaken by Ottoman Army officers. Early construction work was unsuccessful due to mutinies by construction crews who were complaining of maltreatment (Ochsenwald 1980:29), and Ottoman control over the technical aspects of construction was abandoned and work progressed under the leadership of the German engineer, Heinrich August Meisner. The railway reached Ma'an in 1904 and Medinah in 1908.

The railway's 79 stations were not built at regular intervals, and distance between varies from 4 km to 28 km with a mode (most common interval) of 12 km, and a median value of 17 km (derived from Nicholson 2005: 184). The railway was, however delineated by kilometre markers, denoting the distance from Damascus. Large-town stations, such as Ma'an, were modelled on traditional Turkish houses from Istanbul and small-town stations were distinctive single or double storey structures with flat roofs (Fahmy 2001: 5–6) and adopted a standardised design.

Between the towns of Amman and Mudawwara, the railway closely followed the *Darb Al-Hajj* – the Syrian Hajj route. Railway stations were constructed in close proximity to existing Ottoman forts (e.g. Qatrana, Uneiza, Ma'an, Fassu'ah, Mudawwara) that had been built in the first three centuries of Ottoman rule to protect water supplies on the Hajj route (Petersen 1989: 97).

During the Great Arab Revolt of 1916–1918, the railway was the target of frequent and numerous attacks by the Northern Arab Army and Bedouin guerrilla forces inspired and often lead by T.E Lawrence (Lawrence 2003; Nicholson 2005: 100–141; Wilson 1989: 495–499). Much of the railway infrastructure to the south of Ma'an was damaged beyond repair, and railway station buildings that have survived continue to be damaged and suffer from the opportunistic digging of pits in the attempt to find buried gold that is erroneously believed to have been deposited by the Ottomans in 1918.

Today, the railway is derelict for much of its length within Jordan and Saudi Arabia. However, short sections have been refurbished, and operate for the transportation of phosphates from open cast mines north of Ma'an and from Eshidiya to the south. During the 1960s, attempts were made to re-engineer and repair sections of the line to the south of Ma'an, but this work was halted at the start of The Six Day War in 1967 and was never completed (M. Schofield, pers. comm. 2010) (Figure 13.2).

In many areas, the railway was constructed in close proximity to the Syrian Hajj route used for 'thousands of years by nomads traders, pilgrims, invaders and migrants' (Shqiarat *et al.* 2011). It is an example of both industrial archaeology and railway archaeology – the latter being described as 'the study of railways in terms of surviving traces and relics of the past' (Ransom 1981: 15).

Figure 13.2: The line of the Hejaz Railway as a linear feature in Wadi Rutm. (© author)

If a typical industrial archaeology approach was applied then the route and track bed would be recorded together with a standing building recording of station buildings and bridges. Collections of artefacts might include sections of surviving rails, sleepers, rail-shoes, and spikes together with whatever railway paraphernalia might exist. These could be usefully catalogued, but such an empirical approach would be limited in what it could tell us about the social, cultural, and military 'biography' of the railway.

Industrial archaeology can focus on the production, distribution and consumption of commodities, and recent scholarship has also 'emphasised the very transnational nature of industrialisation by considering the technologies themselves' (Symonds and Casella 2009: 149). This is demonstrated by the supply of rails from Belgium, Austria, Russia, Britain, and Germany together with locomotives from six suppliers in Belgium and Germany and (Shqiarat *et al.* 2011: 101) and roof tiles from Marseilles (Figure 13.3). Similarly, in 1914, the construction of another MLF – the Western Front – brought men from five continents to dig and fight in trenches (Dendooven and Chielens 2008).

The construction of Hadrian's Wall and the Hejaz Railway required large work forces and skilled labour that was brought to their respective areas from the empire and Europe. They are examples of how empires muster men and materials from across the world to dominate and control landscapes. These examples demonstrate that MLFs are products of highly organised states with access to manpower and resources. They not only fulfil their primary function but provide an insight in the organisations that constructed them.

Figure 13.3: The roof tiles from Marseilles and the rail tracks from Belgium. (© author)

An alternative approach is to examine the railway from the perspective of landscape archaeology. A cartographic analysis accompanied by fieldwork focused on the passage of the railway through the landscape enables a more nuanced appreciation of why this particular route was chosen. An examination of how the Ottomans interacted with the landscape and the people who occupied it would also be valuable, though perhaps might not reveal much new information about the railway.

A more comprehensive understanding of the railway requires a step back from its obvious and self-evident aspects as a transport system. Emerging from two quite separate studies of the Hejaz Railway and Hadrian's Wall, the idea of a comparative analysis of the 'railway as frontier' was developed.

One approach to investigate a complex structure is to 'dis-assemble' it into its component parts. As an archaeological monument, the railway consists of embankments, bridges, cuttings, buildings, track, and ties built along a generally linear route. The most under-rated aspect of railway engineering has always been the earthworks (Morriss 1999: 35) and yet it is the earthworks, mainly the track-bed, of the Hejaz Railway that are its largest and most extant feature – and it is this salient characteristic which will be analysed.

Between 2006 and 2010, 113 km of the route of the Hejaz Railway from Ma'an to Mudawarra (on Jordan's present-day border with Saudi Arabia) was surveyed, mainly on foot. In November 2010, an aerial photographic sortie was flown along the route of the railway between Ma'an, Batn Al-Ghoul, and Tel el Shahm stations (Winterburn 2011). This enabled the macro-linear aspects of the railway to be explored within a wider landscape context, and its spatial configuration with respect to fortified hill-tops to be visualised. Other short sections of the railway have also been walked in the Shobak, Uneiza, Jerdun, and Menzil areas north of Ma'an, bringing the total surveyed length of the railway to about ten percent. This is considered to be a representative sample of the entire line enabling comparisons to be made with other MLFs.

Walls and frontiers

Walls are familiar features of conflict landscapes, and from antiquity to the modern period, they are often a defining MLF within contested spaces. Ancient examples include the Great Wall of Gorgon, in Iran (Nokandeh *et al.* 2006: 121), the Great Wall of China (Meijer 1956), and Hadrian's Wall (Breeze and Dobson 2000). Modern examples include the notorious Berlin Wall which stood as a 'symbol of the Cold War and a tangible marker of the geopolitical division of Europe'(Feversham and Schmidt 1999: 10) and the 2500 km long sand-wall known as 'The Berm', which geographically and politically divides the Western Sahara (Bhatia 2001: 291).

Frontiers are complex features and where they incorporate walls there are usually other landscape elements that complement the wall's function. Banks, ditches, armed militia, and fortified gateways are elements common to most frontiers; modern examples can also include minefields, electrified fences, and other mechanisms to deter unauthorised crossing. The wall itself may be a narrow single component, but the frontier zone, either side of the wall may be several hundred metres wide.

The Berlin wall produced a 'conflict zone' within a largely urban environment. Constructed by the East German government to stem the flow of migrants from East to West Berlin, it created a frontier and associated conflict landscapes. It was a kind of 'reverse frontier', designed not to keep people out, but to prevent people from leaving, and thus became a political, economic, and ideological barrier within the landscape. By defining the frontier precisely, border guards could patrol along the wall. Those wishing to cross the frontier had to do so at defined and authorised crossing points or risk certain death by attempting an unauthorised crossing.

Frontiers are generally linear features. In the modern world, precisely positioned and delineated by satellite navigation systems, frontiers can be virtual. They can follow lines of latitude; the Mason-Dixon Line, following the 40th parallel and acting as a demarcation between the US state of Pennsylvania with Maryland and West Virginia is one example (Cope 1946: 545), or lines of longitude, as is the case in the Antarctic. Frontiers or boundaries can also be natural features such as rivers, but in many case they are delineated by man-made structures. They are rarely neutral but are frequently charged with multiple layers of meaning.

Frontiers mark the edge of one territory with another, but with Hadrian's Wall, they also mark the edge of the empire or the known world. Crossing the frontier from the known to the unknown world transforms the perception of the individual from a citizen, subject to the laws and protection of the empire, to a potential barbarian, enemy, and outcast. Crossing a frontier, from the inside out, can change the status of the individual from safe and compliant to ambiguous and seditious.

The Ottoman Empire in what is today southern Jordan had no precisely defined boundaries on its eastern extremity. There was a nominal boundary which enclosed the area of southern Jordan and the Hejaz region, and this was loosely defined as areas of Ottoman administration (see Mansfield 2003: 116). In constructing the railway, an eastern frontier to the empire was unintentionally created, and it marked the practical, eastern, extent of the Ottoman Empire in this region. Beyond its zone of influence lay nothing but desert (sparsely populated by Bedouin) and the uninhabitable *Al-Houl* (The Terror) desert region. The railway-as-frontier, was maintained and controlled via a series of small fortified railway stations along its length, and two larger garrison stations (at Ma'an and Medinah). Control of the frontier was accomplished too by patrolling from garrisons and fortified stations along the railway line together with redoubts and trench systems guarding railway infrastructure.

The designers of Abdülhamit's Hejaz Railway drew lines on maps to plot its course and thereby delineate the Sultan's territory. A ruler is a homonym for a measuring instrument used to draw straight lines and for a sovereign or emperor who controls and governs territory. In making political and strategic decisions – his rulings – a course of action for his subjects is also plotted (Ingold 2007: 160) and the action of ruling demonstrates the imperial ability to control both landscape and subjects. The Sultan is ruling to impose order on ungoverned peoples and landscapes.

Between Ma'an and Mudawwara, the majority of the 113 km railway track comprises long straight sections with some minor changes in direction. Linearity or straightness is an 'unambiguous index of masculinity as curvature indexes femininity' (Ingold 2007: 153). Straightness of posture, expected of men but not necessarily of women, also carries connotations of moral standing and social position, an attribute that can also be applied to *civilised* people (*ibid.*). There may be engineering and fiscal reasons for designing a railway or building a wall with long straight sections, but linearity also confirms the attributes of control, power, masculinity and modernity for the empire.

There is however one section of railway where linearity cannot be maintained for topographic reasons. The railway encounters the *Ras al Naqb* escarpment at Batn Al-Ghoul, 53 km south-east of Ma'an. From the station at Aqabat al Hejazia the

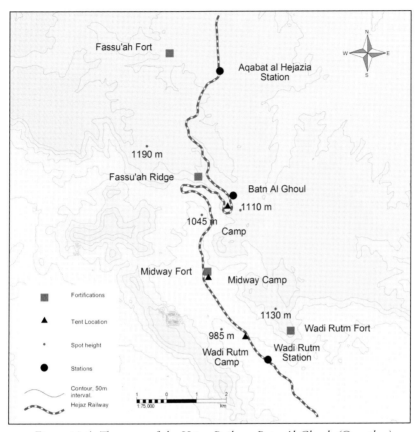

Figure 13.4: The route of the Hejaz Railway Batn Al-Ghoul. (© author)

line descends 100 m to the floor of Wadi Batn Al-Ghoul through a series of sinuous curves culminating in two 180° bends (Figure 13.4). At this point, the *Darb al-Hajj* and the railway intersect, tradition and modernity collide, and the linear concepts of masculinity, power, and control are diminished.

Here, the railway landscape is in a liminal state between straightness and curvature, and as not being representative of a single gender, it becomes ambiguous. The name Batn Al-Ghoul means 'Belly of the Beast', and refers to the mythical and shape-shifting ghoul, 'betwixt genera, ambiguous and indeterminate' (Stetkevych 1984: 668) lurking in the desert to lure travellers to a horrible death; the trans-gendered nature of the early twentieth century landscapes mirroring those of pre-Islamic poets.

This toponym reinforces the ambiguity and danger of the landscape described as '… the strangling place: a sink of desolation …' (Doughty 1888: 23). There are real physical reasons why this area can be considered dangerous. Before the railway was built, pilgrimage caravans would have slowly descended the escarpment making them vulnerable to attack. Trains, likewise, would have been slow to descend or ascend the steep incline. To counter the physical dangers and the intangible aspects of non-linearity this area became one of the most heavily fortified landscapes along the railway.

A series of defended camps, fortified station buildings and hill-top fortifications linked to 'smaller satellite positions along the escarpment' (Saunders and Faulkner 2010: 524) contribute to the defence of this landscape. The two hill-top forts of Fassu'ah Ridge and Wadi Rutm (*ibid*.: 523) contain systems of elaborate pathways defined on the desert floor by carefully placed deposits of gravel. These features are yet more evidence of the Ottomans countering ambiguity in the landscape and non-linearity on the railway with excessive order and control within their fortifications.

Hadrian's Wall

Hadrian's Wall was the north-west frontier of the Roman Empire for over 400 years – a frontier which stretched 4000 km eastwards to Mesopotamia (Iraq) and southwards 2400 km to the Sahara desert (Breeze 2009: 3). The sole surviving comment on the reason for building Hadrian's Wall is provided by Hadrian's biographer: 'Hadrian was the first to build a wall, eighty mile long, to separate the Romans from the barbarians.' (Breeze and Dobson 2000: 1).

The wall is 117 km (73 miles) long and crosses northern Britain from Bowness-on-Solway in the west to Wallsend east of Newcastle upon Tyne – an area known as the Tyne-Solway isthmus (Figure 13.5). The original plan was that it was constructed as a turf wall in the east and a stone wall to the west with protected gates (milecastles) at one Roman mile intervals with two observation towers between each milecastle. It is not certain how high the wall was but estimates indicate somewhere between 3.6 m and 4.4 m. The width of the stone wall was 3 m in places, and it has been suggested that Hadrian may have been influenced in his decision to build such a massive structure by travellers accounts of the Great Wall of China (Breeze and Dobson 2000: 32). Immediately to the north of the wall lay a broad, deep ditch except where topography made this unnecessary. To the south of the wall lay the *Vallum*, a great flat bottomed ditch with two earth banks to either side that ensured the security of the wall from the rear (*ibid*.: 57).

It is generally accepted that the wall was built from 122 CE on the instructions of Emperor Hadrian following his visit to Britain in the same year. The wall was abandoned from 142 when the frontier moved 130 km north and was established on the Antonine Wall. This new frontier was abandoned in 160, and Hadrian's Wall re-established as the frontier.

There has been criticism of the traditional tendency to regard linear features in Roman frontier areas as impenetrable barriers primarily defensive in nature and intended to repel external threats (Hodgson 2000: 12). These lines are now being interpreted as frontier zones, and where they occur are being explained as other than cordons to keep people out (*ibid.*). The provision of milecastles, acting as gateways through the wall, provides further evidence to support the view that Roman linear features were not closed barriers but were probably used to control movement across the frontier zone.

Prior to the building of Hadrian's Wall, the Tyne Solway isthmus area was subject to Roman militarisation. In the central and western areas a road known as the Stanegate linked important river crossings on the routes to Scotland at Corbridge and Carlisle. This linear, east–west military road, protected at regular interval by forts appears to have operated as a means of controlling the movement of the native population through observation and patrolling (Breeze and Dobson 2000: 16–24).

Hadrian's Wall was a massive structure and the longest man-made feature in Britain. It would have been a site of wonder and amazement to the native population, and an expression and symbol of the power and achievements of the Roman Empire. The wall was also a symbol of power and achievement

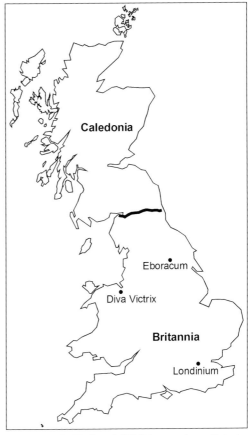

Figure 13.5: Hadrian's Wall in northern Britain. (© author)

for the Emperor Hadrian who had not gained military honours as there had been few major conflicts during his reign. The wall can also be seen as the abandonment of the first Roman ambition for the total control of Britain (*ibid.*: 247) and the realisation that there were practical limits to the expansion of the empire (Figure 13.6).

In the sixth century, the wall was still acknowledged as a frontier, and Bede, writing in the eighth century, comments on the great wall and earthwork banks of the *Vallum*. For 300 years until 1603 the area through which the wall ran continued to be a conflict landscape and became known as 'The Debatable Lands', controlled by local clans who resisted all attempts by Scotland and England to assert authority over the area (HWHL n.d.)

Hadrian's Wall is now a World Heritage site, and forms the principal attraction in 'Hadrian's Wall Country' (HWHL n.d.), spanning the counties of Northumberland and Cumbria. With over 14 million tourist days spent in the area, it is responsible for generating more that £500 million (2006) for the economy (*ibid.*).

Figure 13.6. Hadrian's Wall and Milecastle No. 39, near Steel Rig. (© author)

Modern roads follow the line of the wall, most notably the A186 road through Newcastle, and the B6318 road is constructed on top of the *Vallum* at the village of East Twice Brewed. A long distance footpath closely follows the line of the wall for 135 km (Natural England n.d.) and all major visitor attractions are served by the special bus service, the 'AD 122', that's runs from Newcastle to Carlisle (NNP n.d.).

Roads and pathways are often associated with pilgrimage. The act of walking along a linear feature with a group of like-minded individuals and enduring hardships along the way leads to a state of collective effervescence and communitas (Olaveson 2001). For many scholars, historians, and archaeologists, the wall is regarded as a place of pilgrimage. The first 'modern' pilgrimage was held in 1849 by John Collingwood Bruce, and subsequent pilgrimages have been held at 10 year intervals. In 2009, 220 pilgrims were guided along the wall by David Breeze, who described himself as the Head Pilgrim (Breeze 2010: 13). Pilgrimage is a liminal phenomenon (Turner 1973: 191–192) and the modern pilgrims along the wall are re-engaging with the lost liminality of the wall through their collective endeavours.

These modern track ways, roads, and transport, together with the decennial pilgrimage, illustrate that a Roman frontier, abandoned 1600 years ago, still has relevance and meaning within a modern society. A military frontier is being re-used as a recreational facility for walkers, a site of pilgrimage for scholars, and a linear tourist attraction for millions of visitors which is served by a dedicated transport infrastructure.

During the 2009 Hadrian's Wall pilgrimage, 'the pilgrims lined up on the ramparts of Moresby fort, admiring the acrobatic display of the [Cold War-era] Vulcan bomber' (Selkirk 2010: 16) which coincided with their visit; a serendipitous encounter with iconic symbols of superior military force from the recent and distant past that appears to have gone un-recognised.

Asymmetry, linear features, and degrees of freedom.

When examining the movement of troops along linear features it is informative to consider the concept of *degrees of freedom*. This allows a useful hierarchy of conflict space to be developed that helps illustrate how military forces with higher degrees of freedom are enabled to move more freely within the landscape, and to have significant advantages over troops constrained to linear conflict zones.

A single static military installation such as a pill-box, bunker, or fox-hole can be considered to be a point within the landscape. The dimensions of the fortification, measured in metres, are miniscule compared to the surrounding landscape, making them essentially dimensionless – the equivalent of a mathematical point. The occupying forces are rooted to a single location on the earth's surface, an example of having zero degrees of freedom.

If military forces are constrained to only move along a line, which can be considered to be one-dimensional (the length being many times greater than the width as in the case with a railway line) then they have two degrees of freedom with the ability to move backward and forwards along the line. A body of men in the landscape is operating within a two-dimensional space as they have the ability to move across the surface of the earth in all directions, forward and backward, and to the left and right, giving them four degrees of freedom. The development of the aeroplane in the early twentieth century allowed conflict to occupy three-dimensional airspace, as pilots can fly forward and turn around to go back, move left and right as well as up and down, providing them with six degrees of freedom. (The submarine is also an example of a military force operating within three-dimensional subaquatic space).

Military forces that are confined to linear features are generally at a disadvantage within a conflict landscape, as they have restricted mobility – only able to move freely in one dimension, along the railway, wall, or road. Any forces attacking or attempting to traverse a linear feature generally have four degrees of freedom, and the ability to move in any direction on the earth's surface. Aerial conflict allows the enemy to move in three dimensions with six degrees of freedom. This can be viewed as a hierarchy of conflict spaces, and indicates that forces operating within a conflict-zone 'volume' will generally be at an advantage to those confined to a conflict surface and those constrained on a conflict-zone 'line' will generally be at a disadvantage. It is for this reason that airpower, operating in a conflict-zone volume, is always considered to be the superior force, similarly for submarines in naval conflict.

Conflict Space	Example	Degrees of Freedom
Conflict Point	Bunker	0
Conflict Line	Railway	2
Conflict Surface (Area)	Battlefield	4
Conflict Volume	Airspace	6

The corollary of this feature is that for those seeking to hide forces within the landscape then the more degrees of freedom available the more successful they will be. Attempting to hide forces on a linear feature will be the least successful because the enemy will always know that they are somewhere along the line of the feature.

These concepts accentuate the asymmetrical nature of conflict in a number of ways. If the military force is restricted to occupying a linear feature such as a railway or wall, then their forces can only be dispersed along a line. Enemy forces operating in the landscape, by contrast, can be dispersed on a surface that has area providing them with opportunities for concealment and manoeuvring that increases with the square of the conflict dimensions.

Airpower takes this one stage further with the attacking forces able to disperse their weapons within a volume that grows with the cube of the dimensions of conflict. These concepts are demonstrated in the case of Bedouin guerrilla forces attacking the Hejaz Railway during episodes of the Great Arab Revolt. Ottoman forces guarding the railway were tied to fixed installations along the railway line or in close proximity to it.

The use of linear military features further accentuates the asymmetry of conflict by virtue of the mono-dimensional characteristic of the deployment of forces. The location of forces and *matériel* has to be on the line of the feature providing the enemy with a means of location. When operating in a terrain where there are no maps, the communication of positional information to comrades and allies becomes a major problem. Today, military forces have access to accurate mapping, aerial photography and GPS navigation systems allowing location to be precisely specified in three coordinates.

However, in southern Jordan in 1918, there were no accurate maps and limited aerial photography. British and Arab forces attacking the Ottomans on the railway line were able to locate them with relative ease. If they were to the west of the line then they travelled east until they encountered the line, and then had to move north or south in order to locate the enemy. Similarly, the British Royal Flying Corps (RFC[1]) pilots were able to find the Ottoman forces by first locating the line in the desert and following it north or south. The railway line, as a linear earthwork, was a discernable landmark within the desert environment, its man-made morphology starkly contrasting with the natural landscape components, and providing one of the axes that western, Cartesian coordinate navigational methods rely upon.

Conclusions

Gazing at the dead horizon can tell us nothing new about conflict landscapes. We need to engage with these complex features and, using a multi-disciplinary approach, divine new meaning from apparently self-evident structures. Where a conflict landscape includes an MLF, it provides a tool for examining and engaging with the landscape in ways that can produce new insights and narratives.

The characteristics of MLFs invite peregrination by those who explore them. The railway was initially built for pilgrimage, replacing a route walked by many over hundreds of years. Today, the railway, the iron path, is walked by archaeologists interested in modern conflict, who, through collective endeavours and communitas are an analogue of pilgrims. Hadrian's Wall was not designed for pilgrimage, but has become the site of decennial archaeological pilgrimages, and many hundreds of walkers follow the long-distance footpath along the route of the wall. In the twenty-first century, MLFs in conflict landscapes are facilitating new discourses through walking engagements.

Hadrian's Wall has become a modern linear tourist attraction bringing financial benefit to the local economy and facilitating recreational and educational engagements with historic landscapes. The Hejaz Railway, located within an economically impoverished region, has the potential to attract western tourists interested in military history, walking, and desert adventure. Hadrian's Wall has enhanced the tourism economy of its hinterland, and the Hejaz Railway could do the same for southern Jordan. This potential has been recognised further south in Saudi Arabia (Orbasli and Woodward 2008) but appears to have passed unnoticed in Jordan.

The railway was the dying act of modernity for a failing empire. It became a *de facto* frontier for the Ottoman Empire, delineating the eastern limit of their control, and replacing the *Darb Al Hajj* that had performed a similar function for hundreds of years. Intended to be the focus of support in the cause of a pan-Islamic Caliphate it however became the focus for conflict. The linearity of the railway contributed to its engineering, operational and fiscal objectives, and was a statement of power, control and moral authority for the Ottoman Empire. However, it was this linearity that contributed to its demise through resulting asymmetrical warfare.

A linear feature within a seemingly featureless desert becomes an obvious navigational aid for pilots. In this case it also guided pilots towards their intended targets – which highlights the asymmetrical conflict and disadvantages of limited mobility. The attacks by the RAF pilots on the railway are among the first examples of aircraft being used in this way and prefaced similar actions in later conflicts.

Hadrian visited the area through which the Hejaz Railway is routed, and his legacy in Britain has provided a tool with which to examine the railway and other MLFs in conflict and frontier landscapes. Examining MLFs within conflict landscapes has enabled the concepts of a hierarchy of conflict space to be developed which can be used to examine other areas of military conflict.

Note
1. The Royal Flying Corps (RFC) became the Royal Air Force (RAF) on 1 April 1918.

Bibliography

Barker, G., Gilbertson, D. and Mattingly, D. (eds) (2007) *Archaeology and desertification: The Wadi Faynan Landscape Survey, Southern Jordan.* Oxford: Oxbow Books.

Bhatia, M. (2001) The Western Sahara under Polisario Control, *Review of African Political Economy* 28: 291–298.

Breeze, D.J. (2006) *J. Collingwood Bruce's Handbook to The Roman Wall,* Newcastle: Society of Antiquaries of Newcastle upon Tyne.

Breeze, D.J. (2009) *Hadrian's Wall.* London: English Heritage.

Breeze, D J. (2010) The Pilgrimage of Hadrian's Wall 2009. *Current Archaeology* 240: 12–13.

Breeze, D.J. and Dobson, B. (2000) *Hadrian's Wall.* London: Pelican.

Cope, T.D. (1946) Charles Mason and Jeremiah Dixon. *The Scientific Monthly* 62: 541–554.

Dendooven, D. and Chielens, P. (2008) *World War 1, Five Continents in Flanders.* Tielt: Lannoo.

Doughty, C.M. (1888) *Arabia Deserta.* Cambridge: Cambridge University Press.

Fahmy, A. (2001) Between Mystical amd Military: The Architecture of the Hejaz Railway (1900–1918). *Proceedings of the 11th International Congress of Turkish Art,* 1–22.

Feversham, P. and Schmidt, L. (1999) *The Berlin Wall Today.* Berlin: Verlag Bauwesen.

Finkel, C. (2005) *Osman's Dream. The Story of the Ottoman Empire 1300–1923.* London: John Murray.

Hodgson, N. (2000) The Stanegate: A Frontier Rehabilitated. *Britannia* 31: 11–22.

HWHL (n.d.) *Hadrian's Wall Country.* http://www.hadrians-wall.org Accessed 3 May 2011.

Ingold, T. (2007) *Lines: A Brief History.* London Routledge.

Lawrence, T.E. (2003) *Seven Pillars of Wisdom.* Fordingbridge: Castle Hill Press.

Mansfield, P. (2003) *A History of the Middle East.* London: Penguin.

Maunsell, F.R. (1908) The Hejaz Railway. *Geographical Journal* 32: 570–585.

McOmish, D., Field, D. and Brown, G. (2002) *The Field Archaeology of the Salisbury Plain Training Area.* Swindon: English Heritage.

Meijer, M.J. (1956) A Map of the Great Wall of China. *Imago Mundi* 13: 110–115.

Morriss, R. (1999) *The Archaeology of Railways.* Stroud: Tempus.

Natural England (n.d.) *Hadrian's Wall Path.* http://www.nationaltrail.co.uk/hadrianswall/ Accessed 5 May 2011.

Nicholson, J. (2005) *The Hejaz Railway.* London: Stacey International.

NNP (n.d.) *Hadrian's Wall Bus.* http://www.northumberland-national-park.org.uk/VisitorGuide/ Visiting/ Travel/hadrianswallbus.htm Accessed 5 May 2011.

Nokandeh, J., Sauer, E.W. and Rekavandi, H.O. (2006) Linear Barriers of Northern Iran: the Great Wall of Gorgan and the Wall of Tammishe. *Iran* 44: 121–173.

Ochsenwald, W. (1980) *The Hijaz Railroad.* Charlottesville: University Press of Virginia.

Olaveson, T. (2001) Collective Effervescence and Communitas: Processual Models of Ritual and Society in Emile Durkheim and Victor Turner. *Dialectical Anthropology* 26: 89–124.

Orbasli, A. and Woodward, S. (2008) A Railway 'Route' as a Linear Heritage Attraction: The Hijaz Railway in the Kingdon of Saudi Arabia. *Journal of Heritage Toursim* 3: 159–175.

Petersen, A. (1989) Early Ottoman Forts on the Darb al-Hajj. *Levant* 21: 97–117.

Ransom, P.J.G. (1981) *The Archaeology of Railways.* Tadworth: The Windmill Press.

Saunders, N.J. and Faulkner, N. (2010) Fire on the Desert: Conflict Archaeology and the Great Arab Revolt in Jordan, 1916–1918. *Antiquity* 84: 514–526.

Selkirk, A. (2010) Walking the Wall Backwards. *Current Archaeology* 240: 14–17.

Shqiarat, M., Al-Salameen, Z., Faulkner, N. and Saunders, N.J. (2011) Fire and Water: Tradition and Modernity in the Archaeology of Steam Locomotion in a Desert War. *Levant* 43(1): 98–113.

Stetkevych, S.P. (1984) The Su' luk and His Poem: a Paradigm of Passage Manqué. *Journal of the American Oriental Society* 104: 661–678.

Symonds, J. and Casella, E.C. (2009) Historical Archaeology and Industrialisation. In D. Hicks and M.C. Beaudry (eds), *The Cambridge Companion to Historical Archaeology,* 143–167. Cambridge: Cambridge University Press.

Tourett, R. (1976) *The Hejaz Railway.* Abingdon: Tourret Publishing.

Turner, V. (1973) The Center Out There: Pilgrim's Goal. *History of Religions* 12: 191–230.

Wilson, J. (1989) *Lawrence of Arabia. The Authorised Biography of T.E. Lawrence.* London: Heinemann.

Winterburn, J.B. (2011) 'Flying the Line', *Current World Archaeology* 46: 54–57.

14

Churchill's 'Silent Sentinels': an archaeological spatial evaluation of Britain's Second World War coastal defences at Weymouth, Dorset, *c*. 1940

Philip R. Rowe

With the withdrawal of the British Expeditionary Force (BEF) and Allied forces from the Low Countries completed by early June 1940, the subsequent capitulation of France heralded a new chapter of the Second World War. Preparations for a possible invasion of Britain were now evident on both sides of the English Channel.

In response to '*Unternehmen Seelöwe*' (Operation Sealion) – the proposed German seaborne invasion of Britain – a vast programme of constructing anti-invasion defences was swiftly set in motion, with more than 28,000 defensive structures erected throughout Great Britain by early 1941 (Ruddy 2003: 2). This system of anti-invasion defences began at the coast and continued inland with defensive linear 'Stop Lines' and 'Anti-Tank Islands' hastily constructed during the summer of 1940. Planned initially on policies and tactics of First World War vintage, the anti-invasion defences soon evolved, following lessons learnt in defensive countermeasures during the withdrawal of the BEF from the Low Countries.

Hitler's great seaborne invasion of Britain of course never materialised, yet the huge investment of time and effort by the British does raise the hypothetical question – 'Could the anti-invasion defensives erected during the Second World War ever have halted a German invasion force?' This is a question which archaeological investigation is well suited to help answer.

Despite their size and distribution across the landscape, our knowledge and understanding of these defences have long been over shadowed by the events of the 'Battle of Britain', with the (albeit short-lived) reality of invasion consequently being underestimated, and attracting only limited archaeological attention. The general perception of Britain's anti–invasion network is that of a hastily conceived and constructed defence, short of men and equipment, and most likely ineffective in the face of invasion; an observation epitomised by the BBC comedy *Dads Army*. But how accurate is this view?

With primary documentary evidence for Britain's anti-invasion defence network surviving at various locations (e.g. The National Archives and Local Records Offices), construction information is fragmented, with records listed under a multitude of sub-headings that require lateral thinking from any potential researcher. Thus, it is not surprising that previous studies of the location of these defences are somewhat meagre, with few archaeological studies conducted to date.

In an attempt to redress this situation, Lacey (2003) used geographical information system software (GIS) to conduct a spatial analysis of a section of linear defences along the 'Taunton Stop Line', applying a 'fireshed' analysis – his own variant of the 'viewshed' technique. This is a comparable approach to that adopted by the author, who employed archaeological field techniques and GIS in his investigation of 'Stop Line Green' near the city of Bath (Rowe 2005). Using a variety of archaeological techniques, this paper aims to demonstrate that the spatial evaluation of part of the anti-invasion defensive landscape – the coastal defence battery – can add descriptive and analytical precision to evaluating their potential effectiveness. The analysis will focus on the Weymouth area of Dorset (south-west England), previously identified as a possible point of entry for a second wave of German forces.

Operation Sealion

A German invasion of Britain was initially regarded as unlikely, due to the extensive Allied fortifications sited along the borders of the Low Countries. However, with the unexpected ending of the 'Phoney War', and the defensive stalemate which developed between Allied and German forces, the threat of invasion became suddenly more real.

Launching a *Blitzkrieg* campaign on 10 May 1940, the main German assault bypassed the majority of Allied defences in the Low Countries. The Germans exploited their advantage also in the Ardennes Forest, an area previously considered unsuitable for tank warfare, and consequently only lightly defended by the Allies.

On the defensive from the start, and with no ability to defend France 'in depth', the BEF and Allied forces were forced to withdraw to the area around the French port of Dunkirk, with the order to evacuate as many men as possible. In late May 1940, this operation was given the codename *Dynamo*. The English Channel was the only remaining obstacle between Britain and the German armed forces; on 4 June 1940, the newly-elected Prime Minister, Winston Churchill, addressed Parliament with a now-famous speech

> '… we shall defend our island whatever the cost may be. We shall fight on the beaches; we shall fight on the landing grounds; we shall fight in the fields and in the streets; we shall fight in the hills. We shall never surrender.' (HC Deb 1940)

Deciding upon an invasion force that would land on a narrow front along the south–south-east coast of southern England (i.e. from Worthing in Sussex to Folkestone in

Kent) (Lowry 2004: 9), the *Wehrmacht's* Army Group A's intention was to advance northwards, destroying the main British reserve forces, before encircling London. Additional mechanised forces were then to advance through the counties of Wiltshire and Berkshire, engaging any remaining forces (Marix Evans 2004: 101), while seizing the main industrial centres and principal seaports as they did so.

Held in reserve, German Army Group B, sailing from Cherbourg to the west, would execute a landing in Lyme Bay, Dorset, and occupy the Weymouth and Lyme Regis areas, moving north and eastward, isolating Cornwall before advancing onto Taunton, Bristol, and Gloucester – with an added eastern advance towards London, should the situation dictate it. The campaign timetable had been formulated one year before war began – and included the actual date for invasion – 'S' Day – 21 September 1940 (Longmate 2004: 25).

Defence of Britain

The initial role of Britain's newly created 'Local Defence Volunteers', later renamed the 'Home Guard', was to counter the threat of airborne attack, by undertaking static defence of villages and road blocks.

Formed on 14 May 1940, with nearly a quarter of a million men quickly answering the call to arms (Lowry 2004: 10), it was not until late June that a report was made to the War Cabinet by General Ironside, the newly appointed Commander-In-Chief Home Forces, outlining his aims for Britain's home defence. The coastline was to be defended with a 'crust' of infantry that were expected to disrupt an enemy landing long enough to allow the arrival of reinforcements.

Home Forces Operational Instruction No: 3 dictated that any enemy breakout from a beachhead should be delayed in advance by a series of linear stop lines and defended localities that extended deep inland. Once suitably impeded, and the direction of attack established, a counter-attack using reserve forces could then be efficiently co-ordinated, with the enemy's ability to manoeuvre inhibited by anti-tank obstacles, defended pillboxes, and strong-points (nodal points). This strategy was seen as favouring the defender (Lowry 2004: 25), and its success had been previously demonstrated during the battle for Warsaw in September 1939, where one Panzer regiment lost 57 of its 120 tanks to these concentrated 'killing fields' (Rowe 2005: 11).

'Coastal crust'

The shortage of men and equipment in the British Army after their heroic but chaotic evacuation from France had a direct bearing on the organisation of southern England's defense. The loss of armour, artillery, motor transport, and small arms required a plan which delayed any invasion on the beaches long enough for two responses to occur – and both revolved around buying time. First, the Royal Navy would have to deploy from bases in Scotland and disrupt the cross-Channel passage of invasion forces and supply lines. Second, British army reinforcements inland needed to move to the appropriate areas to counterattack (Osborne 2004: 33).

Based on a War Office directive of 5 July 1940 that stated that '… The policy is to stop the enemy on the beaches or before he reaches them … There will be NO withdrawal from forward posts; they will be held to the last.' (TNA: WO 166/605/1), fixed defences on the beaches were in the form of scaffolding poles, minefields, anti-tank ditches and cubes, with pillboxes and field gun positions hurriedly sited alongside previously established Counter-Bombardment (CB) and Close-Defence (CD) coastal batteries, upgraded in preparation of the expected invasion (Figure 14.1).

Reinforcing the coastal crust further, a number of additional 'Emergency Coastal Defence Batteries' (ECBs) were constructed at minor ports and landing points, using large naval guns from existing Royal Navy stocks and recycled from obsolete First World War ships. Complementing the ECB's were heavy booms, strung out across river estuaries such as the Thames, Medway, and Humber, to prevent the movement of German warships, and landing barges. Concrete pillboxes, machine gun emplacements, and improvised self-propelled guns were located to guard beach exits and slipways (Rowe

Figure 14.1: Extent of the archaeological remains of coastal pillboxes, anti-tank wall, and beach scaffolding, recorded during the fieldwork in the Weymouth area. (© Author).

2005: 13). Eight out of the 15 available infantry divisions assigned to home defence were devoted to coastal defence, with the remaining seven divisions stationed further inland in order to act as a mobile reserve, and counter any threatened breakout from a beachhead or airborne attack (Saunders 1997: 101).

The final part of this coastal crust armoury was the 'Royal Air Force Coastal Command', whose *Scarecrow* patrols of 'Tiger Moth' biplanes and 'Miles Trainer' aircraft (armed only with light bombs and machine guns), were to be used in repelling any beach landing (Lowry 2004: 26), including, potentially, the deployment of mustard gas if all else failed (Longmate 2004: 49). Further inland, behind the coastal crust, there was a series of defensive linear 'stop lines' and 'nodal points'. These defended locations were regarded as being of strategic importance within the landscape, and were sited accordingly across the country, utilising natural topographic features in order to hinder any German advance, allowing valuable time for reserves forces to mobilise.

Study area and investigative methodology

In order to carry out a viable topographical assessment of the siting of the defensive counter-measures within the Weymouth study area, primary locational data were obtained to assist the production of a GIS spatial (viewshed) analysis, and so demonstrate that the coastal batteries were, arguably, strategically well-sited within the landscape, and therefore ideally located to engage the enemy invasion forces. In 2006, the author began a field investigation to obtain 'primary' survey data on the defence's topographical locations within the surrounding environment, and to verify existing entries in English Heritage's 2002 *Defence of Britain* (DoB) site register.

A photographic record was made as part of the documentation of sites – a 'Basic Standing Building Record' – and this was supplemented by an Earth Resistance Survey, using a Geoscan RM15 Resistance Meter (to measure the resistance of sub-surface features to an electrical current). This offered additional 'original' data to that already in the Historic Environment Record (HER) and DoB databases.

The positional locations of the defence sites were recorded with a Garmin Etrex 12 channel handheld '*Navigation Grade*' GPS system, and entered into an Excel spreadsheet. To help compensate for any latent inaccuracies of the GPS positional data, spatial readings were taken from the middle of the site wherever possible, alleviating, as a result, the known inherent 3–4 m inaccuracy of navigational-grade GPS systems.

Finally, to realise a theoretical analytical conclusion as to the strategic siting of the Weymouth area coastal batteries, geo-referenced digital cartographic data, analysed using Esri's ArcGIS v.10 software, was used to create a GIS spatial evaluation (multiple viewshed) of the topographical locations of the batteries within the landscape. Depicting a three-dimensional cartographic contour elevation of the Weymouth landscape (Digital Terrain Model or DTM) the resultant analysis was fundamental to establishing the coastal defence sites' probable arcs of fire (viewsheds), and so any suggested 'strategic siting'.

Site selection

To facilitate a successful examination of the defensive structures in the Weymouth area, sites selected for analysis were chosen using the following English Heritage criteria (Foot 2006: 35).

1. Areas/sites that represent a particular coherent defence construction.
2. Areas/sites with good surviving documentary and/or published sources.
3. Areas/sites with good inter-visibility, where the defence works can be seen within clear viewsheds.
4. Areas/sites with very good survival of defence works, enabling them to be understood easily in their landscape context.
5. Areas/sites with differing types of defence works.
6. Areas/sites that include rare types of defence works.
7. Areas/sites that represent the different strategies of anti-invasion defence employed.

The battery sites chosen for analysis were selected due to their high quality of survival within the archaeological record, and were taken from data entries in the DoB database. Additional documentation, both primary as well as secondary, was sourced from the National Archives (TNA), as well as Historic Environments Record (HER) entries. The information concerning the defence site locations comprised war diaries, unit records, and War Office directives. When combined, they enable a comparatively literal representation of the coastal defensive landscape of the Weymouth area in 1940 to be established.

The coastal defence of Weymouth, Dorset – an archaeological spatial evaluation

The case study area extends for about 41 km in a north-west to south-east direction, along the Chesil Beach coastline to Portland Bill, before following Weymouth Bay to Osmington Mills (Figure 14.2). Beginning at Langton Herring, about 4 km south-east of the village of Abbotsbury, and terminating at 0.7 km south-east of Osmington Mills, the section of defended coastline chosen for archaeological analysis begins at Chesil Beach, a pebble-sand bar that connects the Isle of Portland to the mainland.

Forming a natural topographical barrier between the coastal fringes and the sea to create a large salt water lagoon locked between the mainland and the sea, the hinterland adjacent to the Chesil can be seen to gradually rise from the water's edge and its associated

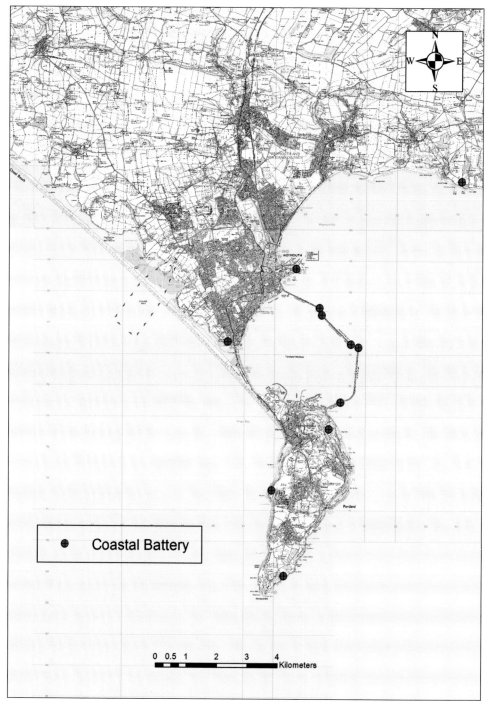

Figure 14.2: Site cartography with Coastal Battery sites denoted (© Digimap © Crown copyright/ database right 2009, generated in © ArcGIS). (© Author).

metal scaffold defensive beach obstacles, infantry pillboxes (Type's FW 3/24 and 25, as defined by Wills (1985: 17)) and slit trenches, to *c.* 45–55 m above sea level (ASL) and the undulating ridges of high ground located to the north-west around the areas of West and East Fleet.

Providing a dominant vantage point over the defended coastline, south-east of the case study area, around the village of Wyke Regis and the site of an ECB, the landscape rises to a plateau *c.* 50–60 m ASL, before gradually descending into the low lying basin of Weymouth Bay and sea level.

Extending from the Nothe promontory north-eastwards to Bowleaze Cove and the adjacent village of Osmington Mills, Weymouth Bay (including Weymouth Town itself) was protected by a CD coastal battery sited at Nothe Fort, a CB coastal battery at Upton, infantry pillboxes (Type FW 3/24; *ibid.*: 17) and associated slit trenches sited along the coastline between Bowleaze Cove and Osmington Mills, in addition to beach scaffolding defences.

Due south, across the deep anchorage of Portland Harbour, the Isle of Portland, classified as a 'tied island' due to it being connected to the mainland by the Chesil bank, rapidly ascends in height from *c.* 9 m ASL at the north end and the village of Chiswell, to *c.* 146 m ASL at the Victorian citadel of 'The Verne', and East Weare batteries, north-east of the village of Fortuneswell.

Progressively descending in height southwards, infantry pillboxes (Type FW 3/25; *ibid.* 1985: 17) and associated slit trenches, can be found east of the village of Easton, with the site of an ECB located at the Old Lighthouse, *c.* 800 m north-east of the southernmost promontory of Portland Bill.

Figure 14.3: Extant remains of East Weare Battery, as viewed today. (© Author)

Archaeological field survey
Working with data sourced from the DoB database, in addition to primary documentation in the 50th Division War diaries (NA WO 166/605/1), six coastal batteries were chosen for brief archaeological field survey.

East Weare Battery(s)
Originally an extension of the Victorian-period 'Verne Fort' citadel, and designed to guard the newly-constructed Portland harbour, the East Weare batteries comprised two counter-bombardment (CD) 9.2-inch (234 mm) guns at the outset of hostilities in 1939. Their operative range, as noted in the armament table of the 31 August 1943, was recorded as being 19,700 yards, *c.* 18 km (NA WO 78/5075, quoted in Andrews and Pinsent 1981: 19).

Throughout the course of the war, various alterations and building additions were made, including the siting of a Battery Observation Post (BOP), Coast Artillery Searchlight (CASL) emplacements, as well as an additional battery ('E') comprising two 90 mm guns in 1941 (*ibid.* 1981:19). Decommissioned in the 1950s, the site today is fairly well preserved within the former Naval base (now the Portland Harbour Authority), and is accessible by public footpath, whereas the main battery site can only be accessed with prior permission from the Port authority (Figure 14.3).

Breakwater Fort (including 'Inner Pier Head Battery' and 'A' and 'C' Pier-Head Batteries)
Locally known as 'Chequer Fort', the site was originally named 'North Head Fort', and was constructed during the latter half of the nineteenth century; it housed two 6-inch (152 mm) guns during the Second World War (Pomeroy 1995: 21) (Figure 14.4).

Classified as a 'Close Defence' (CD) battery, with a suggested maximum range of 14,000–24,500 yards (*c.* 13–22 km), dependent on gun mounting (Brown *et al.* 2002: 94), the fort was modified during the Second World War, with the additions of BOP and CASL emplacements. The site today is well preserved, with the majority of external fortifications still standing, with seaborne access by permission of Portland Harbour Authority.

Sited at the end of the attached pier enclosing the south side of Portland harbour, the *c.* 1862 Inner Pier Battery is located in an excellent position to assist the East Weare Battery(s), and during the Second World War was armed with a Light Anti-Aircraft (LAA) 40 mm *Bofors* gun (Andrews and Pinsent 1981: 22). Predominately used for low level air defence (with a recorded maximum rate of fire of 120 rounds per minute to an altitude of *c.* 5000 ft (*c.* 1.5 km)), it is possible that it could have lowered its barrel sufficiently to engage targets at sea in the event of invasion.

Constructed by the beginning of the twentieth century, 'C' Pier Head battery was sited at the end of the north arm breakwater. It faced 'B' Pier Head battery, located on the middle arm breakwater, with 'A' Pier Head battery located at the opposite end of the middle arm breakwater, facing the Chequer Fort.

Regimental records and plans for the batteries, dating to the early 1940s (NA WO 78/5077 – Parts 6 and 7; quoted in Andrews and Pinsent 1981: 23), suggests that both 'A' and 'C' batteries, sited in association with coastal searchlights, comprised two 12-pounders (5.44 kg) guns, whereas 'B' Pier Head Battery was not installed until after the war. These locations are classified by Brown *et al.* (2002: 94) as being 'Anti-Motor Torpedo Boat Batteries' (AMTB), and the effective range of their 12-pounder guns was 10,000 yards (*c.* 9 km).

The Nothe Fort

In 1939, Nothe Fort, which commanded the entrance to Weymouth harbour, comprised two 6-inch (152 mm) guns, and was classed as a CD battery with an effective range similar to that of the Chequer Fort. Its origins were as a Victorian 'Palmerston Fort', but it was now re-inforced with a Battery Observation Post (BOP), a Light Anti-Aircraft position (LAA), and a Coastal Artillery Searchlight emplacement (CASL), and its underground magazines served as the central depot for anti-aircraft shells. On the glacis adjacent to the fort was a semi–mobile anti-aircraft battery of two 3-inch (76 mm) First World War guns, though these were soon replaced by a permanent four gun 3.7-inch (94 mm) Heavy Anti-Aircraft (HAA) battery, complete with magazines and a command post.

Today, Nothe Fort is a 'Museum of Coastal Defence', having undergone restoration funded by the Heritage Lottery. While all surface traces of the HAA battery have disappeared beneath the heavily-landscaped Nothe Gardens and its adjacent car park, the subterranean remains survive almost intact, according to a recent Resistance Survey (Rowe and Price 2006) (Figure 14.5).

Blacknor Fort (West Weares Battery)

Located midway along Portland's west side, and occupying a commanding position above Lyme Bay and the western approaches, Blacknor Fort (originally built in 1901), was armed with two 9.2-inch (234 mm) Mk 10 Breech-Loading guns (Pomeroy 1995: 91) during the Second World War, each with a maximum range of 36,700 yards (*c.* 33 km) (Lowry 2004: 28). Classified as a CB battery, the BOP was located on the south side of the fort in order to provide excellent command and control visibility, and thus provided protection against landings along the Lyme Bay area (Figure 14.6).

Despite this, there existed a potential 'dead water zone' at the foot of the cliffs where the guns could not be lowered sufficiently to defend it (Andrews and Pinsent 1981: 29). Perhaps for this reason an 'Emergency Coastal Defence Battery' (ECB) was built at Wyke Regis (NA WO 192/301), providing an arc of fire which covered the approach to the dead water zone. Today, Blacknor Fort is in private ownership, and so a complete field recording could not be made.

Figure 14.4: Chequer Fort, with associated Coast Artillery searchlight emplacements and auxiliary buildings, as viewed seawards. (© Author)

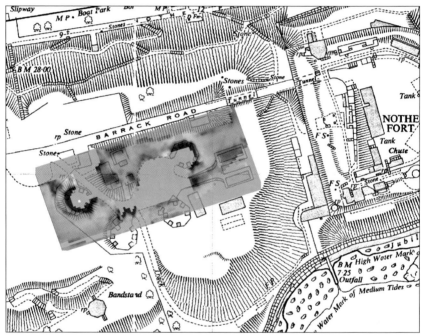

Figure 14.5: RM15 Resistance Survey overlaying 1:1250 1958 National Grid Map (© Digimap © Crown copyright/database right 2009, generated in © ArcGIS). (© Author)

Figure 14.6: Battery Observation Post (BOP) sited south of Blacknor Fort

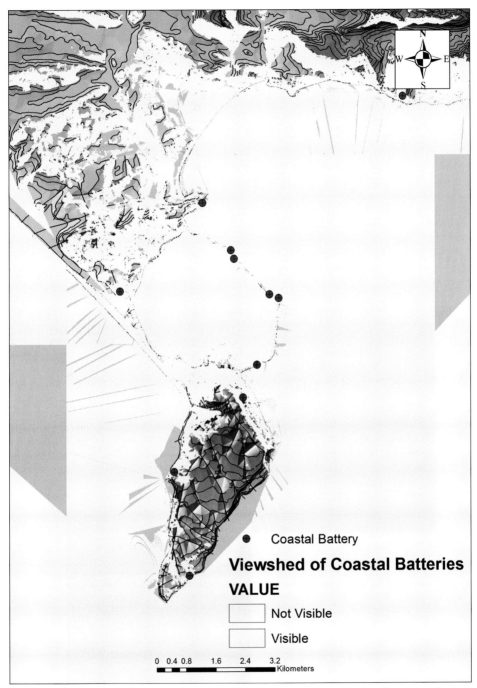

Figure 14.7: Theoretical viewshed (fields of fire) of the coastal batteries for the case study area of Weymouth (© Digimap © Crown copyright/database right 2009, generated in © ArcGIS). (© Author)

'Spatial' analysis and conclusions

When observing the DTM of the Weymouth area with the coastal batteries overlaid, it is apparent that by siting batteries at the key positions of the Nothe Promontory, Portland breakwaters, East Weare, Upton, Wyke Regis, Portland Bill, and Blacknor, excellent strategic use was made of both pre-existing Victorian fortifications, in addition to local topographic conditions (Figure 14.7).

Computing a multiple viewshed in order to illustrate the batteries' arcs of fire, the results clearly reveal that excellent visibility of the surrounding coastal waters and shoreline was afforded to the battery locations within the landscape. Observing dead water zones beneath both Blacknor Fort (despite the siting of an ECB at Wyke Regis), as well as along a large section of coastline immediately south-east on the Isle of Portland, it is not unreasonable to suggest that these coastal zones could have been areas regarded as potential landing zones for German troops. Examining the natural topography of the coastline at those points, it soon becomes apparent that any infantry landing in these zones would have encountered steep slopes and high cliff faces, and so it can be assumed these dead water zones posed no threat with regard to enemy landing.

Accepting that the generated viewshed is comparable to that of a coastal battery gun's arc of fire, compensation for any possible digital inaccuracy of 'computational' range was factored into the results. Limited by the size of the digitally created DTM (see Appendix) and therefore not a factual representation of a weapons maximum 'operational' range of fire, the computed edge of the depicted DTM for this study was purposely created smaller than the maximum given range of the coastal guns, and so plausibly does represent the batteries effective arcs of fire.

The cartographically-calculated measurements for the viewshed clearly demonstrate that excellent theoretical fields of fire were afforded to the guns. Thus, it is reasonable to assume that the coastal batteries could have engaged an advancing enemy flotilla from its effective maximum range, and so hindered a German landing.

In conclusion, this research shows that by employing archaeological field investigation and GIS 'spatial' analysis to Second World War defence sites, the resulting data can contribute significantly to the analysis of the siting of defensive structures within the landscape, and thereby assist our understanding of the hypothetical strategic effectiveness of these defences.

Bibliography

Andrews, E.A. and Pinsent, M.L. (1981) The coastal defences of Portland and Weymouth. *Fort: Fortress Study Group* 9. Liverpool: Fortress Study Group.

Archaeological Data Service '*On Line Catalogue – Defence of Britain database*' www.ads.ahds. ac.uk/catalogue/specColl/dob Accessed 1 December 2010.

Brown I, Burridge, D., Clarke, D., Guy, J., Hellis, J., Lowry, B., Ruckley, N. and Thomas, R.

(2002) *20th Century Defences in Britain – An Introductory guide*. York: Council for British Archaeology.

Conolly, J, and Lake, M. (2006) *Geographical Information Systems in Archaeology*. Cambridge: Cambridge University Press.

©Digimap: © Crown copyrights/database right (2009) – Ordnance Survey/Edina Supplied Service to the University of Bristol (Educational Licence).

©Esri: ArcGIS v.10 – Geographical Information System Software Supplied Service to the University of Bristol (Educational Licence).

Fisher, P. (1991) First Experiments in Viewshed Uncertainty: the Accuracy of the Viewshed Area. *Photogrammetric Engineering and Remote Sensing* 57: 1321–1327.

Foot, W. (2006) *Beaches, Fields, Streets, and Hills… the Anti-Invasion Landscapes of England, 1940*. York: Council for British Archaeology.

HC Deb (1940). *House of Commons Debate, 4 June 1940*. Vol 361, cc787–798. *http://hansard. millbanksystems.com/commons/1940 /jun/04/war-situation* Accessed 1 December 2010.

Lacey, C. (2003) *The Application of GIS Techniques to Historic Military Data*. Southampton: University of Southampton (unpublished MSc dissertation), Department of Archaeology.

Longmate, N. (2004) *If Britain Had Fallen – The Real Nazi Occupation Plans*. London: Greenhill Books.

Lowry, B. (2004) *British Home Defences 1940–45*. Oxford: Osprey.

Marix Evans, M. (2004) *Invasion! Operation Sealion 1940*. Harlow: Pearson Education.

Osborne, M. (2004) *Defending Britain – Twentieth Century Military Structures in the Landscape*. Stroud: Tempus.

Pomeroy, C.A. 1995. *Military Dorset Today – Second World War Scenes and Settings that can Still be Seen 50 years on*. Peterborough: Silver Link Publishing.

Rowe, P.R (2005) *A Landscape Study into the Perceived Effectiveness of the 'Stop Line Green' Anti-invasion Defence*. Bristol: University of Bristol (unpublished MA dissertation), Department of Archaeology and Anthropology.

Rowe, P.R. and Price, C.J. (2006) *Geophysical Survey Report for Nothe Fort Public Car Park, Weymouth*. Bristol: Department of Archaeology and Anthropology, University of Bristol, unpublished report 06/04.

Ruddy, A. (2003) *British Anti-Invasion Defences 1940–1945*. Storrington: Historic Military Press.

Saunders, A. (1997) *Channel Defences*. London: Batsford.

Star, J. and Estes, J. (1990) *Geographic Information Systems: an Introduction*. New Jersey: Prentice-Hall.

The National Archives Document: WO 78/5075.

The National Archives Document: WO 78/5077 – Parts 6 and 7.

The National Archives Document: WO 166/605/1.

The National Archives Document: WO 192/301.

Wheatley, D. and Gillings, M. (2002) *Spatial Technology and Archaeology – the Archaeological Application of GIS*. London: Taylor and Francis.

Wills, H. (1985) *Pillboxes: a Study of U.K Defences 1940*. London: Leo Cooper.

Appendix

Expressing fundamentals of the 'real' world by way of visually presenting cartographic data in either two (x, y easting's/northings plan), or three (x, y plan plus z elevation/ height data) dimensional information, the vector datasets were analysed using a 'Digital Terrain Model' to a scale of 1:10,000, and were initially converted into a 'Triangulated Irregular Network' in order to show elevation data (Wheatley and Gillings 2002: 112).

Employed in the planning/civil engineering industries, as well as increasingly by the military (Fisher 1991: 1321), the multiple 'viewshed' is the combination of individual areas of visibility (viewshed themes), with cells to the value of 1 (colour coded Green) denoting areas visible from any of the entered observation points, whilst cells to the value of 0 represent area that are not visible (colour code set to Transparent) (Wheatley and Gillings 2002: 207).

Illustrating therefore the visibility afforded to a given site, the analysis, however, can potentially be not without complications, with the following two variables factored for when presenting the analytical results:

Computational – How the software calculates visibility, taking into account issues such as the 'curvature of the earth', a factor Conolly and Lake (2006: 228) define as being a *c.* 7.86 m reduction in elevation per 10 km from viewpoint.

Envisaging there is a maximum horizontal distance between an observer and target beyond which the earth's curvature inhibits visibility, in most cases the software does not take this into consideration, instead creating infinite calculations limited only to the size of the two-dimensional grid data set.

Substantive – Parameter/data values selected for visibility analysis calculations. Of those cited by Conolly and Lake (2006: 230–232), the main potential concern is that of 'height of observer'.

Allowing only one observer height to be entered into the feature attribute table (OffsetA), the height of observer does not take into account differing statures of the coastal defences, and so could potentially produce an inaccurate 'viewshed'. For this research, an arbitrary height of 1.5 m was chosen as OffsetA to represent the average height of the coastal defences.

15

Landmark, Symbol, and Monument: public perceptions of a Cold War early warning site in Germany

Gunnar Maus

Wasserkuppe radar station is a landmark, an 'object in the landscape, which, by its conspicuousness, serves as a guide in the direction of one's course' ("landmark, n." 2010), in the true sense of the word. Sitting atop the Rhön mountain range, *c.* 120 km north-east of Frankfurt, at 950 m above sea level, its golfball-like radome dominates the

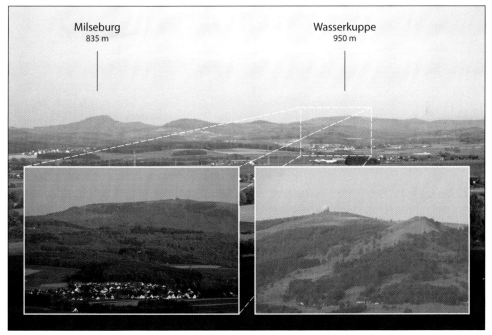

Figure 15.1: The remaining radome on Wasserkuppe prominently identifies the mountain in the panorama of the Rhön mountain range as seen from Fulda. Milseburg, in contrast, is known for its distinctive shape. (© author, 2009)

landscape for miles. In clear conditions, travellers on the Hamburg to Munich mainline train, or motorists speeding along the parallel *Autobahn 7,* enjoy a good view of the station's distinctive silhouette in the distance (Figure 15.1). Personally, I remember Wasserkuppe mostly for the orange fairy lights of the compound's nightly security floodlighting. They would be assuring me when returning from a family gathering that we would finally be home soon. Yet, the lights were turned off years ago, and the lamp-posts soon dismantled. The chain of lights is now but a memory.

I will argue here that such distinctly local memories of the shapes and lights on Wasserkuppe have made the remaining radome building an integral part of the Rhön panorama, and a permanent landmark imbued with meaning. While its shape might offer an acute yet fleeting impression to passers-by on the national road and rail routes, many locals have come to see it not only as a conspicuous landmark, but as a symbol and a monument in its own right. I address how memories and quotidian practices on Wasserkuppe can complement assessments of such military sites by the Heritage industry. To this end, I suggest 'interrogating' material gained from archives, the press, oral histories, public polls, and the archaeological record to investigate wider perceptions of the site's conspicuousness, 'militariness', and significance (Figure 15.1).

Just another Cold War early warning site

Wasserkuppe radar station was an aircraft control and early warning station, some 7 km from the former inner-German border – the frontier between East and West Germany. Originally established by the British Royal Air Force as an experimental station in 1945, the US Air Force operated it for most of its existence, and by 1979 the German *Luftwaffe* had assumed sole responsibility. After more than 50 years of service, conducting air surveillance on the Iron Curtain, the site was decommissioned in 1998, and all equipment and personnel finally redeployed by 2004 (see Maus in press for a more detailed history).

Strategically, Wasserkuppe was one element in the chain of NATO aerospace defence emplacements in Cold War Europe (Morbach *et al.* 2008), and stood for a multitude of identical sites along the territorial perimeter of the western world during that era. Many studies in modern conflict archaeology have dealt with iconic Cold War sites, such as the Berlin Wall (e.g. Klausmeier *et al.* 2004), a Soviet nuclear missile site in Cuba (Burström *et al.* 2009), 'Cold War archetype' Greenham Common, Berkshire, England (Fiorato 2007), or the Nevada Test Site, USA (Beck *et al.* 2007; Powell, this volume).

Why, then, study Wasserkuppe? By comparison to the aforementioned sites, the history and archaeology of this Cold War military establishment appears mundane. The study of a site which is rather unimportant in the global history of the Cold War becomes a worthwhile endeavour only if it chooses to investigate 'those aspects of contemporary life … which are constantly being overwritten by dominant narratives' (Harrison *et al.* 2009: 191), and consequently adopts a bottom-up approach. This is what I take Buchli and Lucas (2001: 171) to mean when they point out that an archaeology of the recent past takes a 'qualitatively different' approach to the study of recent history by focusing on the 'critical consequences of presencing absence … – bringing forward or indeed materialising that which is excessive, forgotten or concealed'.

When the Hessian Monument Protection Authority listed the last remaining radome at Wasserkuppe (Figure 15.2), as a monument in 2009, the authority stated that it is not only the best known landmark of the Rhön, it also reminds us of the long military use of the summit, and is symbolic of Germany's division and Cold War confrontation. It is a cultural monument for historical, technological, and academic reasons' (LfDH 2009. my translation). Their brief characterisation already hints at two powerful strands of narrative evident in discourse on many western Cold War relics. First, an obsession with the technological within heritage practice, and second, a discourse framing such relics as symbols of a profoundly western and establishment perspective on the Cold War.[1] (Figure 15.2).

Questioning dominant narratives

Cold War heritage practice reduces military sites virtually to their strategic and technological military aspects. One example of this approach is the recording project by The Royal Commission on the Historical Monuments of England (now English Heritage (EH)), and which led to the publication of *Cold War: Building for Nuclear Confrontation* (Cocroft *et al.* 2004b). The main goal of the study was 'to determine the most significant sites for conservation and preservation' (Cocroft 2007: 107), and thus the focus was on 'structures built, or adapted, to carry out nuclear war between the end of the Second World War and 1989' (Cocroft *et al.* 2004b: 2).

To that end, the authors offer a classification system for Cold War structures in the UK which largely focuses on military structures as well as civil emergency stores and civil government buildings (Cocroft 2007: 112). There is emphasis also on explaining Cold War relics in their historical context (cf. Cocroft 2007: 121–126), and 'as a reflection of a unique national experience of the political and military stand-off between the Superpowers' (*ibid.*: 107). Notwithstanding this clear focus on technology, organisation, and strategy, EH has also studied aspects of 'military culture', such as military wall art (*ibid.*: 117; Cocroft *et al.* 2004a), as a part of this recording exercise.

While EH has carried out this comprehensive assessment of Cold War structures in England, the German situation is ambiguous. Heritage protection is devolved to the state level in Germany, which results in sixteen similar yet different state 'monument protection acts', and even more responsible heritage protection authorities. The Bavarian authority is among the most active heritage bodies in former West Germany concerning Cold War relics.

Figure 15.2: The remaining radar tower with protective radome encasement stands 25 m high. Construction began in 1990, the radome was fitted to the tower in 1994. (© author, 2009)

In 2002, it conducted a systematic assessment of Cold War pre-constructed obstacles in a case-study area in northeastern Bavaria (Ongyerth 2007). As a result, five examples of these defensive structures intended to block roadways were listed. They are two bridges with demolition fixtures, two falling block obstacles, and a munitions bunker. Assessment criteria for these Cold War fortifications were 'their strategic location and military engineering agency in the landscape' while the more commonly used assessment criteria of 'age, amenity value, or structural integrity' (Ongyerth 2007: 103, my translation) were only of subordinate importance.

These two examples from heritage practice in the UK and Germany are not intended to prove heritage professionals wrong. Instead, I want to show that they think about Cold War relics in a very specific way as monuments. As Cresswell and Hoskins (2008) have argued in a different context, monument protection bodies tend to attribute significance to the material fabric of a site, rather than to the (historic) practice it is saturated with. Researchers need to be wary of 'the apparent obviousness of the material remains [of the Cold War, G.M.] that seem to need no interpretation' (Fairclough 2007: 20). I will pick up this theme later, suffice to say now that – making a structure a monument – in this way, powerfully presences its materiality in the landscape.

A second line of a dominant narrative is that, in a Western context, Cold War sites are often represented as sites of Western victory over the East. In the case of Wasserkuppe, a notion of determination is often bestowed on the radome, as I will show later. If

Western politics, the military, and wider society can be seen as romanticising the Cold War as a war won, then subaltern narratives also spring to mind. Schofield and Anderton (2000) have presented a convincing study of Greenham Common Airbase, Berkshire, in southern England, as a site of discord just by stretching the extent of their area of interest literally by only a few metres to include the women's peace camps adjacent to the perimeter fence (see also Beck *et al.* 2009 for peace camps at the Nevada Test Site). These studies are necessary, but I prefer to follow Fairclough (2007: 26) who argues that in the context of the Cold War '[t]here is a real risk that [interpretative] closure will oversimplify and in the process understanding will be lost along with complexity.' Categorising fluid memories and perceptions as originating in neat and tidy interest groups ranging from peace activists to conservatives appears too simple.

Public perceptions: an empirical approach

I wish to adopt an exploratory methodology which focuses on the wealth of available source material, rather than unwittingly singling out the material that serves anticipated narratives. I also want to avoid reducing the site's materiality to its military technological applications. Instead, the aim is to capture local perceptions of the site through its entire history by looking at its agency in the landscape, as well as sourcing representations of how locals experience it. More formal representations include histories written on Wasserkuppe and newspaper analysis. Collecting ephemera such as postcards and souvenirs also yields data and insight. Arguably, narrative biographical interviews with actors involved with the site, and a press-based call for public opinion, provided the densest contemporary source material (cf. Maus in press for more detail on sources).

   While not exhaustive, this research is sufficient to describe and problematise perceptions of Wasserkuppe. My analysis of the material follows the question of how Wasserkuppe is or was perceived by locals. To that end, I will present the material as contributing to three ways of perceiving the site: conspicuousness, militariness, and significance. These are informed by interdisciplinary theoretical debates on ideas of place and landscape (Tilley 2006, for an overview).

Conspicuousness

> 'Who is supposed to recognise Wasserkuppe, if the mountain's landmarks, the domes, are missing?' (Kirschbaum 1997, my translation)

The idea here is that the way the site is seen as conspicuous corresponds to Denis Cosgrove's (2003) work on landscape as a way of seeing. Referring to Wasserkuppe radome(s) as conspicuous objects in the landscape appears appropriate when drawing on sources that tell of Wasserkuppe as a landscape element seen from afar. The sources help us to understand how something as alien to 1960s rural Germany as those huge spherical structures on a mountaintop eventually became a factor in local identity. Cosgrove summarises:

> '[w]e accept geographical reality because we can see it. To *see* something is both to observe it and to grasp it intellectually. The way people see their world is a vital clue to the way they understand that world and their relationships with it.' (Cosgrove 1998: 8–9)

How people see and grasp the radome(s) on Wasserkuppe can be sketched from sources that relate notions of high visibility, of *pars pro toto* in the landscape, and of naming the object as a way of knowing it.

It is common knowledge in the region that looking for the summit with the 'dome' in the mountainous Rhön panorama easily identifies Wasserkuppe. The one remaining radome is frequently described as 'a distinctive mark of Wasserkuppe, which is difficult to recognise or point out to strangers, since it has no distinctive shape, especially compared to Milseburg'[2] (cf. Figure 15.1). During discussions on whether all the radomes should be demolished when the military left, statements such as the following probably speak for a majority of local opinion: 'Without the hallmark domes, the mountain [i.e. Wasserkuppe] would be a mountain like any other' (Weber 1997, my translation). As a navigational marker, the radomes identify Wasserkuppe, and have become an integral part of the landscape.

Visual representations of the region reinforce these statements. Local corporations now frequently use photographs and sketches of Wasserkuppe showing the remaining radome. Nevertheless, the radome(s) on Wasserkuppe compete for prominence with another feature of the mountain. Internationally, Wasserkuppe is probably best known as 'the cradle of glider flying' (Figure 15.3). Most souvenirs (like the glass, top left) and postcards (bottom left) show the *Fliegerdenkmal* or aviation monument.

Interestingly, most postcards[3] depicting a close-up view of Wasserkuppe's summit are similar to the souvenir glass. The 1980s postcard shown here is a rare exception, showing how close to each other are the aviation monument and the military compound. Local shopkeepers either did not commission souvenirs showing the radomes because they thought they spoilt the mountain, or they stopped doing so when, during the 1990s, they had reason to believe that all military structures on Wasserkuppe were soon to be demolished. Recently, however, the radome appears to be incorporated into an iconographic programme of Wasserkuppe (and the Rhön mountain range more generally).

It has taken a long time for the radome to be recognised as an integral part of the landscape, as is evident from the names the radomes were initially called. Originally, they were referred to as 'a cold, ugly egg', a disgrace to the natural landscape of the Wasserkuppe plateau. When the first radomes were built in the 1960s, newspaper comments would be infrequent and rather matter-of-fact:

> 'The five big radar sets on Wasserkuppe have become a new landmark of the mountain in the last years. While the radars were once visible to everyone on the Rhön's highest mountain, spherical fibreglass gowns have now enclosed them. The encasement is designed

primarily to protect the radar sets from the rigour of the harsh Rhön weather.' (Anon. 1966)

Only when the radomes gradually began disappearing during the late 1980s (due to a technical upgrade that led to their demolition and replacement by the last and much bigger radome), did newspapers start to comment on the 'bumps', 'domes', 'spheres' or 'radar towers' – terms already common among locals. More creative variants included 'footballs' or 'mushrooms'.[4] The term *Radom* (German usage of 'radome', short for *ra*dar *dome*) or the compound noun *Radarkuppel* (German for radar dome) was not common with locals until the 1990s, as noted in contemporary newspapers. Thus, during the past two decades, the name of the structures has changed from a description of what people saw, to the technical term radome, previously an engineering term. Although the aesthetic value of the radome(s) in the landscape is (still) a matter of taste, I consider the way people talk about the radomes as an important sign of how they 'took possession' of them, and incorporated the last radome into their landscape.

Militariness

'The stream of visitors is focused on the central area of Wasserkuppe between the main road and the military compound, a place that is a parking area for cars and coaches at the same time and surrounded by stalls and inns. From here … the streams of visitors lead alongside the northern face of the military compound to the summer bobsleigh track on the north-eastern slope and along the southern face of the military area to the *Fliegerdenkmal* [i.e. aviation monument].' (Evers *et al.* 1982: 48, my translation)

This description of an observation exercise, conducted as part of a state government landscape plan, may sound rather dull, but it is clear evidence that there are other themes of perception of Wasserkuppe radar station than just its conspicuousness. The focus here is on Wasserkuppe as a practiced landscape, and I want to argue that the military compound on the mountain was (and to a certain extent still is) an essential part of this.

The perception of a conspicuous object like the radome as seen from afar must clearly be complemented by perceptions of it as experienced up close. Whereas above I followed an idea of landscape put forward by Cosgrove (1998) to analyse sources on the site, I now wish to explore Cresswell's (2003) critique of that term. Cresswell, who would rather do away with landscape in favour of place, pleads for:

'geographies that are lived, embodied, practised; landscapes which are never finished or complete, not easily framed or read. These geographies should be as much about the everyday and unexceptional as much as they are about the grand and distinguished.' (Cresswell 2003: 280)

Others have drawn on their own experiences as a methodological approach. Davis (2008), for instance, has explored the military research site of Orford Ness in Suffolk in Britain in a descriptive essay on walking that landscape, while Reynolds and Schofield

Figure 15.3: The Fliegerdenkmal is a landmark commonly associated with Wasserkuppe and it is shown on most souvenirs and postcards. (background and top left, © author, 2009)

(2010) have contributed a photo essay to the interpretation of Greenham Common Airbase. Here, I want to operationalise the embodied experience of Wasserkuppe radar station by looking at those aspects in the sources that refer to it, both explicitly and implicitly, as a military site. It appears to me that some kind of militariness is a defining factor that frames many practices associated with such sites.

Oddly, common knowledge has it that most visitors to Wasserkuppe thought the radomes were actually water towers. A former radar technician stated that in his opinion:

> 'the public never saw this [the radar station, G.M.] as a threat or as a danger. Quite contrary, partly they were absolutely blue-eyed, they didn't even know what lay quiet beneath the domes.'[5]

Wasserkuppe radar station can indeed be seen as unusual for a military site – there were few personnel to be seen, there was no firing practice – especially in a region which saw frequent NATO training exercises and was heavily militarised as a part of the infamous Fulda Gap. However, the material agency of the fences, the barbed wire, and unambiguous signs that security staff were authorised to use firearms, made it obvious that the enclosed area on Wasserkuppe's peak was indeed a military emplacement.

Surprisingly, neither in interviews nor in the call for public opinion did anyone comment on the perimeter fence that literally determined people's movement around the site (Figure 15.4). The evidence is largely non-vocal. One participant described how

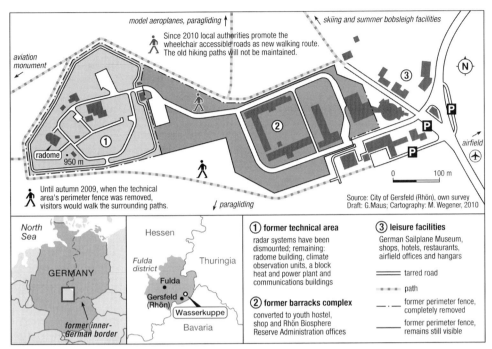

Figure 4: The relics of Wasserkuppe radar station are in the midst of a busy tourist destination that offers a range of leisure activities. The map also shows the main walking routes around the summit (next to the radome) before and after the perimeter fence was removed. (© author, 2011)

he felt like 'doing something forbidden' when he entered the compound for the first time after a gap had appeared in the fencing. The perimeter fence of the technical area, where the radome stands, was removed in 2009, but people will (albeit many probably unconsciously) iterate the emplacement's dimensions when walking the former guard track that the local authority promotes as the new footpath on the summit (Figure 15.4).

The remaining radome has been open to the public as a viewing platform since 2009. The military nature of the building is now probably more apparent than ever as visitors can walk up close to it and can even enter the building. A local architect described the radome as an example of what she called military logic. The massive concrete, the high quality and redundant utility systems were just so unlike anything civilian to her eyes. Feelings of fascination, especially for technology, and eeriness, apparent for example in the all-embracing security measures, are evident in many personal reflections on Wasserkuppe.

Significance

'I think that Fulda and the Wasserkuppe are symbols for preventing the Cold War from turning into a hot war. Because it showed determination.' (Former US Air Force officer at Wasserkuppe, pers. comm.)

Hitherto, my interpretation has focused on how people visually integrate the Wasserkuppe radome into the landscape (i.e. their perceptions of conspicuousness), and how they experience and react to it in a more embodied way when present on site (perceptions of militariness). I now turn to more straightforward statements like the above.

When people voice their opinion on a place this has to be accepted more or less at face value. The kinds of sources highlighted now are mostly such conscious expressions of why the radome is significant to an individual. Therefore, I now draw on Doreen Massey's concept of places:

> 'as constantly shifting articulations of social relations through time; and to think of particular attempts to characterise them as attempts to define, and claim coherence and a particular meaning for, specific envelopes of space-*time*.' (Massey 1995: 188)

Massey uses the phrase 'envelope of space-time' to express how, in her view, time and space are inseparable, because places are not only thought of as geographical area, but are continually constructed through multi-vocal interpretations of their pasts (*ibid.*).

I expected that interpretations of Wasserkuppe radar station would be either the dominant narrative of winning the Cold War or the peace movement's opposing views. Indeed, a local left-wing peace activist helped to organise nuclear disarmament demonstrations at Wasserkuppe in the 1980s. Another member of the local peace movement acknowledged that Wasserkuppe was one spot amongst many of militarisation in the region. The former US Air Force officer quoted above, describes the radome as a site that is almost sacred:

> 'I wouldn't like to see the radome as a disco. You know it kind'a means more, it's gotta be more than that. And it can't be an event.' (Former US Air Force officer at Wasserkuppe, pers. comm.)

The radome is now part of the landscape, but also carries meaning beyond being a symbol of geopolitical conflict. It is also emblematic of (other) local identities. A local historian has highlighted how the population of the wider region embraces Wasserkuppe as its *Hausberg* (i.e. a 'local mountain', Kramm 1998: 110). Besides being a place of military utilization including some forty years of Cold War history, it accommodates many identities and histories in a rich palimpsest: as a traditional hiking location, as a place within a UNESCO biosphere reserve, as the highest peak in Hessen and of the Rhön Mountains, and as an internationally acclaimed centre of aviation.

In addition, the radome is sometimes probably more closely associated with its vicinity than with its apparent history. A local musician has locked himself in the space beneath the radome's protective hull for a week to compose a musical album: 'You know, you stand upon the highest point in Hessen, that's an elevated emotion in the true sense of the word to be able to work up there' (local musician, pers. comm.). When asked to what extent he thought about Cold War history while engaging artistically with the site, he said:

'Well, first I thought about whether I should incorporate something in the music that would remind of the Cold War. For example consciously put in radio communications or radar sounds, but I didn't do it. Because I thought, that that would bring some coldness, a matter-of-fact attitude to the music, that I didn't want to have.' (*ibid.*)

This is one example of why the heritage authority's characterisation of the Wasserkuppe radome's significance falls short of locals' appropriation of the site. Schofield (2006) has argued that artists can contribute to characterisations and interpretations of cultural heritage in a way which complements the work of archaeologists, historians, and geographers, since they 'may sometimes be better able to capture the essence of the place, and people's contemporary perceptions of and interactions with it' (Schofield 2006: 22). I am uncomfortable with the term 'essence', but a number of artistic engagements with Cold War sites have shown how they are creative enhancements to scholarly interpretations of public perceptions and interactions, which are at the heart of this paper (e.g. Bäuml *et al.* 2006; Boulton 2006; Cocroft *et al.* 2006; Cooper *et al.* 2001; Wilson 2009).

Conclusions

The Cold War has been a new and exciting field for modern conflict archaeology in the last two decades. Cold War relics abound – they are preserved exceptionally well, and they may also be seen as special 'inasmuch as they are often not in themselves scenes of conflict and death. Their importance and value lies in what they represent and what they could have been' (Uzzell 1998:18) – at least as far as much of the Western world is concerned. But this enthusiasm has arguably led to a bias towards iconic sites, and has likewise produced a strange dichotomy of subaltern narratives of peace protest vs. dominant narratives of technological superiority or fascination and military success.

The case of Wasserkuppe radar station presented here has been an attempt to work exploratively from the source material rather than from preconceived narratives. The focus has been on the quotidian perceptions of the Cold War in the past and today. While sketching the evolution and change of perceptions over time is beyond the remit of this paper, I have tried to operationalise concepts of place and landscape. Cresswell (2003) has criticised the concept of landscape as a way of seeing as materialist and lifeless, but I argue that such an approach can order some of the relevant data, and thereby reveal its contribution to public perceptions of the site's conspicuousness.

Here, this focuses on the profound visual impact of the Wasserkuppe radome and its conceptualisation as a local landmark. More embodied experiences of the military sites under consideration can be unveiled by questioning the sources for perceptions of its militariness. The eeriness and material force associated with the 'concrete' Cold War relics appears a theme so powerful that this category could be developed further to explain this particular object of conflict archaeology. Finally, the category of significance should not be left to essentialist accounts that often characterise the literature on monument protection, but extended to include multi-vocal perceptions of place.

Following such avenues, modern conflict archaeology can really free itself from the straitjacket of traditional 'Battlefield Archaeology' (Saunders 2010; this volume) and integrate itself further into established, interdisciplinary studies of place and identity.

Acknowledgements

I would like to thank Nick Saunders who supervised this work as an MA thesis. I am also grateful to Pia Groß of the Wasserkuppe Radome for her support.

Notes
1   Construction of this last remaining radome on Wasserkuppe commenced in 1990 and it was actually never in active service as an early warning emplacement. Since the site's official characterisation (LfDH 2009) specifically addresses the radome as a technological and historical monument despite the fact that it was never used, it is arguably listed as a symbol of western militarisation and defence technology.
2   This is from a written statement by a participant in the call for public opinion that was sent in to the author. All unreferenced quotes are from the body of these responses and thereby made anonymous.
3   I am indebted to Joachim Jenrich, Gersfeld (Rhön), who kindly let me go through his impressive collection of postcards from Wasserkuppe and the Rhön in general.
4   The image of 'golfballs' is unfamiliar in the region (cf. Spinardi 2007 for the well-known British example of the Golfballs on the Moor, a.k.a. as the Fylingdales site of the Ballistic Missile Early Warning System).
5   Quote from the oral history interview conducted as part of the project. As with participants in the call for public opinion, these are made anonymous. My translation.

Bibliography

Anon. (1966) Der Radarstrahl verrät den Feind. In jedem Augenblick 'tags und nachts' ist die Radarstation auf der Wasserkuppe über die Situation in unserem Luftraum im Bilde. 400 Amerikaner bedienen die Geräte (1966). *Fuldaer Volkszeitung*, 11/06/1966.
Bäuml, L., König, E. and Feuerer, T. (2006): *Der Bunker*. Berufsverband Bildender Künstler Niederbayern/Oberpfalz. Available online at http://www.kunst-in-ostbayern.de/upload/col/27/broschuere.pdf Accessed 23 September 2010.
Beck, C., Drollinger, H. and Schofield, J. (2007) Archaeology of Dissent. Landscape and Symbolism at the Nevada Peace Camp. In Schofield and Cocroft (eds) 2007, 297–320.
Beck, C., Schofield, J. and Drollinger, H. (2009) Archaeologists, Activists and a Contemporary Peace Camp. In C. Holtorf and A. Picinni (eds), *Contemporary Archaeologies. Excavating Now*, 95–111. Frankfurt: Peter Lang.
Boulton, A. (2006). Film Making and Photography as Record and Interpretation. In J. Schofield,

A. Klausmeier and L. Purbrick (eds), *Re-mapping the Field. New Approaches in Conflict Archaeology*, 35–38. Berlin: Westkreuz-Verlag.

Buchli, V. and Lucas, G. (2001) Presencing absence. In V. Buchli and G. Lucas (eds), *Archaeologies of the Contemporary Past*, 171–174. London: Routledge.

Burström, M., Acosta, T., Noriega, E., Gustafsson, A., Hernández, I. and Karlsson, H. (2009) Memories of a World Crisis: the Archaeology of a Former Soviet Nuclear Missile Site in Cuba. *Journal of Social Archaeology* 9(3): 295–318.

Cocroft, W. (2007) Defining the National Archaeological Character of Cold War Remains. In Schofield and Cocroft (eds) 2007, 107–127.

Cocroft, W. and Wilson, L. (2006) Archaeology and Art at Spadeadam Rocket Establishment (Cumbria). In J. Schofield, A. Klausmeier and L. Purbrick (eds), *Re-mapping the Field. New Approaches in Conflict Archaeology*, 15–21. Berlin: Westkreuz-Verlag.

Cocroft, W., Devlin, D,. Gowing, R., Schofield, J. and Thomas, R. (2004a) *Military Wall Art. Guidelines on its Significance, Conservation and Management*. Swindon: English Heritage.

Cocroft, W., Thomas, R. and Barnwell, P. (2004b) *Cold War. Building for Nuclear Confrontation. 1946–1989*. Swindon: English Heritage.

Cooper, E., Durden, M., Wells, L. and Hipperson, S. (2001) *Cold War Pastoral. Greenham Common*. London: Black Dog Publishing.

Cosgrove, D. (1998) *Social Formation and Symbolic Landscape*. (2nd edn) Madison: University of Wisconsin Press.

Cosgrove, D. (2003) Landscape and the European Sense of Sight: Eyeing Nature. In K. Anderson, M. Domosh, S. Pile and N. Thrift (eds), *Handbook of Cultural Geography*, 249–268. London: Sage.

Cresswell, T. (2003) Landscape and the Obliteration of Practice. In K. Anderson, M. Domosh, S. Pile and N. Thrift (eds), *Handbook of Cultural Geography*, 269–281. London: Sage.

Cresswell, T. and Hoskins, G. (2008) Place, Persistence, and Practice: Evaluating Historical Significance at Angel Island, San Francisco, and Maxwell Street, Chicago. *Annals of the Association of American Geographers* 98(2): 392–413.

Davis, S. (2008) Cultural Geographies in Practice: Military Landscapes and Secret Science: the Case of Orford Ness. *Cultural Geographies* 15(1): 143–149.

Evers, O. and Heintze, G. (1982) *Landschaftsplan Wasserkuppe/Rhön*. Wiesbaden: Hessische Landesanstalt für Umwelt.

Fairclough, G. (2007) The Cold War in Context: Archaeological Explorations of Private, Public and Political Complexity. In Schofield and Cocroft (eds) 2007, 19–32.

Fiorato, V. (2007) Greenham Common. The Conservation and Management of a Cold War Archetype. In Schofield and Cocroft (eds) 2007, 129–154.

Harrison, R. and Schofield, J. (2009) Archaeo-Ethnography, Auto-Archaeology: Introducing Archaeologies of the Contemporary Past. *Archaeologies: Journal of the World Archaeological Congress* 5(2): 185–209.

Kirschbaum, I. (1997) Kuppeln als Wahrzeichen. Briefe an die Redaktion. *Fuldaer Zeitung*, 30 April 1997: 12.

Klausmeier, A. and Schmidt, L. (2004) *Wall Remnants – Wall Traces. The Comprehensive Guide to the Berlin Wall*. Bad Münstereifel: Westkreuz-Verl. Berlin/Bonn.

Kramm, H. (1998) Wasserkuppe – gestern, heute und am Tag danach. Bevölkerung in der Region identifiziert sich mit ihrem 'Hausberg'/vorläufiges Nutzungskonzept sieht Umwandlung des militärischen Teils in Jugendbildungsstätte vor. *Jahrbuch des Landkreises Fulda* 25: 105–110.

"landmark, n." (2010) Oxford English Dictionary Online. Oxford University Press. http://www.oed.com/viewdictionaryentry/Entry/105499 Accessed 22 March 2011.

LfDH (Landesamt für Denkmalpflege Hessen) (2009) *Bescheinigung der Denkmaleigenschaft des Radoms auf der Wasserkuppe gem. § 2 Abs. 1 des Hessischen Denkmalschutzgesetzes*. Letter to Radom Flug gGmbH. Wiesbaden, 16 November 2009.

Massey, D. (1995) Places and Their Pasts. *History Workshop Journal* 39(1): 182–192.

Maus, G. (in press) Archaeology of Cold War Early Warning Sites. The Case of Wasserkuppe, Germany. In B. Fortenberry and L. McAtackney (eds), *Modern Materials: the proceedings of CHAT Oxford, 2009*. Oxford: British Archaeological Reports/Archaeopress.

Morbach, G. and Sudhoff, G. (2008) Der Einsatzführungsdienst der Luftwaffe. Gestern – Heute – Morgen. *Strategie & Technik* 10: 39–46.

Ongyerth, G. (2007) Fortifikationen des Kalten Krieges in der Denkmalliste – Methodische Ansätze der flächenbezogenen Denkmalforschung in Bayern. In *Denkmalpflege an Grenzen – Patrimoine sans frontiers?*, 103–107. With assistance of A. Bock. Saarbrücken (Denkmalpflege im Saarland, Arbeitsheft 1).

Reynolds, L. and Schofield, J. (2010) Silo Walk: Exploring Power Relations on an English Common. *Radical History Review* 108: 154–160.

Saunders, N.J. (2010) Worlds Apart: Modern Conflict Archaeology and Battlefield Archaeology. *Arheo* 27: 45–55.

Schofield, J. (2006) *Constructing Place. When Artists and Archaeologists Meet* (Liquid Geography). Available online at http://diffusion.org.uk/liquid/D_LG_Schofield_A4.pdf Accessed 12 May 2009.

Schofield, J. and Anderton, M. (2000) The Queer Archaeology of Green Gate. Interpreting Contested Space at Greenham Common Airbase. *World Archaeology* 32(2): 236–251.

Schofield, J. and Cocroft, W. (eds) (2007) *A Fearsome Heritage. Diverse Legacies of the Cold War*. Walnut Creek (CA): Left Coast Press (One World Archaeology 50).

Spinardi, G. (2007) Golfballs on the Moor. Building the Fylingdales Ballistic Missile Early Warning System. *Contemporary British History* 21(1): 87–110.

Tilley, C. (2006) Introduction: Identity, Place, Landscape and Heritage. *Journal of Material Culture* 11(1/2): 7–32.

Uzzell, D. (1998) The Hot Interpretation of the Cold War. In J. Schofield (ed.) *Monuments of War. The Evaluation, Recording and Management of Twentieth-Century Military Sites,* 18–20. London: English Heritage.

Weber, P. (1997) Hotels und Gaststätten reichen aus. Briefe an die Redaktion. *Fuldaer Zeitung*, 2 May 1997: 10.

Wilson, L. (2009) Notes on a Record of Fear: On the Threshold of the Audible. In C. Holtorf and A. Piccini (eds.) *Contemporary Archaeologies. Excavating Now*, 113–128. Frankfurt: Peter Lang.

16

America's Nuclear Wasteland: conflict landscape, simulation, and 'non-place' at the Nevada Test Site

Liam J.S. Powell

It was ecstasy city, but we blew it
the way we blew everything, the pink
skin of pigs that was almost human,
the clothes that covered its nakedness like ours,
the hollow torsos of redheads that never got it
so the Russians, the Chinese, the aliens in silver ships
wouldn't get it either, even if they laid
down their arms among us, their bodies burning
for one another in the wild sodomies
of everything and light. (Goldberg 1991: 21)

Beckian Fritz Goldberg's poem *Survival Town* is a hauntingly vivid description of the destruction of a simulated civilian environment at the Nevada Test Site at the height of Cold War nuclear weapons testing. The site was established as the Nevada Proving Ground in 1951, in response to the perceived need for a continental nuclear testing facility following the successful testing of the Soviet Union's first nuclear weapon in 1949 (Fehner and Gosling 2000: 37–48). Between its inception and a unilateral testing moratorium in 1992, the Nevada Test Site witnessed some 100 atmospheric and near-surface, and over 800 underground nuclear weapons tests (Department of Energy 1994: viii). Ironically, this made the United States the most heavily bombed country in the world.

Along with the equivalent Soviet sites at Semipalatinsk in Kazakhstan and Novaya Zemlya, the Nevada Test Site became a geographic centre of the Cold War – itself arguably the single most culturally influential event in the second half of the twentieth century – a conflict driven by international competition to develop and apply new technologies to establish and maintain military superiority (Beck 2002: 65). The Cold War was, as are all modern conflicts, a war of *matériel*, defined by its technologies (Saunders 2004: 5). The nature of the Cold War's technologies – nuclear weapons systems – created entire landscapes as a part of the conflict-related archaeological record of the period.

Although intended primarily as an artistic commentary on the paranoid and bizarrely self-destructive behaviour of US military and political leaders during the Cold War, Goldman's poem, perhaps unintentionally, touches upon an important but so far largely neglected aspect of the study of the material culture of conflict; the experience of controlled military landscapes as simulacra and 'non-places'.

New worlds: a phenomenology of modern conflict landscapes

Traditional 'bullets and buttons' Battlefield Archaeology has tended to regard landscapes in terms of their historical military significance – as exclusively physical, fixed geographical backdrops within which military events occur. The dominance of academic understandings of landscapes as 'the assemblages of real world features' (Roberts 1987: 79), as palimpsests of meaning, to be 'read' in much the same way as an historic text (Hoskins 1955; Yamin and Metheny 1996), has informed a disciplinary methodology which focuses on official records (e.g. Beresford 1957) and cartography. Increasingly in recent years, aerial photography (e.g. Aston 1985; 2002), through the practice of 'reading' landscapes, has consistently re-presented a particular, historically constituted, and distinctly 'top-down' understanding of landscape as 'seen from everywhere' (Merleau-Ponty 1962: 59).

This 'Western Gaze' conception of landscape, as discussed by Bender (1999; 2002a), serves to control and order the experience of the physical world according to a particular, dominant, political worldview, i.e. of boundaries, of ownership, of centre and periphery. It 'seeks a total view of social reality' (Thomas 1993: 23), and requires the historian to stand apart from history (Foucault 1977: 152), presenting a landscape that is insular and dislocated, except through distinct highways and lines of communication. It is essentially bounded, singularly functional, and devoid of people as anything other than the hypothetical occupiers of a central focal point.

The terminological and methodological exclusivity of Battlefield Archaeology sees landscape as implicitly and explicitly restricted to the physical geographic location of a specific instance of military antagonism (e.g. Lynch and Cooksey 2007), to the exclusion of an understanding of how such sites relate culturally to others, and to the experiences of the *real* people to whom those places 'belong'.

To acknowledge the partiality and politicisation of traditional archaeological understandings of landscape does not require abandoning the use of aerial photos and mapping, but rather, suggests Thomas (1993: 27): 'that we should recognise that this way we have of looking down on the past as a map laid out for simultaneous perception is only one among many ways of looking'.

Schofield *et al.* (2002: 4) recognise the importance of landscape as a distinct kind of twentieth-century conflict *matériel*, physically and conceptually shaped by warfare. Bender (2002a: 136) argues that the established view of landscape as an archaeological palimpsest, whereby past activities leave a multi-layered archaeological record, fails to appreciate the continuing conceptual volatility of that record to those that continue to interact with it. If, as Gosden (1999: 2) asserts, reprising Lewis Binford's famous dictum, that 'Archaeology is anthropology or it is nothing', then landscape is to be understood as a conceptually dynamic cultural artefact, and places 'as they are experienced by a subject' (Tilley 1994: 12). According to Tilley (*ibid.*: 12–13), 'places *constitute* space as centres of human meaning', and 'The meaning of place is grounded in the existential or lived consciousness of it'. Landscape as space is made of places as they are experienced, subjectively and personally, by human agents.

Unlike the landscapes of traditional Battlefield Archaeology, these essentially anthropocentric landscapes 'as experienced' are conceptually complex, and are not confined to the physicality of specific places. Rowlands (1996), for example, has discussed the 'financial landscapes' of modern economic systems, while Layton and Ucko (1999: 1) suggest that as much as referring to physical entities, landscapes are 'particular ways of expressing conceptions of the world'.

The establishment of the Nevada Proving Ground and the beginning of nuclear weapons testing in 1951 meant that globalised landscapes of modern industrial conflict were no longer a new concept. However, the exigencies and cultural intensity of a nuclear Cold War, fought on home territory against an invisible and politically fetishised enemy, created new experiences of conflict landscapes that re-defined twentieth century realities of warfare, nationality, and identity.

This is not to negate the materiality of landscape. According to Bender (2002b: 104), 'To say that landscape and time are subjective does not require a descent into a miasma of cultural relativity'. While engagement with landscape is subjective, the materiality of the physical world is affective on humans, making experiences and meanings possible or not possible (Bender 2006: 303). But the personal and highly subjective nature of interaction with and experience of 'being in' one's landscape (Saunders 2003: 127–128) demands an understanding of the social-cultural significance of landscape beyond a traditional archaeological interpretation of its physical characteristics. Neither do humans simply create the world, physically and conceptually, and then live out our lives within but untouched by it; nor are landscapes mere physical spatial 'containers' for temporal human action.

All persons have, according to Heidegger (1962), the existential characteristic of 'being-in-the-world'. A distinction is drawn between this sense of 'being in place' and the category-defining physical inclusion of objects as 'being in' one another. Heidegger's existential quality of 'being-in-the-world' is, according to Dreyfus (1991: 43), characterised by concern; by a personal and self-defining involvement as opposed to a merely spatial or logical inclusion. It is a distinction analogous to that between 'being at work (at the place of work)' and 'being at work (in the sense of being occupied by it)' (*ibid.*).

People experience not only physically being in a place, but 'inhabiting' (*ibid.*: 44), *their* world; that is, 'being in' (Saunders 2003: 127–128; 2004: 7) the world such that it is no longer an object, but becomes an inalienable 'part' of our own self-conception.

In this way, space is socially produced; an involved medium for self-aware human action, from which it cannot be divorced. Landscapes then are the de-totalised social constructions of the experience of space and place.

Facsimile, simulation and the Nevada Test Site as a 'non-place'

The creation of modern conflict landscapes is always metaphysically unstable, entailing the destruction of prior traditional landscapes as 'a re-ordering of existence' (Saunders 2004: 8–11). However, where other twentieth century conflict landscapes have later become reclaimed and renegotiated by civilians following the end of hostilities (see Saunders 2001) the landscapes of the Cold War are the landscapes of a conflict that never was, and due to the nature of nuclear weapons systems, has never truly 'ended'. The Nevada Test Site today continues to represent a landscape variously and simultaneously destroyed, recreated, imagined, contested, lost, stolen and denied.

From its initial acquisition by the Atomic Energy Commission (AEC) in 1951, the Nevada Test Site has been a landscape considered lost and even stolen by those that lay claim to it. AEC officials at the time determined that there was 'only one legitimate property owner' connected to the site; a rancher who held a grazing lease for approximately two-thirds of the original test area, while a 'herdsman and wife' residing in Tippipah Spring were also relocated by officials. 'Illegal people', such as 'a miner that [lived] in the ground that the Air Force [had] not been able yet to smoke out of his hole' (Fehner and Gosling 2000: 51), were known to be occupying the area. For these people, life and landscape were inherently connected, and the deprivation of the latter was a deprivation of the former.

The withdrawal of the Nevada Test Site from its traditional landscape has transformed it into what Marc Augé (1995: 77–78) refers to as a 'non-place': 'a space which cannot be defined as relational, or historical, or concerned with identity'. No space, or place, or landscape can be considered to be value-free, especially where they are the product of an intense cultural trauma. Nevertheless, the concept of the 'non-place' appears to capture the sense in which the nuclear landscape of twentieth century America was a privation of reality as experienced prior to the initiation of nuclear weapons testing at the Nevada Test Site.

The Nevada Test Site has become a 'non-place' precisely because the area's former inhabitants are denied their relational, historical, and identity-forming connections with the landscape. Through its removal, restrictions, and, ultimately, nuclear destruction, the Nevada Test Site has become a void in the landscape as experienced by those excluded from it.

Inside the test site's boundary, the landscape, for many, represents the coalescence of simulation and reality. The role of the site as a military simulacrum (*pace* Baudrillard 1994) simulating the nuclear warfare of the Cold War, became central in both political and cultural developments in Cold War-era America. If, as William Gray Johnson (2002:

227) suggests, the defining characteristic of the Cold War was a sense of fear, then the purpose of nuclear testing at the Nevada Test Site was to capitalise on that dread. In proudly and aggressively displaying nuclear capabilities in simulated combat landscapes (at their respective test sites), Americans and Soviets fought a psychological war where fear was the weapon in a 'placeless war, [whose] effects are now everywhere' (*ibid.*). For many, this was the reality of the Cold War, and the multi-vocal material cultural landscape of the Nevada Test Site and its environs, serve as witness to the reification of the Cold War through simulation.

The key to understanding the Nevada Test Site landscape lies in a cross-disciplinary examination of the material culture significance of the site *as experienced*. It is a landscape of simultaneous, multi-vocal, and continually contested experiences, realised as 'non-place' and simulacrum by those individuals and groups to whom the landscape 'belongs'.

'Deterritoriality' of the Native American landscape

Few experiences of the Nevada Test Site as a 'non-place' have been so intense as for the Native American community. From the initial 1500 sq km area of the Proving Ground in 1951, the Test Site increased to over 3500 sq km by 1992, encompassing areas of the Mojave Desert and the Great Basin. Petroglyphs indicate that both these areas had once been occupied by Native American communities (Department of Energy 1994: 6).

The test site is situated within the area known to the Western Shoshone/*Newe* community as *Newe Sogobiahg*, 'the People's Land'. Indigenously claimed as ancestral lands, the region is regarded as having been 'illegally seized from the tribe' by the United States Government during the 1940s (Shundahai Network n.d.). The acquisition and use of the Nevada Test Site for nuclear weapons testing has consistently served to marginalise the experience of Native American communities of 'being in' their traditional desert landscape.

The Department of Energy (1994: 6–7) has noted the ethnocentricity of Lt. George M. Wheeler in 1869 when he encountered the *Newe* community. He described how they 'roamed at pleasure, eking out a purposeless existence', and described their lifestyle as 'a subsistence strategy designed to cope with a severe and unforgiving environment' (*ibid.*) Wheeler demonstrated a continuing and profound misunderstanding of the *Newe* engagement with and experience of 'being in' their landscape.

Corbin Harney (1992: 14), leader of the *Newe* and a prominent anti-nuclear activist, describes the Native American experience of the desert landscape as one of co-operative and co-dependent symbiosis:

> 'The Native way is to pray for everything, to take care of everything. Our Mother Earth is very important. We can't just misuse her and think she's going to continue. We can see what's taking place: the animal life, the tree life, even the water is telling us, but we're not paying attention to it.'

Members of the Shundahai Network consider the Nevada Test Site a 'National Sacrifice Area', permanently damaged by the effects of nuclear weapons testing.

Valerie Kuletz (1998) has examined the role of cartography in removing the Nevada Test Site from the traditional Native American desert landscape and transforming it into a 'non-place'. Official maps depict the site as a physical and conceptual space, clearly apart from the surrounding landscape. It is neatly divided by straight borders that bear no particular relation to the physicality of the landscape which they serve to fragment. 'Unofficial' maps of the area by contrast, are often inconsistent in the drawing of boundaries, focusing rather on the centrality of the *Newe Sogobia* in the landscape of the American South-west. Kuletz (1998: 7) names this process of constructing the Nevada Test Site as a sacrificial landscape by the US government as 'deterritoriality'. For Kuletz, it represents a 'dramatic form of disembodiment – the perceived separation between self and nature' (*ibid.*).

For Native American societies, for whom landscape is connected not only to economic subsistence, but also to cultural and religious identity, the construction of the Nevada Test Site as a sacrificial landscape has served to create the archetype of the 'non-place'. Fragmented within the wider traditional Native American desert landscape of the *Newe Sogobiah*, and therefore stripped of its relational, historical, and identity-forming significance, the site has become an inverted form of non-landscape for the Shundahai Network, whereby its significance is negative, consisting in the experience of what the landscape is *not*, rather than what it *is*.

'Survival Town' and Las Vegas in the American nuclear landscape

Forming a major part of the testing programme at the Nevada Test Site during the 1950s was a number of 'civil effects programmes' – atmospheric detonations of nuclear weapons on simulated civilian settlements. Spearheaded by the Federal Civil Defense Administration, the civil effects programmes were organised to teach the population how to survive a nuclear attack.

Unlike other testing at the site, the results of the civil effects programmes were intended for public dissemination – to 'create' an American nuclear landscape in the psyche of the American people. The physical remains of these settlements, such as 'Survival Town' and 'Doom Town' are extensive. They include restored residential structures, outfitted with posed mannequins, furniture and fully stocked kitchens, industrial facilities such as a parking garage, hangars, a bank vault, bomb shelters (Johnson 2002: 228–230; Beck 2002: 68–70), and the effects of nuclear warfare upon civilians available for all to see. However, it is in America's urban centres that the cultural legacy of the civil effects programmes is most apparent and most complex, and nowhere more so than in Las Vegas.

Some 65 miles (105 km) from the Nevada Test Site, Las Vegas served as 'the host city to America's atomic weapons testing programme' (Johnson 2002: 231). It was apparently the ideal city for this role, with its reputation as 'The Great American Playground' (McCracken 1997), and a tolerant city. But, it also enthusiastically embraced a patriotic role in ensuring America's continued status as a world military power by adopting the Nevada Test Site as part of its landscape.

Titus (2001: 93–94; also Johnson 2002: 231–232; Beck 2002: 75; Green and Penn 2006: 55) comments on the ubiquity of the word 'atomic', used as a prefix in naming cocktails, entertainers, car sales, beauty pageants, souvenirs, motels, and even hairstyles. The *Atomic View Motel* in particular capitalised on its situation within the nuclear landscape, boasting that its guests could view the test explosions without leaving their poolside loungers.

The positive identification with nuclear testing in Las Vegas in the 1950s was so strong that the Clark County official seal featured a stylised atomic mushroom cloud. Even as late as 1993, the demolition of the *Dunes Hotel and Casino*, built in 1955, was flanked by two miniature dynamite 'mushroom clouds' in true Las Vegas pyrotechnic style, harkening back to the casino's Cold War nuclear heyday.

However, the architectural legacy of Cold War-era Las Vegas appears out of step with this 'heretical atmosphere at the gateway to the nuclear age' (Johnson 2002: 232). Johnson (*ibid.*: 233) suggests that, despite the patriotic enthusiasm for American nuclearism in Las Vegas, and its physical and conceptual proximity to the civil effects programme at the Nevada Test Site: 'the message from the [Federal Civil Defense Administration] was not only ignored, but appears to have been castigated'. The adoption of a distinctive suburban style of architecture that favoured open, thin-walled buildings with large glass windows was, according to Johnson (*ibid.*), 'the antithesis of the brutish, survival-minded lessons taught by civil effects testing'. The reason for this apparent incongruity is not entirely clear.

Johnson (*ibid.*: 233–234) suggests a connection between the adoption of suburban-style architecture and the development of semi-utopian International Geophysical Year (Fagan 1982) philosophy – according to which limitless energy from nuclear sources would provide health, wealth, and justice for all – in capturing a reactionary response to the threat and fear of nuclear warfare. However, Johnson's connection appears to rest solely upon the chronological coincidence of this peculiarly American utopianism and an apparently ideological architectural movement, and the suggestion of any real ideological connection appears premature. It seems more likely that in the simple (albeit highly ironic) disparity between experiences of the fear and survival-centric landscape created by the civil effects programs, and of Las Vegas as the American nuclear-age economic boom town, the latter experience won out.

The experience of Las Vegans of 'being in' their landscape was predicated on the light of the atom and the neon sign, rather than living in the shadow of the mushroom cloud; and the light, luxurious, high-modern, suburban architectural legacy of the city from the 1950s appears to reflect this. According to Johnson (2002: 234), the Las Vegans' experience of their nuclear landscape 'coalesced into an anti-Communist, xenophobic, extremely patriotic cultural landscape … that allowed the deliberate adoption of an architectural style least likely to withstand the effects of atomic war'. Rather than being a reification of the post-apocalyptic American nuclear wasteland, the simulated landscape of the civil effects programmes became a symbol of the threat of nuclear war against which to rebel, and which simultaneously ensured against its own realisation.

However, the reality of simulated nuclear warfare within the fences and borders of the Nevada Test Site could not have been farther from the futuristic, glamorous, and heavily sanitised image that was permitted, and no doubt perpetuated by the Department of Energy and AEC in Las Vegas (Gearey 1989; Dvorchak 1994).

Downwinders and the 'Big Lie'

Those that lived in nearby downwind areas, described by the AEC as 'a low-use segment of the population' (Gallagher 1993: xxiii), soon became all too aware of the effects of nuclear testing in Nevada. Jay Truman, a 'downwinder' from Enterprise, Utah, recalled his childhood experiences of this American nuclear landscape.

> 'I remember in school they showed a film once called A is for Atom, B is for Bomb … I think most of us who grew up in that period, we've all in our own minds added C is for Cancer, D is for Death. I think that's what I see for the future.' (Gallagher 1993:xvi)

Ken Pratt (Gallagher 1993: xvi) who lived in southern Utah in the 1950s, and worked as a stuntman, described his son's birth shortly after the commencement of atmospheric testing in Nevada:

> 'His face was a massive hole and they had to put all these pieces of this face back together. I could see down his throat, everything was just turned inside out, his face was curled out and it was horrible. I wanted to die. I wanted him to die.' (*ibid.*)

For those that lived immediately downwind of the test site, the landscapes in which they and their families lived became an insidious threat. The environmental damage wrought by nuclear weapons in the American desert landscape inverted even itself. Atmospheric phenomena; the wind and the rain; the dust of the American desert, became 'weaponised' against their inhabitants; upon the citizens of a nation that had turned its delusions of a nuclear utopia, its military paranoia, and its greatest capacity for destruction upon itself. Within this landscape, living bodies became artefacts not of a past remembered, but of a future denied to them; a temporal disruption of personal realities. They were no longer places in which people lived, but in which they died.

The reality of combat on the simulated battlefield

According to Jean Baudrillard (1994), the distinction between simulacra and reality can no longer be drawn at all: the reproduction of reality in the post-modern condition is now so commonplace that simulacra take on a meaning and a reality of their own. 'Something has disappeared', argues Baudrillard (1994:2): 'the sovereign difference, between one and the other ... It is no longer a question of imitation, nor duplication, nor even parody. It is a question of substituting the signs of the real for the real'. That a simulacrum is experienced makes it as real as that which it simulates.

For none is this more true than those that call themselves the 'atomic veterans' of the Cold War, for whom weapons of fear, and the simulated combat landscapes of the Cold War in which they were deployed, became real weapons and landscapes of physical destruction and injury and, for many, the inescapable reality of death.

Parallel to the simulations of the FCDA's civil effects programmes, the US Defense Department during the 1950s undertook a programme of simulated nuclear warfare within the Nevada Test Site. The stated goal was to train 'troops to function with confidence on nuclear battlefields and ... [to study] ... their performance and psychological reactions under such conditions' (Kalven 1983:26). For some 57,000 US soldiers ordered to take part in simulated military exercises at or near ground zero sites here, nuclear warfare in the Cold War became a personal and unavoidably real experience. Where the frontline soldiers of the First World War emerged from the 'real' combat landscape of the Western Front, and were often figuratively and literally 'remade' (Saunders 2004: 9), so too were the veteran soldiers of America's simulated nuclear battlefield irreversibly changed by their experience of 'being in' their own very modern conflict landscape.

Herb Stradley recalled to Mary Manning (1995: 55) his experience of America's nuclear war. In 1953, at 20 years old, he felt 'indestructible'. A Private First Class in Battalion A of the US Army, he was at Camp Desert Rock at the Nevada Test Site to take part in a combat exercise immediately following the detonation of the weapon 'Shot Simon' during 'Operation Upshot-Knothole'. In the one pre-shot orientation session, the trainer jokingly told them: 'Don't worry. It takes 27 rems [a measurement of radiation dosage] to kill you and 35 rems to make you sterile'. Aside from the fact that the majority of US Army privates would be extremely unlikely to fully understand the relevance of measurements of radiation doses in rems, this quip was obviously intended to calm the nerves of any soldiers that (justifiably) felt nervous about the prospect of walking into the mushroom cloud of a nuclear device. Such advice was woefully inadequate preparation for the experience of a nuclear battlefield.

Stradley described the fireball from 'Shot Simon', viewed from trenches some 10,800 ft (*c.* 3290 m) away, as being 'like a bright light bulb going off in your face. Then the earth shook like a bowl of Jell-O'. He broke his nose against the bottom of the trench, and was then ordered to move towards the mushroom cloud once the shockwave had passed, through a rain of pea-sized gravel and falling birds. The AEC ordered a retreat, as ground zero was still too 'hot' (Manning 1995: 55). They were then 'decontaminated' by 'some guy with a broom brushing the dust off' (*ibid.*). Two months later, Stradley's gums started bleeding. Then his teeth fell out.

Thomas H. Saffer described his own experience of training in America's simulated nuclear landscape: 'when the bomb was exploded, the light was so bright that I saw the bones in my forearm … It was displaying every color I'd ever seen, and those I hadn't too' (LeBaron 1998: 39). The experience of 'being in' these landscapes was not only a reality in itself, but a new sort of reality, in which both the body and prior experiences of subjective realities were redefined. To call the reality of the atomic veterans a 'simulation' of nuclear warfare is to grossly misrepresent that experience – with no point of reference by which to compare the experience of 'being in' a nuclear landscape there is no 'reality' to be simulated. The experience and the landscape are real in and of themselves.

Furthermore, they represent a hyper reality: a reality beyond prior understanding of the real. Experience of 'being in' the nuclear landscapes of the Nevada Test Site fundamentally reshaped essential properties of reality for atomic veterans, whereby the human body could not just be seen, but could be seen *into*; where one could see not only all the colours that 'existed', but those that 'didn't' as well; and where the physical effects of that landscape, that reality, were intangible yet real, and still dangerous, years later, far away, and across generations. The American nuclear landscape was, and continues to be for the atomic veterans, a landscape that transcended spatial and temporal limitations: the first truly universal battlefield.

Conclusion

As a distinctive form of material culture, the landscape of the Nevada Test Site represents the battlefield of the Cold War, a war defined, as are all modern conflicts, by *matériel*. As a controlled military landscape, the Nevada Test Site is variously and simultaneously a simulacrum and a 'non-place' in the experiences of individuals and groups. Beyond merely an archaeological palimpsest, whereby remnants of the past are 'laid down', the Nevada Test Site is a continually changing, multi-vocal, and metaphysically volatile cultural artefact. A cross-disciplinary understanding and methodology of material culture studies reveals the 'reality' of the landscape of the Nevada Test Site as infinitely mutable and negotiable.

For Native American individuals and communities, such as Corbin Harney and the Shundahai Network, for whom life and land are inextricably linked, the Nevada Test Site represents a lost landscape: an inverted 'non-place' removed from its own reality, and whose significance lies in its negative conceptual impression of a traditional Native American desert landscape. For residents of Las Vegas during the 1950s and later, the simulated landscapes of the civil effects programmes became simultaneously and ironically a symbol to reject, and the catalyst for that rejection: a mirror image of the city of Las Vegas which became the patriotic antithesis of Cold War paranoia. For the atomic veterans of the Nevada Test Site, for whom the experience of the American nuclear landscape was perhaps most extreme, it became a landscape in which simulacra superseded reality to create a hyper reality, in which essential conceptions of landscape, of the body, of the self, and ultimately of reality itself were transformed.

Bibliography

Aston, M. (1985) *Interpreting the Landscape: Landscape Archaeology in Local Studies*. London: Batsford.

Aston, M. (2002) *Interpreting the Landscape from the Air*. Stroud: Tempus.

Augé, M. (1995) *Non-places: Introduction to an Anthropology of Supermodernity*. (trans. J. Howe). London: Verso.

Baudrillard, J. (1994) *Simulacra and Simulation*. (trans. S.F. Glaser). Michigan (IL): University of Michigan Press.

Beck, C.M. (2002). The Archaeology of Scientific Experiments at a Nuclear Testing Ground. In J. Schofield, W.G. Johnson and C.M. Beck, (eds), *Matériel Culture: the Archaeology of Twentieth Century Conflict*, 65–79. London: Routledge.

Bender, B. (1999) Subverting the Western Gaze: Mapping Alternative Worlds. In P.J. Ucko and R. Layton (eds), *The Archaeology and Anthropology of Landscape: Shaping your Landscape*, 31–45. London: Routledge.

Bender, B. (2002a) Landscape and Politics. In V. Buchli (ed.), *The Material Culture Reader*, 135–140. Oxford: Berg.

Bender, B. (2002b). Time and Landscape. *Current Anthropology* 43(4): 103–112.

Bender, B. (2006) Place and Landscape. In C. Tilley, W. Keane, S. Küchler, M. Rowlands and P. Spyer (eds), *Handbook of Material Culture*, 303–314. London: Sage.

Beresford, M. (1957) *History on the Ground*. Stroud: Sutton.

Department of Energy (1994) *United States Nuclear Tests 1945–1992*. Springfield (VA): National Technical Information Services.

Dreyfus, H.L. (1991) *Being-in-the-World: a Commentary on Heidegger's Being and Time, Division I*. Cambridge (MA): MIT Press.

Dvorchak, R. (1994) What They Knew, What They Said About Radiation. *The Sunday Courier*, 27 March 1994.

Fagan, D. (1982) *The Nightfly, Track 1*. Los Angeles (CA): Warner Brothers.

Fehner, T. and Gosling, F. (2000). *Origins of the Nevada Test Site*. Washington D.C.: United States Department of Energy.

Foucault, M. (1977) Nietzsche, Genealogy, History. (trans. D.F. Bouchard and S. Simon). In D.F. Bouchard (ed.), *Language, Counter-Memory, Practice: Selected Essays and Interviews*, 139–164. Ithaca (NY): Cornell University Press.

Gallagher, C. (1993) *American Ground Zero: The Secret Nuclear War*. Cambridge (MA): MIT Press.

Gearey, R.R. (1989) Nevada Test Site's Dirty Little Secrets. *Bulletin of the Atomic Scientists* 45(3): 35–38.

Goldberg, B.F. (1991) *Body Betrayer*. Cleveland (OH): Cleveland State University Poetry Center.

Gosden, C. (1999) *Archaeology and Anthropology: A Changing Relationship*. London: Routledge.

Green, M.S. and Penn, E. (2006) *Las Vegas: A Pictorial Celebration*. New York (NY): Sterling.

Harney, C. (1992) *The Way It Is: One Water, One Air, One Mother Earth*. Nevada City (CA): Blue Dolphin.

Heidegger, M. (1962) *Being and Time* (trans. J. Macquarrie and E. Robinson). Oxford: Blackwell.

Hoskins, J. (2006) Agency, Biography and Objects. In C. Tilley, W. Keane, S. Küchler, M. Rowlands and P. Spyer (eds), *Handbook of Material Culture*, 74–84. London: Sage.

Johnson, W.G. (2002) Archaeological Examination of Cold War Architecture: a Reactionary Cultural Response to the Threat of Nuclear War. In J. Schofield, W.G. Johnson and C.M. Beck (eds), *Matériel Culture: the Archaeology of Twentieth Century Conflict*, 227–235. London: Routledge.

Kalven, J. (1983) The Legal Quandary. *Bulletin of the Atomic Scientists* 39(1): 26–29.

Kuletz, V.L. (1998) *The Tainted Desert: Environmental Ruin in the American West*. New York (NY): Routledge.

Layton, R. and Ucko, P.J. (1999) Introduction: Gazing on the Landscape and Encountering the Environment. In P.J. Ucko and R. Layton (eds), *The Archaeology and Anthropology of Landscape: Shaping your Landscape*, 1–20. London: Routledge.

LeBaron, W.D. (1998) *America's Nuclear Legacy*. Commack (NY): Nova Science Publishers.

Lynch, T. and Cooksey, J. (2007). *Battlefield Archaeology*. Stroud: Tempus.

Manning, M. (1995) Atomic Vets Battle Time. *Bulletin of the Atomic Scientists* 51(1): 54–60.

McCracken, R.D. (1997) *Las Vegas: The Great American Playground*. Reno (NV): University of Nevada Press.

Roberts, B.K. (1987) Landscape Archaeology. In J.M. Wagstaff (ed.), *Landscape and Culture: Geographical and Archaeological Perspectives*, 77–95. Oxford: Blackwell.

Rowlands, M. (1996) Looking at Financial Landscapes: a Contextual Analysis of ROSCAs in Cameroon. In S. Ardener and S. Burman (eds), *Money Go Rounds: The Importance of Rotating Savings and Credit Associations for Women*, 111–124. Oxford: Berg.

Saunders, N.J. (2001). Matter and Memory in the Landscapes of Conflict: the Western Front 1914–1999. In B. Bender and M. Winer (eds), *Contested Landscapes: Movement, Exile and Place*, 37–53. Oxford: Berg.

Saunders, N.J. (2003). *Trench Art: Materialities and Memories of War*. Oxford: Berg.

Saunders, N.J. (2004). Material Culture and Conflict: The Great War, 1914–2003. In N.J. Saunders (ed.), *Matters of Conflict: Material Culture, Memory and the First World War*, 5–25. Abingdon: Routledge.

Schofield, J., Johnson, W.G. and Beck. C.M, (2002) Introduction: Materiel Culture in the Modern World. In J Schofield, W.G. Johnson and C.M. Beck (eds), *Matériel Culture: The Archaeology of Twentieth Century Conflict*, 1–8. London: Routledge.

Shundahai Network (n.d.) Shundahai Network. http://www.shundahai.org Accessed 25 March 2010.

Thomas, J. (1993) The Politics of Vision and the Archaeologies of Landscape. In B. Bender (ed.), *Landscape: Politics and Perspectives*, 19–48. Oxford: Berg.

Titus, A. (2001) *Bombs in the Backyard: Atomic Testing and American Politics*. Reno (NV): University of Nevada Press.

Tilley, C. (1994) *A Phenomenology of Landscape: Places, Paths and Monuments*. Oxford: Berg.

Yamin, R. and Metheny, K.B. (eds) (1996) *Landscape Archaeology: Reading and Interpreting the American Historical Landscape*. Knoxville (TN): University of Tennessee Press.

Signs, Signals and Senses:
the soldier body in the trenches

Melanie Winterton

'In the Great War eight million people were destroyed because two persons, the Archduke Ferdinand and his Consort, had been shot.' (Fussell 1977: 7–8)

History overflows with facts and figures, but it is cross-disciplinary approaches such as those adopted by modern conflict archaeology that allow us to look beyond the statistics of the First World War to the reality of life for soldiers in the trenches (Saunders 2011). This reality acknowledges that the arrival of global industrialised warfare in 1914 exposed soldiers to living nightmares, from which the only escape often seemed to be wounding or death. In the trenches, the 'soldier body' endured conditions beyond any experienced by humans before – they lived in a technologically-defined state of 'unstructured liminality' (Turner 1995: ix; Leed 1979). As 'liminal entities', soldiers were 'betwixt and between' (*ibid*.: 95) as they endured trench life, and the possibility of random death or injury at any time. Soldiers who came from:

'[a] generation that had gone to school on a horse-drawn streetcar now stood under the open sky in a countryside in which nothing remained unchanged but the clouds, and beneath these clouds, in a field of force of destructive torrents and explosions, was the tiny, fragile human body.' (Benjamin 1999 [1955]: 84)

The agents of industrialised warfare wreak havoc, physically and mentally, on the fragile human body, for this is their purpose. The intention of war is 'injuring … to alter (to burn, to blast, to shell, to cut) human tissue' (Scarry 1984: 63). This paper explores the cultural, experiential, and sensorial aspects of being a soldier in the trenches of the First World War. It is informed by primary evidence – the published memoirs and letters of soldiers and nurses; such texts in themselves may be viewed as material culture, for they represent a dimension of human creativity integral to the social production of reality (Moreland 2001: 83). Soldiers wrote of their 'truths' about their experiences during the war, such writings representing the 'authority' of their direct experiences (Winter 2006: 113).

Since landscapes are cultural productions (Daniels and Cosgrove 1992; Hirsch 1995), the trenches of the First World War may be interpreted through human experience. Landscape should not be viewed as merely a backdrop to human activity, and, in adopting a phenomenological approach, the view cannot be static because we exist within it. As Bender has observed, 'landscapes are not just "views" but intimate encounters. They are not just about seeing, but about *experiencing* with all the senses' (Bender 2002: 136). Indeed, Merleau-Ponty argues that human consciousness and knowledge of the world is dependent upon the senses, and on experiences mediated through the body, the senses representing a 'unit of experience' (2002 [1958]: 3–14) making all the associated elements of senses and feeling a prominent feature of cultural analysis (Howes 2005).

However, Ingold (2000: 284) argues that Howes' approach 'reduces the body to a locus of objectified and enumerable senses'. Nevertheless, war is man-made, and the resultant horrors would be unimaginable experiences within the peaceful society that people and their ancestors are accustomed to. In wearing a uniform and being placed in the trenches – a hitherto alien environment – the soldier body is an artefact *in extremis*.

After experiencing the Western Front for only three weeks, the English war poet, Wilfred Owen, wrote to his mother: 'I have not seen any dead. I have done worse. In the dank air, I have *perceived* it, and in the darkness, *felt*'. (Owen and Bell 1967: 429).

It is clear that the First World War created a new landscape of the senses (Eksteins 1989; see also Saunders 2007: 68; 2009: 5), and the term 'sense-scape' is thus introduced here as a tool with which to study sensation in a cultural context (Howes 2005: 143–145). Hence the neologism 'scape', when annexed to 'sense', is used to represent a subjective means of perceiving the 'trench world' through the soldier body and, therefore, represents a significant method of interpretation within the young discipline of modern conflict archaeology. The soldier body experienced the trench world through its senses, its emotions, its movements, gestures, and bodily signs and signals. Such is the importance of the study of the senses and experiences through the body, that we can come to know and understand the trench world of the soldier body as it is exposed to a totally new environment.

Vision has hitherto been prioritised over other senses in the Western world (Howes 1991: 3–5; Hamilakis 2002a: 100), although others maintain that we have never been obsessed with the eye (Ingold 2000: 245). However, it is clear that sight was not always the most dominant sense in the trenches of the First World War (Saunders 2007: 68; 2009: 5), for the enemy, on the whole, was an unseen presence, with snipers offering instant oblivion to any soldier who momentarily raised his head above the parapet. A sniper looked through a gun sight to enable his eyes to see into the distance, such technological magnification of sight presenting sentience as an artefact (Scarry 1985: 255). However, as we shall see below, for soldiers at close quarters in the trenches, sight, in some circumstances, was an important sense in that the body unconsciously emits both physical and mental signs and signals in terms of its well-being.

The experiential action of 'feeling through the body' is particularly relevant to the trench world of the Western Front (Das 2005: 100). This focus on the tactile senses is an area which has been given increasing archaeological attention (e.g. Hamilakis 2002b), especially since the 'culture of touch involves all of culture' (Classen 2005: 1). Nevertheless, we should be cautious about concentrating on singular senses, for the experiences of the soldier body in the trench world of the Western Front were multi-sensorial, as men were constantly assaulted by the sounds, sights, and smells of war. Simultaneously, they bore witness to the extreme bodily consequences of life in the trenches, and felt the effects of conflict in a tactile and emotional sense. On occasion, feeling even substituted for sound, as Barbusse, in describing being under fire, observed that the noise was so 'monstrously resounding that one feels himself annihilated by the mere sound of the downpour of thunder' (Barbusse 2010 [1933]: 206).

The war correspondent Philip Gibbs, describes being in the trenches as:

> '[B]odies and bits of bodies, and clots of blood, and green metallic looking slime, made by explosive gases, were floating on the surface of that water below the crater banks … Our men lived there and died there within a few yards of the enemy, crouched below sandbags and burrowed in the sides of the crater … Human flesh, rotting and stinking, mere pulp, was pasted into the mud banks.' (Gibbs 1920: 56)

Such first-hand accounts embody the experience of being a soldier in the trenches of the First World War and, on reading them, we are able to make present that which is absent (Buchli and Lucas 2001: 3–18). The reality of industrialised warfare was a living nightmare, and, even with eyes shut, its presence could still be felt, smelt and heard. Indeed, it was a 'synaesthetic' nightmare (Saunders 2002: 193). Within this sense-scape, the greatest instinct for the soldier body was to survive – listening for, and reacting to, auditory signals of warning; remaining alert for, and reacting to, visual signals or indications of danger, and, in darkness, using the body to feel and know the immediate environment.

Being in a gas attack

In an attempt to break the stalemate on the Western Front, chemical warfare in the form of gas attacks was introduced. A gas attack provides the catalyst for a series of experienced bodily and sensorial events. An observer sees the cloud of gas approaching, and shouts a warning; a soldier runs to strike the gas gong – another auditory warning (Figure 17.1). The thudding sound of the gas shells together with the noise of high explosives informs the soldiers of its arrival.

Gas can be smelt – an olfactory warning. The odour of gas is often likened to the smell of familiar and tangible 'things' on the home front. Chlorine smells like bleach (Cook 2003: 48); phosgene recalls freshly mown hay (Cook 2003: 49). The soldier

Figure 17.1: A gas sentry ringing an alarm. (Crown © IWM Q669)

searches frantically for his gas mask, hoping to avoid an untimely death, as the confines of the gas mask become the soldier body's safe breathable space.

If the soldier is exposed to gas, there are bodily consequences, as he becomes a liminal being – 'betwixt and between' (Turner 1995) in a state between life and death. Through vomiting, frothing at the mouth, and gasping for air, the soldier 'spew[s] up [his] burned-out lungs, bit by bit' (Remarque 1994 [1929]: 47) as his mouth becomes an 'organ of disgust' (Miller 1997: 93–98). As the soldier succumbs to a dreadful death, he is watched and cared for by a nurse, the final witness to his suffering; a suffering that the nurse has, out of necessity for her own sanity, grown both hardened and accustomed to.

Before gas masks were supplied, a soldier urinated on his puttees, or on a handkerchief, held over his face, thus using his own bodily secretions to save himself, even though such polluting substances would be considered 'matter out of place' on the home-front of ordered Edwardian society (Douglas 2002 [1966]: 44–45).

Mustard gas was also used, and this burned both the skin and the lungs. The First World War nurse and author Vera Brittain, writes in *Testament of Youth*:

> '[I] could see the poor things burnt and blistered all over with great mustard-coloured suppurating blisters, with blind eyes – sometimes temporally [*sic*], sometimes permanently – all sticky and stuck together.' (Brittain 2004 [1933]: 360)

Figure 17.2: British troops blinded by gas. (Crown © IWM Q11586)

It was a common sight on the Western Front to witness gassed blindfolded soldiers moving slowly and dejectedly in single file, trying to understand and navigate a new sensory world. They moved as one, touching the shoulder of the man in front, enabling them as a group to be guided through touch as their hands and fingers substitute for their eyes, feeling their way forward whilst perceiving the all-encompassing noisy and stench-filled darkness of their sudden war-inflicted blindness (Figure 17.2).

John Singer Sargent's painting, *Gassed* – exhibited in the Imperial War Museum – reveals how real it is, for, as a war artist on the Western Front, Sargent witnessed the scene he painted (Figure 17.3). Sargent's painting serves as a 'marker of human activity' (Renfrew 2003: 144), capturing the futility of the aftermath of a gas attack. Thus, Sargent has: 'seen the world, experienced it, and acted upon it, embodying and expressing that experience, and thereby offering us as viewers further experiences' (Renfrew 2003: 8), as his multi-sensorial past mingles with our visual present so that we might understand and know *his* past.

Today, 30 tons of gas shells are unearthed each year by French bomb disposal experts (*demineurs*). The shells still contain poisonous liquid, which, on exposure to air, turn

Figure 17.3: Aftermath of a mustard gas attack. Painted by John Singer Sargent. (Crown © IWM ART 1460)

to a deadly gas thus instilling the feeling of fear among the *demineurs* (Cook 1999: 3). The slow and painful deaths experienced by the troops of the Great War are still a possibility today as legacies of the Great War live on, thereby promoting an archaeology of cultural association.

Experiencing a battle against the elements

Soldiers on the Western Front fought a harsh battle against the elements. The trenches were often ankle or knee-deep in mud. An officer in the Ypres Salient reported how it once took him three hours to feel his way along a muddy communication trench that was only 400 yards (366 m) long (Ellis 1976: 44).

Nightmares of being buried alive came true. In *Undertones of War*, Edmund Blunden writes of a man buried alive in mud who 'only had time to reach out his arm' (1937 [1928]: 298). Duckboard tracks were laid over the mud for soldiers to walk on. The narrowness of these tracks, together with the weight of rucksacks, guns, and equipment carried by the soldiers, enabled the vestibular sense of the soldier body as it balanced precariously, legs wobbling and body swaying, trying desperately to avoid falling into the mud. Towards the end of his life, Harry Patch, the longest-surviving First World War veteran, clearly recalls the consequences of walking over duckboards: 'We were always told … that, if a fellow slipped into a shell hole filled with water, to leave him there because it was liquid mud; if you tried to get him out you'd go in yourself' (Patch 2009: 80).

Enduring life in the trenches was not just about waiting to be shot, blown up, or gassed by the enemy. Winters on the Western Front felt painfully cold. Fur undercoats were distributed in an attempt to keep warm (Ellis 1976: 52). The soldiers' daily rum ration was deemed of great importance and, for Harry Patch, rum 'burnt all the way down … it warmed you up beautifully' (2009: 76). However, on occasion, the sun did actually shine, and the German officer, Ernst Jünger, somewhat surreally, recalls sunbathing in a huge crater, working on his tan, 'disturbed, on occasion, by shells or whizzing fragments of metal coming too near' (2003 [1920]: 260), signifying that Jünger had grown accustomed to, and was at ease with his trench world.

Soldiers were ordered to care for their feet to remain fit for fighting. One of Wilfred Owen's letters reports: '… I have to take a close interest in feet, and this very day I knelt with a candle and watched each man perform his anointment with Whale Oil; praising the clean feet, but not reviling the unclean' (Owen and Bell 1967: 426).

Soldiers standing in the muddy trenches for hours at a time with wet boots and socks were prone to 'trench foot' which caused loss of sensation in their feet. They saw their feet turn red and blue, a bodily sign they had no control over, but a useful warning signal to seek medical attention. In extreme cases, gangrene set in, necessitating the amputation of toes or feet, such cruel alterations being symbols of war, and thereby affording the soldier body cultural meaning.

Knowing no-man's land

Encouraged to adopt an offensive spirit, small patrols of soldiers ventured out into no-man's land during darkness, each soldier's night-blindness forcing him to know his immediate environment though his senses of touch, hearing, and smell. In particular, the haptic senses were crucial to his embodied existence and survival. A soldier would cautiously feel his way forward, crawling on his stomach, to get within earshot of enemy trenches. In such instances, the soldier body consciously controls its soldier world of sensory experience. The soldier controls every inch of his body, straining his muscles and joints, such concentration causing him to unconsciously hold his breath as he crawls in a muscular way, actively engaging his haptic senses as he feels his way through no-man's land. He simultaneously and silently gags from the smell of rotting corpses that he senses are there, but which he cannot see, though which he feels as he crawls over them. Whilst the soldier body could shut its eyes to block out visual horrors, tactile and olfactory senses do not deceive.

Being under fire

In *Under Fire*, Henri Barbusse tells how the incessant and diabolical din of war constantly bombards the soldier body with the unendurable noise of bursting shells, causing pain to the ears, the sound alone causing feelings of annihilation (Barbusse 2010 [1933]: 207) whilst materialising in an 'invisible bodily assault' (Leed 1979: 124). The *Wipers Times* poems written by soldiers (Roberts 1928) indicate the practised ease with which the soldier body identifies the noise of the various lethal projectiles, an example of heightened senses, and an indication that the soldier has been on the Western Front for some time. There are also instances of soldiers objectifying their sense of hearing whilst under bombardment from artillery shells. Ellis, in *Eye-Deep in Hell*, quotes a Canadian soldier who describes his experience during the barrage that preceded the assault on Vimy Ridge: '… I felt that if I lifted a finger I should touch a solid ceiling of sound, it now had the attribute of solidity' (Ellis 1976: 64). Another artillery officer describes the sensation of artillery fire as 'not that of sound. You feel it in your ears than hear it' (*ibid.*: 63). Feeling and hearing somehow intermingle in this multi-sensorial sense-scape.

Jünger describes a scene of soldiers caught in the midst of an explosion – they are reduced to a pile of charred bodies, writhing in agony and crying out for help. His attention is drawn to a young soldier, who, only days ago, he had witnessed being mocked by his comrades, and who had cried on exercises, weeping under the weight of the big munitions boxes he was carrying.

Following the explosion, Jünger witnessed the young soldier loyally carrying his comrades out of the crater. Jünger writes: 'Seeing that did for me. I threw myself to the ground and sobbed hysterically' (2003 [1920]: 226). Thus, after experiencing such a horrific initiation into manhood, the boy-soldier transforms into a man (van Gennep 1960 [1909]). Whilst Jünger was unable to control his emotions, even though he had managed to control both his body and his emotions when engaging in night patrols, his tears, as they traverse the boundary of his body, symbolise the vulnerability of his soldier body (Douglas 2002 [1966]: 150).

Even when war concludes, the noise of war is remembered, for the human body may be viewed as a 'central recording device' in terms of bodily memory (Hamilakis 2002b: 124). Harry Patch, on arriving home injured, remembers: 'I was jumpy for a while. The least noise and I wanted to dive for cover – you couldn't help it' (Patch 2009: 114).

Being injured

Soldiers injured in the trenches were hospitalised, their suffering witnessed by nurses. The effects of an industrialised war caused the soldier body to change its form – to become an artefact of conflict through its horrific injuries. The First World War nurse, Mary Borden, describes how:

> '… there are heads and knees and mangled testicles. There are chests with holes as big as your fist, and pulpy thighs, shapeless; and stumps where legs once were fastened. There are eyes … blind eyes, eyes of delirium; and mouths that cannot articulate, and parts of faces – the nose gone, or the jaw.' (Borden 2008 [1928]: 43–44)

French soldier, Louis Walser, wrote to Sister Mabel Jeffreys informing her that he was 'completely cured and ready to go back to war' (Wenzel and Cornish 1980: 44). Although bodily experience is subjective, it is clear that the soldier body becomes an object of war, an object to be broken, an object to be mended and recycled to return to being a human agent of conflict.

From mid-1916, for every wound received in combat, an allied soldier was permitted to wear a gold-coloured wound stripe on his lower left sleeve; the stripe representing a cultural message symbolising the creation of a group of wounded soldiers, identified visually by a gold flash of colour. Ironically, the left side of the human body, in anthropological terms of polarity and dexterity, is perceived to be the 'side of death and weakness' (Hertz 1973: 12). There was no limit to how many stripes wounded soldiers could wear; indeed, Neville Lytton had occasion to see a sergeant wearing 'no less than eight wound stripes' (Lytton 1920: 109).

Wound stripes, however, were not awarded to sufferers of 'shell-shock', because those afflicted were, incorrectly, deemed to be malingerers or suffering from hysteria (Simpson 2003: 509). Edwardian society on the home front demanded that the soldier body, in a show of manliness, accustom itself to the horrors of industrialised warfare. Gibbs witnessed the effects of shell-shock on the soldier body:

> 'shaking in every limb in a palsied way … his mouth is slobbered and two comrades could not hold him down. These badly shell shocked boys clawed their mouths ceaselessly. … Others sat in the field hospitals in a state of coma, dazed, as though deaf, and dumb. I … turned my eyes away from them, and yet wished that they might be seen by bloody-minded men and women who, far behind the lines, still spoke of war lightly, as a kind of sport, or heroic game, which brave boys liked, or ought to like.' (Gibbs 1920: 31)

After two years as a nurse on the Western Front, Mary Borden had learned to feel bodily signs of impending death, as bodily extremities become progressively colder as a person is dying. Borden's hands 'could instantly tell the difference between the cold of the harsh bitter night and stealthy cold death' (2008 [1929]: 124).

Many soldiers died of tetanus, the body emitting signals that such sufferers were near the end of their lives, for the skin of the soldier body visibly pales and is unable to feel as its limbs stiffen. At the end, only the eyes remain alive – for a long time (Remarque 1994 [1929]: 179); the sense of sight, for a while, outliving the other senses.

If it was not enough to endure life in the trenches under threat of being drowned in mud, gassed, bitten by lice, or blown to pieces, a soldier had to endure punishment and discipline, often enforced through brutalising the fragile soldier body in an effort to induce feelings of humiliation and thereby to enforce conformity. Siegfried Sassoon describes the treatment of a conscientious objector by a fellow officer: '… the Major had him tied to the back of a wagon and dragged along a road until he was badly cut about. "After a few hundred yards he cried enough, and afterwards turned out to be quite a decent soldier"' (Sassoon 1931: 169).

Robert Graves describes 'Field Punishment No. 1' being carried out on his servant as a punishment for drunkenness in the field. This involved the body being tied by the ankles and wrists in the form of a cross (2000) [1929]: 147). This was yet another punishment designed to impart feelings of humiliation on the soldier body and to set an example to those who witnessed the incident, thereby creating a 'sensory structure of witnessing' (Das 2005: 206).

Wipers Times and feelings of comradeship

Finally, since this paper uses the direct evidence of publications written by soldiers and nurses who experienced the Great War at first hand, mention should be made of soldiers writing in the trenches. The *Wipers Times* is the best known of the many trench newspapers written and published by soldiers during the First World War. Produced with a mix of sarcasm and black humour, it is representative of soldiers' views and experiences of their trench world.

In the words of the paper's editor after the war: 'Remember that the hilarity was more often hysterical than natural' (Roberts 1928: vii). The *Wipers Times* is full of in-jokes, for it was written by 'insiders' for 'insiders' – for those who experienced the stark realities of the trench world. Evidently, it was produced and sustained by the feelings of comradeship it created amongst the troops, who never knew from day to day whether they would have the chance to write, print, read, or be read again. The acts of writing copy, being part of the production process, as well as reading the published result, reflect the construction of an identity that offers momentary feelings of relief from the experienced hells – for a moment in time, the soldier body is in control of what it experiences in its contested space in the trenches.

Conclusion

We have explored the effects of industrialised warfare on the fragile soldier body. Its war-induced multi-sensory experiences did not cease with the armistice and the stillness of the battlefields. Soldiers that survived were haunted by their memories of war. Injuries suffered from gas attacks remained; soldiers had to come to terms with missing limbs, facial disfigurement, the effects of shell-shock, and recurring nightmares as they remained artefactual objectifications of the consequences of war (Reznick 2004). Ernst Jünger, feeling haunted by shooting a young British soldier, wrote: 'the state, which relieves us of our responsibility cannot take away our remorse … Sorrow [and] regret pursued me deep into my dreams' (2003 [1920]: 241).

A phenomenological account of being in the trenches generates an awareness of material agency by exploring the dialectical relationship between the experiential soldier body, its senses, and the man-made trenches – thereby promoting an intimate and emotional understanding of what it was like to be in a First World War sense-scape.

The multi-disciplinary study of modern conflict archaeology, therefore, provides an important contribution to archaeological discourse – it is another way of telling the story through highlighting the significant and non-obvious.

It is evident that such a study highlights cultural transformations as the subjective experiential soldier body becomes an object of war – to be injured, mended, and recycled in order to return to the fight. Being in the trenches was a waking nightmare. Even with eyes shut tight, you could still feel, hear, and smell the war for the sense-scape of the soldier body was all-encompassing and multi-sensorial with manifestations of sensory substitution and sensory objectification.

Acknowledgements

With thanks to the Imperial War Museum for permission to use its photographs, and to Dr N.J. Saunders for his encouragement and comments on this paper.

Bibliography

Barbusse, H. (2010) [1933] *Under Fire*. Radford: Wilder Publications.

Bender, B. (2002) Landscape and Politics. In V. Buchli (ed.), *The Material Culture Reader*, 135–140. Oxford: Berg.

Benjamin, W. (1999 [1955] The Story Teller. In H. Arendt (ed.) (trans. H. Zorn) *Illuminations*, 70–82. London: Pimlico.

Blunden, E. (1937) [1928] *Undertones of War*. London: Penguin.

Borden, M. (2008) [1929] *The Forbidden Zone*. London: Hesperus Press.

Brittain, V. (2004) [1933] *Testament of Youth*. London: Virago.

Buchli, V. and Lucas, G. (2001) The Absent Present. In V. Buchli and G. Lucas (eds), *Archaeologies of the Contemporary Past*, 3–18. Oxford: Routledge.

Classen, C. (ed.) (2005) *The Book of Touch*. Oxford and New York: Berg.

Cook, T. (1999) *No Place to Run: The Canadian Corps and Gas Warfare in the First World War*. Toronto: UBS Press.

Cook, T. (2003) Dying like so many rats in a trap. *The Army and Doctrine Training Bulletin* 5(4): 47–56. http://www.army.forces.gc.ca/caj/documents/vol_05/iss_4/caj_vol5.4_09_e.pdf Accessed 2 April 2010.

Daniels, S. and Cosgrove, D. (1992) Introduction: Iconography and Landscape. In D. Cosgrove and S. Daniels (eds), *The Iconography of Landscape*, 1–10. Cambridge: Cambridge University Press.

Das, S. (2005) *Touch and Intimacy in First World War Literature*. Cambridge: Cambridge University Press.

Douglas, M. (2002) [1966] *Purity and Danger*. London and New York: Routledge.

Eksteins, M. (2000) *Rites of Spring. The Great War and the Modern Age*. London: Papermac.

Ellis, J. (1976) *Eye-deep in Hell*. London: Crook Helm.

Fussell, P. (1977) *The Great War and Modern Memory*. Oxford: Oxford University Press.

Gibbs, P. (1920) *Realities of War*. London: Heinemann.

Graves, R. (2000) [1929] *Goodbye to All That*. London: Penguin.

Hamilakis, Y. (2002a) Experience and Corporality. Introduction. In Y. Hamilakis, M. Pluciennik and S. Tarlow (eds), *Thinking Through the Body. Archaeologies of Corporeality*, 99–103. New York: Kluwer Academic/Plenum Publishers.

Hamilakis, Y. (2002b) The Past as Oral History: Towards an Archaeology of the Senses. In Y. Hamilakis, M. Pluciennik and S. Tarlow (eds), *Thinking Through the Body. Archaeologies of Corporeality*, 121–136. New York: Kluwer Academic/Plenum Publishers.

Hertz, R. (1973) The Pre-eminence of the Right hand: a Study of Religious Polarity. In R. Needham (ed.), *Right and Left: Essays on Dual Symbolic Classification*, 3–31. Chicago and London: University of Chicago Press.

Hirsch, E. (1995) Introduction. Landscape: Between Place and Space. In E. Hirsch and. M. O'Hanlon (eds), *The Anthropology of Landscape. Perspectives on Place and Space*, 1–30. Oxford: Clarendon Press.

Howes, D. (1991) Introduction: To Summon all the Senses. In D. Howes (ed.) *The Variety of Sensory Experience*. London: Routledge.

Howes, D. (2005) Acknowledgements. In D. Howes (ed.), *Empire of the Senses. The Sensual Culture Reader*, ix–x. Oxford: Berg.

Ingold, T. (2000) *The Perception of the Environment. Essays in livelihood, dwelling and skill*. Oxford: Routledge.

Jünger, E. (2003) *Storm of Steel*. Toronto: University of Toronto Press.

Leed, E.J. (1979) *No Man's Land. Combat & Identity in World War I*. Cambridge: Cambridge University Press.

Lytton, N. (1920) *The Press and the General Staff*. London: W. Collins.

Merleau-Ponty, M. (trans. C. Smith) (2002) [1958] *Phenomenology of Perception*. London: Routledge.

Miller, W.I. (1997) *The Anatomy of Disgust*. Cambridge (MA) and London: Harvard University Press.

Moreland, J. (2001) *Archaeology of Text*. London: Gerald Duckworth.

Owen, H. and Bell, J. (eds) (1967) *Wilfred Owen. Collected Letters*. London: Oxford University Press.

Patch, H. (2009) *The Last Fighting Tommy. The Life of Harry Patch, Last Veteran of the Trenches, 1898–2009*. London: Bloomsbury.

Remarque, E. (1994) [1929] *All Quiet on the Western Front*. London: Vintage.

Renfrew, C. (2003) *Figuring It Out. What are We? Where do We Come From? The Parallel Visions of Artists and Archaeologists*. London: Thames and Hudson.

Reznick, J.S. (2004) Prostheses and Propaganda: Materiality and the Human Body in the Great War. In N.J. Saunders (ed.), *Matters of Conflict: Material Culture, Memory and the First World War*, 51–61. Abingdon: Routledge.

Roberts, F.J. (1928) *The Wipers Times. A Facsimile Reprint of the Trench Magazines: The Wipers Times – The New Church Times – The Kemmel Times – The Somme Times – The B.E.F. Times*. London: Herbert Jenkins.

Sassoon, S. (1931) *Memoirs of an Infantry Officer*. London: Faber & Faber.

Saunders, N.J. (2002) Bodies of Metal, Shells of Memory: 'Trench Art' and the Great War Re-cycled. In Buchli (ed.) 2002, 181–206.

Saunders, N.J. (2007) *Killing Time. Archaeology and the First World War*. Stroud: Sutton.

Saunders, N.J. (2009) Introduction. In N.J. Saunders and P. Cornish (eds), *Contested Objects. Material Memories of the Great War*, 1–10. Abingdon: Routledge.

Saunders, N.J. (2011) First World War Archaeology: Between Theory and Practice. In *Archeologia della Grande Guerra: Atti del Conveguo Internazionale 23/24 June 2006*, 37–53. Trento: Stampalith.

Scarry, E. (1984) *The Body in Pain. The Making and Unmaking of the World*. Oxford: Oxford University Press.

Simpson, K. (2003) Dr. James Dunn and Shell-shock. In H. Cecil and P. H. Liddle (eds), *Facing Armageddon. The First World War Experience*, 502–520. Barnsley: Pen & Sword.

Turner, V. (1995) *The Ritual Process. Structure and Anti-Structure*. New York: Aldine de Gruyter.

Van Gennep, A. (1960) [1909] *The Rites de Passage*. London: Routledge.

Wenzel, M. and Cornish, J. (1980) *Auntie Mabel's War. An Account of her Part in the Hostilities of 1914–18*. London: Penguin.

Winter, J. (2006) *Remembering War. The Great War between Memory and History in the Twentieth Century*. New Haven (CT) and London: Yale University Press.

Beneath the Waves:
the conflict seascape of the Baltic

Gabriella Soto

The Potsdam Conference following the Second World War mandated the Allies to inherit the Axis powers' unused munitions, amounting to a approximately 296,000 tons, of which 65,000 tons were considered 'harmful military substances' or chemical agents (CEPA 2008). In response to this unwelcome bequest, the Allies agreed to tow the munitions out into the Atlantic, and cast them into depths of over 1000 m. By so doing, it was expected that these dangerously volatile materials would cease to be a threat to civilians in the post-war era. This legal change of ownership was supposed to have brought a premature end to the 'social life' of these definitively twentieth century conflict objects – but it was not to be.

It is now known that the Allies did not honour their obligation. Instead of the Atlantic, it was the smaller, shallower, and enclosed waters of the Baltic which became the dumping ground of the war's debris and munitions – thereby creating a new and illegal conflict landscape (more accurately seascape) as an enduring legacy of war.

Barges loaded with Axis munitions, containers filled with the same, and even individual items were sunk and jettisoned in the Skagerrak and Kattegat Straits, southwest and east of the island of Bornholm, south-east of Gotland island, and southwest of Liepaja in Lativa (where some munitions set in concrete blocks were also dumped) (CEPA 2008; DEPA 1994). In addition, large quantities of Second World War munitions are often encountered by Russian fishermen within Russian territorial waters, and that may be war damage, rather than the product of post-war dumping (Anon.a. 2010). One German wreck is known to have 10,000 live shells on board, and fishermen often return to port with volatile munitons in their nets (*ibid.*).

The locations used by the United Kingdom and the United States as dumping grounds will not be declassified until 2017 (although those of the former Soviet Union are now in the public domain) (CEPA 2008; DEPA 1994). These locations remain classified despite appeals from the 'Baltic Marine Environmental Protection Agency' (also known as the 'Helsinki Commission' or HELCOM) and other environmental bodies in order to safely map and destroy the weapons (CEPA 2008; DEPA 1994).

Today, the sites at the bottom of the Baltic where the Allies disposed of Axis war *matériel* have been 'accidentally' re-encountered and uncovered by the construction of the Nord Stream pipeline – a project of Russia's Gazprom, the world's largest natural gas exploration and production company (Figure 18.1). The Nord Stream pipeline is conceived by contemporary theorists as a material articulation of Russia's energy monopoly and a physical expression of its power over European consumers who increasingly rely on it (Rodgers 2009; Anon. b 2009; Wingfield-Hayes 2009; de Jong *et al.* 2009; Larsson 2007; Smith 2008).

As an engineering feat, the pipeline is an artefact of contemporary technology. Upon its completion, Nord Stream will be one of the longest underwater pipelines ever constructed, as well as an efficient conduit for transporting natural gas to northern Europe (Figure 18.2). Nord Stream is projected to help the European Community to eventually meet its climate change targets and decrease its reliance on fossil fuels (Cronshaw 2009; de Jong *et al.* 2009; Nord Stream, 2009; 2010a; 2010b). It is one of many ironies that the path which this vehicle for 'green energy' takes runs through a conflict seascape originating in the post-Second World War years which should not be there, and which was created by the Allies themselves in direct contradiction of their international and legally binding Potsdam obligations.

Beneath the Baltic, juxtaposed to the pipeline, lay the discarded remains of the First and (mainly) Second World Wars. Both conflicts were global wars of *matériel*, and today an enduring legacy of the proliferation of industrialised killing scars the seabed. As such deadly materialities of conflict continue to be found, the objects themselves transform into the epitome of modern war – they come to represent 'war beyond conflict', remaining lethal beyond their war-time intention to kill (Saunders 2004: 6).

It is this definitively modern 'intention' which I wish to explore here, as part of the existence of this 'artefact set' (of unexploded munitions) hidden from view for some 50 years, but now dramatically resurrected as a 'newly recognised' legacy landscape/seascape of war.

González Ruibal (2008: 256) defines sites of abjection as those '… whose existence has been erased from collective memory, about which nobody is allowed or wants to speak or whose existence is denied'. The Baltic seabed and the objects deliberately deposited on it surely qualifies as a 'site' of abjection.

The investigation of the Baltic's seabed, and its relationship with the Nord Stream pipeline, necessarily explores the materiality of conflict beyond war, and raises issues of how we conceptualise the post-Cold War era when paradigms of conflict have shifted away from the industrialized production of weapons designed for mass killing (Gaddis 2006).

> 'The Cold War may well be remembered … as the point at which military strength, a defining characteristic of 'power' itself for the past five centuries, ceased to be that. The Soviet Union collapsed, after all, with its military forces, even its nuclear capabilities, fully intact. The advance of technology, together with a culture of caution that transcended

Figure 18.1: Map of the major existing and proposed Russian natural gas transportation pipelines to Europe. Source: Bailey, S. (15 November 2009) Wikimedia Commons (Creative Commons Attribution 3.0 Unported License)

ideology, caused the nature of power itself to shift between 1945 and 1991: by the time the Cold War ended, the capacity to fight wars no longer guaranteed the influence of states, or even their continued existence, within the international system.' (Gaddis 2006: 260–261)

In light of Gaddis' analysis, and using the construction of the Nord Stream pipeline as a case study, we can explore the material articulations of power that are non-lethal, economically productive, and outwardly innocuous.

The Baltic seabed, like any landscape, is a palimpsest – here, a layering of conflict-related material culture – which exhibits, in potentially lethal objects, the changing nature of power in the post-1945 world.

The contested seascape of the Baltic: an overview

The Baltic is a contested seascape, and one of the most polluted bodies of water in the world. As such, it is a focus of attention for supra-national governmental organisations like the Helsinki Committee (HELCOM) whose remit is to protect the environmental integrity of Baltic waters. HELCOM's aim of protecting the Baltic's environment is

Figure 18.2: The Castoro Dieci laying a segment of the Nordstream pipeline. (© Nordstream AG)

Figure 18.3: A marine archaeologist from the Viking Ship Museum in Roskilde investigates the seabed in co-operation with Nord Stream to protect the Baltic's cultural heritage. (© Nordstream AG)

Figure 18.4: Castoro Sei semi-submersible on station in the Baltic Sea south-east of Gotland (Sweden) during pipe-laying for Nord Stream. Source: Philaebuckie. (23 July 2011) Wikimedia Commons. (Creative Commons Attribution 3.0 Unported License)

supported by its co-operation with European Union and non-EU countries (HELCOM 2010). The accumulated debris from the First and Second World Wars has transformed the Baltic seabed not only into a contested area, but also into an arena for international political, economic, and environmental cooperation. The illegally dumped legacy of twentieth century conflict has created a framework for transnational sub-aquatic co-operation stimulated in part by northern Europe's desire for Russian gas.

This conflict dimension is not the only issue, as the Baltic has also become a dumping ground for the material culture of the modern age more generally. The nations bordering it deposit their agricultural run-off and garbage on the sea-bed alongside the jettisoned war *matériel*. Recent surveys conducted on behalf of Nord Stream pipeline construction have detected boulders, shopping trolleys, oil drums, washing machines and refrigerators, among other things (Nord Stream 2010a).

Nord Stream construction planning included detailed surveys of the Baltic seafloor. This was done to mitigate damage to the fragile underwater environment, avoid potentially lethal unexploded munitions, and to preserve the area's subaquatic cultural heritage (in the form of historic shipwrecks) (Nord Stream 2010b: 3) (Figure 18.3). The survey included mapping and imaging with Remotely Operated Vehicles (ROVs), equipped with cameras, side scan sonar systems and gradiometers for the detection of ferrous objects (Nord Stream 2010b: 3). One survey was completed during early construction planning and another directly before pipe-laying '... to ensure that nothing has changed in the installation corridor since previous surveys ...' (*ibid.*) (Figure 18.4).

While the Baltic seabed represents the civil and military dumping activities of the twentieth century, it also contains a more extensive archaeological legacy which relates to earlier episodes of war and peace. Near the pipeline port of Griefswald, Germany, are 20 ships deliberately sunk to prevent enemy ships from entering the bay during the Great Nordic War (AD 1700–1721). These wrecks are historically significant, representing and exemplifying maritime technology of that time (Nord Stream 2010b: 6). The disruption of the cultural integrity of this particular site was minimized where the pipeline route was strategically placed so that only one of the smaller ships needed to be relocated and was ultimately salvaged for study (*ibid.*).

Three additional wrecks were located in German territorial waters, only one of which was in the pipeline corridor. This wreck was re-located 100 m away and buried beneath the sea bottom in order to ensure its preservation. Another of these wrecks was determined to be of 'supra-regional importance', being a cargo vessel dated *c.* AD 1400–1600. Its cargo provided valuable insights into Baltic trade of that era (*ibid.*).

Historical wrecks such as these are a particular concern: seventeen have been located within Russian territorial waters alone by Nord Stream surveys – two of which are within 50 m of the pipeline route (Nord Stream 2010b: 3). Six wrecks have been found within 50 m of the pipeline route in Finnish territorial waters, with an additional 13 within the pipeline anchor corridor. In the planning stages of construction, the pipeline was re-routed and/or re-designed to avoid four wrecks of great historical value (*ibid.*: 3–4).

Additionally, Nord Stream surveys have detected geological change, with several now submerged areas previously having been inhabited dry land. During the Mesolithic period (8000–4000 BC), several areas within the Swedish Exclusive Economic Zone (SEEZ), now submerged, were once land areas used for settlements and seasonal hunting camps. It has thus been acknowledged that Nord Stream pipeline construction may unearth artefacts not immediately visible, especially as sea level changes in the Baltic have not been uniform (Nord Stream 2010b: 4). Danish Sector surveys identified tracts of now-submerged forests, which hold potential data about oceanographic changes in the Baltic over time (*ibid.*: 5).

While my focus here is on the materialities of modern conflict surviving today on the Baltic seabed, the uniqueness of this palimpsest landscape/seascape is also revealed – not least by the realisation that even the land we walk on can be an ephemeral dimension.

Renegotiating the past: First and Second World War ordnance

Ordnance located on the Baltic seafloor is evidence that this area has served as both a barrier to enemy passage and a war zone. In discarding ordnance in Baltic waters after the end of the Second World War, Allied powers turned the sea into a site of abjection (CEPA 2008; González-Ruibal 2008). All this *matériel* has outlived its original purpose, but has not lost original destructive power – it lingers in deadly silence beneath the surface.

'Modern conflicts are defined by their technologies – all are wars of *matériel*' (Saunders 2004: 5; Paarlberg 2004: 122). The First World War offers worrying insights into the ambiguous legacies of such industrialised conflicts (and which set them apart from all pre-twentieth century wars). Unexploded ordnance is recognised, for example, as the 'defining feature of the Western Front' (Saunders 2001: 46) and more generally, as 'the definitive artifact … of industrialized war' (Saunders 2004: 9). On the modern landscape of the Western Front, '… [during] the late 1990s, an average year on the Somme yielded around 90 tons of dangerously volatile "hardware" known as the "iron harvest"… In Belgium, in the area around Ypres, up to 250,000 kgs of such materials can be recovered in a year …' (Saunders 2001: 46–47).

The scale of munitions present in the Baltic is comparable to that surviving today on the Western Front, with perhaps 296,000 tons of chemical and conventional arms lying on the seabed. They remain volatile and deadly, perhaps more so because this submerged cache includes active chemical warfare agents, many in containers which have corroded, enabling sea water to leak in. It is assumed that 10–20% of the known quantities of dumped chemical munitions are active chemical warfare agents. In this figure, dilution/degradation in the sea water is not included (DEPA 1994: 9).

Among the known chemical agents produced by Germany between 1935 and 1945 are Chloroacetophenone, Clark I, Clark II, Adamsite, Arsinic Oil, Phosgene, Mustard

Warfare Agent	Quantity (in tons)	Symptoms/Effects Caused by Agents
Chloroacetophenone (CAP)	7100	Tear gas (lachrimator)
Clark I	1500	Nose and throat irritant
Clark II	100	
Adamsite	3900	
Arsinic Oil (Active ingredients include Clark I)	7500	
Phosgene	5900	Lung irritant
Mustard Gas	25,000	Blister gases (vesicants)
Nitrogen Mustard	2000	
Tabun	12,000	Nerve gas
Lewisite	Production quantity known to be relatively small, but no exact amount figure is available	Blister gas (vesicant)
Total quantity of chemical warfare agents produced	65,000	

Source: Danish Environmental Protection Agency. (January 1994) *15th Meeting of Helsinki Commission: Report on Chemical Munitions Dumped in the Baltic Sea.* Helsinki Commission: Baltic Marine Environmental Protection Commission. Helsinki, Finland

Table 18.1: Types, quantities and effects of chemical warfare agents produced in Germany between 1935 and 1945

Allied Occupation Zone Where Discovered	Amount (in tons)
In the American occupation zone	93,995
In the British occupation zone	122,508
In the French occupation zone	9,100
In the Soviet occupation zone	70,500
Total	296,103

Source: Danish Environmental Protection Agency. (January 1994) *15th Meeting of Helsinki Commission: Report on Chemical Munitions Dumped in the Baltic Sea.* Helsinki Commission: Baltic Marine Environmental Protection Commission. Helsinki, Finland.

Table 18.2 Quantities of chemical munitions and warfare agents confiscated from German territory between the end of the Second World War and 1948

Gas, Nitrogen Mustard, Tabun and Lewisite (DEPA 1994: 8). Table 18.1 shows the effects of each type of warfare agent and the quantity in which they were produced in Germany during this period.

Where Table 18.1 illustrates the total amount of chemical weapons produced by Germany, Table 18.2 quantifies the tonnage of remaining chemical agents, including the weight of munitions containing chemical agents. It also provides a breakdown of the respective quantities of Germany's chemical and conventional stockpiles inherited by Allied countries – the United States, United Kingdom, France, and the Soviet Union – after the Second World War.

Types of Chemical Munitions	Mustard Gas	Other Vesicants	Adamsite	CAP	Others	TOTAL
Aircraft bombs	12.864	1.968	1.284	1.040	X	17.156
Artillery shells	1.458	X	0.132	0.078	X	1.668
High-explosive bombs	0.682	X	X	X	X	0.682
Mines	0.092	X	X	X	X	0.092
Encasements	0.174	0.442	1.506	X	0.16	2.282
Smoke Grenades	X	X	0.142	X	X	0.142
Containers	X	2.008	X	X	X	2.008
Drums	X	X	0.04	X	X	0.04
TOTAL	*15.270*	*4.418*	*3.104*	*1.118*	*0.16*	*24.070*

Source: Danish Environmental Protection Agency. (January 1994) *15th Meeting of Helsinki Commission: Report on Chemical Munitions Dumped in the Baltic Sea.* Helsinki Commission: Baltic Marine Environmental Protection Commission. Helsinki, Finland.

Table 18.3 Types of chemical munitions and quantities (in tons) of warfare agents dumped in the Baltic Sea by the former Soviet Union

Figure 18.5: The Eddya Freya ROV Support Vessel engaged in munitions clearance in March 2010. (© Nordstream AG)

The only dumped weapons accounted for are a portion of the Soviet Union's share of 70,500 tons. Unlike its British and American counterparts, the former Soviet Union released information concerning where they disposed of their weapons. Nevertheless, HELCOM's documentation only records the dumping locations of 24 tons of chemical munitions/warfare agents – a small fraction of the Soviets' total – with approximate locations southeast of the island of Gotland, east of Bornholm island, and just east of the Danish territorial waters that form the Baltic's western boundary. Table 18.3 shows the different kinds of weapons dumped into the Baltic by the Soviets, and specifies the types of chemical agents and munitions in which they were encased.

In light of the figures shown in Table 18.3, it is notable that:

> 'the quantity of chemical warfare agents varies for the individual types of munitions, depending on their purpose. The decisive factor is whether the munitions are artillery ammunition, aerial bombs or other containers which consist only of a thin shell and thus contain a larger amount of warfare agents.' (DEPA 1994: 9)

Of the total tonnage of weapons dumped by the Soviets, based on the munitions casing and types of chemical agents involved, the weapons have had different effects on the Baltic marine environment and represent variable threats to the Nord Stream construction process today.

The ordnance deposited in the Baltic is representative of the industrial capacity of the protagonist nations of both the First and Second World Wars. Similarly, the hugely complex industrial undertaking that is the Nord Stream pipeline project is a contemporary artefact representing the regional reliance on natural gas, reciprocal to the amount of production entailed with the size and scope of the planned pipeline.

Nord Stream's construction is inextricably linked to the material legacy of both World Wars. The failure of the Allies to dispose of dangerous munitions in the Atlantic has created a post-war conflict seascape where volatile ordnance blocks the planned pipeline route. The huge expense of surveying, assessing, and disposing of such objects adds inexorably to the cost of the pipeline – an expense which will be added to the overall price charged for the natural gas which will eventually flow through it. In another ironic twist of this legacy of industrialised war, the gas consumers of present-day northern Europe will be paying for both World Wars every time they use natural gas, and for the foreseeable future.

Due to the potentially lethal complexities of the situation, the ordnance and mine disposal firm, Bactec Global, has played a crucial role in the pipeline project. Since 1991, Bactec has built a global reputation for such work, and has been responsible for the 'clearance of more than 500,000 landmines and 1000s of tons of unexploded ordinance' (Bactec 2010).

For Nord Stream, projections are that it will take Bactec two days to clear each mine. The company has identified 70 specific bombs which inhibit the path of the pipeline. Each bomb contains over 600 lb (*c.* 272 kg) of explosives (Bactec 2010) (Figure 18.5).

Bactec's efforts represent the largest commercial clearing of mines ever attempted (Fox 2010), and, partly as a consequence, their methods are innovatory. They use a team of unmanned robots instead of humans to dispose of the munitions. Thus, state of the art wartime *matériel c.* 1918–1945, is being rendered safe by the latest twenty-first century robotic technology. In the event that any of this equipment is lost or destroyed, the Baltic seascape will accumulate a new layer of material culture.

The Baltic has become a setting where objects have come to define changing meanings and reactions to the past as well as 'new engagements between people and things' (Saunders 2004: 6). As contractors prepare to build Nord Stream, pre-construction seabed surveys have identified and destroyed dumped military ordnance from both World Wars, and categorised them not as information-rich archaeological artefacts, but as objects to be avoided or destroyed (Nord Stream 2010c). The building of Nord Stream is not the first instance where ordnance has been characterised as such, with previous seabed surveys conducted mainly by HELCOM having established a similar terminology to designate weapons – especially chemical agents – as pollutants, posing dangers to the Baltic marine environment (CEPA 2008; DEPA 1994).

On those occasions where such objects from the past are brought to the surface, it seems that they have been investigated solely as matter 'detached from socially significant recollection' (González-Ruibal 2008: 254–257). They are not conceptualised in any of the literature as historical material culture, but rather as dangerous objects to be disposed of (HELCOM 2010; CEPA 2008; DEPA 1994; Nord Stream 2010c). Through the actions of Allied powers, the Baltic has been turned into a vast abject landscape (González-Ruibal 2008: 254–257), a place where munitions could be ostensibly neutralized because their effects could seemingly no longer be viscerally experienced.

Nord Stream

The eventual completion of the Nord Stream pipeline will add a new layer of materiality to the Baltic seascsape. The pipeline materialises the technological infrastructure between states, and the embodies just how such energy technology binds nations, both physically via the pipeline itself, and in the social relationships it creates in the form of contracts attaching people and nations as producers and consumers. It also, irrevocably, ties the present (and possibly the future) to the past.

At 51% ownership of Nord Stream, the state-owned Russian company Gazprom is the prime mover of pipeline construction, and the main beneficiary of the exportation of natural gas to Europe (Bartlett 2008; Anon. c. 2009; Nord Stream 2010b). In fact, Gazprom is the largest supplier of natural gas in the world, owning 65% of Russia's gas reserves and 90% of the country's production and supply (EIA 2010). Gazprom supplies 42% of Europe's total gas imports, where 61% of all European gas needs are imported (Anon. d 2008; Anon. e 2009).

> 'In Europe as a whole, more than three-quarters of power demand growth has been met by gas-fired power since 2000, and these trends look set to continue. Gas has become the default option for power generation because of its advantages – low capital cost and short lead times, plus a low greenhouse gas footprint – as well as the lack of construction of new nuclear and coal-fuelled power stations. At the same time, Europe's gas production is falling... It is clear that Russia, as a holder of the world's largest gas reserves, will remain an important part of the European energy landscape for the foreseeable future.' (Cronshaw 2009)

European reliance on Russian natural gas demonstrates why the Nord Stream pipeline is being built, but also why it has been so controversial: Europe's lack of resource procurement choices make it a vulnerable consumer. The European Commission defines energy supply security as:

> '… geared to ensuring, for the well-being of its citizens and the proper functioning of the economy, the uninterrupted physical availability of energy products on the market, at a price which is affordable for all consumers (private and industrial) while respecting environmental concerns and looking towards sustainable development … Security of

Pipeline	Route and Destination	Capacity in trillions of cubic feet (tcf) OR millions of cubic feet (mcf)
Yamal-Europe I	Carry gas to Eastern and western Europe via Belarus	1tcf
Northern Lights		3tcf
Soyuz	Carry gas to Eastern and Western Europe via Ukraine	
Bratrstvo (also known as its English translation, "Brotherhood")		
Blue Stream	Carry gas to Turkey and Former Soviet Union Republics	3tcf
North Caucasus		
Mozdak-Gazi-Magomed		

Source: Energy Information Administration. (2010) *Country Analysis Briefs: Russia.* Washington, D.C.: U.S. Department of Energy. http://www.eia.doe.gov/cabs/russia/full.html

Table 18.4 Existing natural gas export pipelines in Russia owned by Gazprom

Pipeline	Route and Destination	Capacity in units of tcf	Notes
Yamal-Europe II	Carry gas from Russia to Poland & Germany via Belarus	1tcf	• Duplicates capacity of Yamal-Europe I • Ongoing disputes between Gazprom & Polish government over exact route of pipeline: Gazprom desires route via SE Poland to Slovakia to Central Europe; Poland desires route directly through Poland to Germany
South Stream	Carry gas from Beregovaya, Russia & splits into 2 routes: (1) crossing Serbia & Hungary to link with existing line; (2) SE through Greece & Albania linking Italian gas networks	?	• Same start point as existing Blue Stream at Beregovaya, Russia • Pipeline built as result of Russia/Ukraine gas disputes – pipeline constructed through Turkey's territorial waters, avoiding Ukraine all together
Nord Stream	Carry gas from Russia to Germany underwater through Baltic Sea	1.9tcf	• Pipeline built as result of Russia/Ukraine gas disputes • Longest sub-sea pipeline in world, with 2 parallel pipelines each running 1220 miles (*c.* 1960 km, for total distance of 2440 miles (*c.* 3920 km)

Source: Energy Information Administration. (2010) *Country Analysis Briefs: Russia.* Washington, D.C.: U.S. Department of Energy. http://www.eia.doe.gov/cabs/russia/full.html

Table 18.5 Gazprom proposed pipelines for natural gas export

supply does not seek to maximize energy self-sufficiency or minimize dependence, but aims to reduce the risks linked to such dependence. Among the objectives to be pursued are those balancing between and diversifying the various sources of supply and by geographical reason …' (EC 2000: 2)

Europe's vulnerability to Gazprom has manifested itself on two recent and controversial occasions. Both situations centred on Ukraine, an ex-Soviet state through which two of Gazprom's major export pipelines now pass, and which Nord Stream (and its southern counterpart, 'South Stream') will deliberately bypass (Anon. b 2009; Wingfield-Hayes 2009; Rodgers 2009).

Although the proposed Nord Stream pipeline supplies some of Europe's growing energy needs, it is also '... hugely expensive, fraught with environmental problems and [arguably] unnecessary' (Wingfield-Hayes 2009). In one sense, Nord Stream can be seen as Russia's articulation of power *vis-a-vis* the bypassing of Ukraine, and as a material basis for establishing a monopolistic autonomy over its natural resources which leaves European gas consumers at its mercy (de Jong *et al.* 2009). Figure 18.1 and Tables 18.4 and 18.5 outline Gazprom's existing and proposed pipeline routes and capacities.

Ukraine and Russia have a difficult political relationship, which has been articulated through their arguments over gas exports (de Jong *et al.* 2009; Anon. e 2009; Wingfield-Hayes 2009; Rodgers 2009). In 2006, and again in January 2009, Gazprom turned off the flow of gas travelling through Ukraine bound for Eastern Europe. Theories abound as to why this occurred – whether motives were political or commercial – but it had tangible and devastating results in many Eastern European states, for which imported Russian gas was the main energy supply (de Jong *et al.* 2009; Anon. f 2009).

Several political events were thought to have been the key motivators in the gas dispute. One was Ukraine's Orange Revolution of November 2004 to January 2005 in which the Kremlin-supported presidential incumbent was deposed in a run-off election. After the Ukrainian general public responded with mass protests, a third election brought victory to Viktor Yuschenko. '[This so-named] orange revolution … set a major new landmark in the postcommunist history of Eastern Europe, a seismic shift Westward in the geopolitics of the region' (Karatnycky 2005: 35). This was because under Yuschenko's direction, Ukraine – a former 'part of the Slavic heartland' – attempted to gain membership to the European Union (EU) and North Atlantic Treaty Organization (NATO) (Karatnycky 2005; Wingfield-Hayes 2009). Tensions between Ukraine and the Kremlin rose again in 2008 when Ukraine supported Georgia's war with Russia over South Ossetia (Rodgers 2009).

Former Gazprom chairman and current Russian president Dmitry Medvedev names the building of Nord Stream a direct result of ongoing regional tensions between Russia and Ukraine (Wingfield-Hayes 2009) – an interesting correlation between conflict in former Soviet Union territories and the disturbance of the conflict seascape of the Baltic. On a separate occasion, Medvedev accused Ukraine of 'dancing to the music which is being orchestrated not in Kiev, but outside the country' (Rodgers 2009). Political commentators allege that Medvedev was referring to the United States as the prime mover behind Georgia's military action to retake South Ossetia, as well as encouraging regional support for its actions (*ibid.*).

Whether or not political motives influenced the actions, in early January 2009 Gazprom issued a statement that Ukraine had defaulted on its payments. Gas bound for Eastern Europe still flowed through Ukraine, until Gazprom then accused Ukrainians of illegally siphoning gas from the pipeline and cut off the flow through the country. Gazprom consumers in Eastern Europe were left without heat during the coldest time of year (Anon. e 2009). Eighteen countries were affected by the event in 2009, with conditions so dire in Bulgaria in particular, that the country was forced to close schools and public buildings during the three week gas cut-off (de Jong *et al.* 2009; Anon. f 2009).

The events of January 2009, as well as similar incidents in 2006, highlighted European concerns over gas security, and the suspicion that Gazprom was not above playing a political game with its energy supply (Bartlett 2008; Wingfield-Hayes 2009).

Beyond the missile silos and memories of several generations whose lives were characterised by the imminent fear of 'mutually assured destruction' during the Cold War, the material culture of the Russian natural gas trade is considered by many political scientists as a new breed of power play (Bartlett 2008; de Jong *et al.* 2009; Larsson 2007; Smith 2008). From an archaeological perspective, the materiality of the Nord Stream pipeline construction entails billions of Euros of up-front capital to essentially duplicate an established pipeline route.

Unlike Nord Stream's two overland counterparts (Figure 18.1 and Table 18.4), the undersea pipeline forgoes incursions into any other nations' territorial waters. This autonomises Russia's control of this resource, and following natural laws of supply and demand, makes countries which require the resource rely wholly on one company to set prices and deliver. Furthermore, because the natural gas supply is actually required for basic household services in Eastern Europe, these nations' reliance on Russian fuel further secures Gazprom's control and power base (de Jong *et al.* 2009; Larsson 2007; Smith 2008).

Such geopolitical issues, intricately entwined with Russia's political relationships with its former Soviet possessions, Europe's worries about energy security, and more recent concerns about renewable and alternative energy sources is a volatile mix. In July 2011, German Chancellor Angela Merkel announced that Germany does not now need – and will therefore not build – the third, fourth, and fifth branches of the Nord Stream pipeline (Shabanov 2011). The future of the complete Nord Stream project, the projected South Stream, and a competitor known as Nabucco, remains unclear, though dependent in large part on Russia's relationships with Eastern Europe, Turkey, and Central Asia.

Discussion and conclusions

The Baltic seascape has come to embody both memory and forgetting, building the future while destroying the past, a metaphor in action. In a significant break with the practices of pre-twentieth century conflicts, the industrialied wars of the last 100 years have changed out of all recognition – in their prosecution and their individual and collective legacies (Gaddis 2006: 260; González-Ruibal 2008; Saunders 2001; 2004). The First and Second World Wars left nations bankrupt, and demonstrated that wars of attrition were prohibitively expensive for victor and loser alike (Gaddis 2006: 260). However, the '… memories of casualties and costs in World War II alone would not have ruled out future wars: comparable memories of World War I [had also] failed to do so' (Gaddis 2006: 260).

> 'Prior to 1945, great powers fought great wars so frequently that they seemed to be permanent features of the international landscape … After 1945, however, wars were limited to those between superpowers and smaller powers, as in Korea, Vietnam, and Afghanistan, or to wars among smaller powers like the four Israel and its Arab neighbors' fought between 1948 and 1973, or the three India-Pakistan wars of 1947–48, 1965, and 1971, or the long, bloody, and indecisive struggle that consumed Iran and Iraq throughout the 1980s. What never happened, despite universal fears that it might, was a full-scale war involving the United States, the Soviet Union, and their respective allies. The leaders of these countries were probably no less belligerent than those who had resorted to war in the past, but their bellicosity lacked optimism: for the first time in history *no one* could be sure of winning, or even surviving, a great war. Like the barbed wire along the Hungarian border, *war itself – at least major wars fought between major states – had become a health hazard, and therefore an anachronism.* (Gaddis 2006: 260)

Although in many ways the Cold War period represented hot conflict barely averted, the détente introduced a new paradigm of conflict, in which a large scale battle or any action that might lead to it is unlikely (though not impossible). A poignant aspect of Gaddis's observation is the acknowledgement that the end of large-scale war does not mean that their ideological correlates have disappeared. For those concerned with the archaeology of modern conflict (and its interdisciplinary focus on material culture), it is important to identify and chart the changing manifestations of power. Nord Stream represents food for speculative thought as to what the new materializations of conflict might look like.

The conflict seascape of the Baltic is a material narrative of the evolution of human relationships through time in this region. The sea has swallowed land that used to be inhabited by prehistoric peoples, and its depths have been watery graves to historical warships sunk in German harbors, and which serve as well-preserved reifications of eighteenth century maritime power.

Chemical agents and munitions of the First and Second World Wars represent the legacies of the world's first globalized industrial conflicts, '… the horrendous casualties of [these wars] can only be explained by an imbalance between people and things

– things going way ahead of people' (González-Ruibal 2008: 253). At the bottom of the sea, and as we relate to those objects as relics of our past, these volatile munitions and debris of war define the world's uncomfortable memories of its past conflicts.

Deliberately and illegally dumped, they were put out of sight and mind, alienated as it were from everyday post-war life. As we know now, these actions to cast-off the legacy of that *matériel* proved futile. Objects, once made, endure in the world, and their social life and material effects, often remain beyond our control.

The Nord Stream pipeline represents a new chapter in the history of regional relations. With this vast, transnational piece of modern material culture, we cannot benefit from hindsight as with all of the previous era's material legacies left in the deep. However, this does not preclude our ability to engage with it as archaeologists, and to attempt to define how it might influence the social lives of people today and in the future.

Bibliography

Anon.a. (2010) Baltic sea swimming with WW2 munitions. *Russia Today*. http://rt.com/news/underwater-ww2-ships-baltic/ Accessed 23 July 2011

Anon.b. (20 January 2009) Q & A: Russia Ukraine Gas Row. *BBC News*. http://news.bbc.co.uk/2/hi/europe/7240462.stm Accessed October 2010.

Anon.c. (9 April 2009) Nord Stream Gas Pipeline Underwater Construction Starts. http://news.bbc.co.uk/2/hi/8607214.stm Accessed February 2010.

Anon.d. (13 November 2008) EU Seeks to Expand Energy Grids. *BBC News*. http://news.bbc.co.uk/2/hi/europe/7727028.stm Accessed October 2010.

Anon.e. (1 January 2009) Russia Shuts Off Gas to Ukraine. *BBC News*. http://news.bbc.co.uk/2/hi/europe/7806870.stm Accessed October 2010.

Anon. f. (14 January 2009) EU Warns of Legal Action Over Gas. *BBC News*. http://news.bbc.co.uk/2/hi/7827829.stm Accessed October 2010.

Bactec. (2010) Mine Action. *Bactec Global*. http://www.bactec.com/mine-action.htm Accessed February 2010.

Bailey, S. (2009) *Map of the Major Existing and Proposed Russian Natural Gas Transportation Pipelines to Europe*. Wikimedia Commons. http://en.wikipedia.org/wiki/File:Major_russian_gas_pipelines_to_europe.png Accessed October 2010.

Bartlett, D. (24 February 2008) Russia's Energy Giant Flexes Its Muscles. *BBC News*. http://news.bbc.co.uk/2/hi/business/7259407.stm Accessed November 2010.

CEPA (Council of Europe – Parliamentary Assembly). (2008) *Chemical Munitions Buried in the Baltic Sea*. Committee on the Environment, Agriculture and Local and Regional Affairs. Strasbourg: Council of Europe. http://assembly.coe.int/Documents/WorkingDocs/Doc08/EDOC11601.pdf Accessed February 2010.

Cronshaw, I. (2009) Europe Charts New Gas Future. *BBC News*. http://news.bbc.co.uk/2/hi/7852145.stm Accessed October 2010.

DEPA (Danish Environmental Protection Agency). (1994) *15th Meeting of Helsinki Commission: Report on Chemical Munitions Dumped in the Baltic Sea*. Helsinki Commission: Baltic Marine Environmental Protection Commission. Helsinki, Finland. http://www.helcom.fi/stc/files/Publications/OtherPublications/1994Report-ChemicalMunitionsDumpedInTheBalticSea.pdf Accessed February 2010.

de Jong, S., Wouters J. and Sterkx, S. (2009) *The EU in Multilateral Security Governance: The Case of the Russian-Ukrainian Gas Dispute. Working Paper No. 30*. Leuven: Katholieke Universiteit Leuven, Leuven Centre for Global Governance Studies.

EC (European Commission) (2000) *Green Paper Towards a European Strategy for the Security of Energy Supply*. Brussels: European Commission.

EIA (Energy Information Administration). (2010) *Country Analysis Briefs: Russia*. Washington, D.C.: U.S. Department of Energy.

Fox, S. (2010) Robots to Clear Baltic Seabed of WWII Mines. *Popular Science*. http://www.popsci.com/technology/article/2010-02/robots-clear-baltic-sea-wwii-sea-mines Accessed February 2010.

Gaddis, J.L. (2006) *The Cold War: A New History*. New York: Penguin.

González-Ruibal, A. (2008) Time to Destroy: An Archaeology of Supermodernity. *Current Anthropology* 49(2): 247–279.

HELCOM. (2010) About HELCOM. Helsinki Commission: Baltic Marine Protection Commission. http://www.helcom.fi/helcom/en_GB/aboutus/ Accessed February 2010.

Karatnycky, A. (2005) Ukraine's Orange Revolution. *Foreign Affairs* 84(2): 35–52.

Larsson, R.L. (March 2007) *Nord Stream, Sweden and Baltic Security*. Stockholm: Swedish Defense Research Agency. Report Number: FOI-R-2251-SE. www.foi.se Accessed October 2010.

Nord Stream. (2009). Natural Gas Use Aids EU's Climate Change Challenge. *E-Facts: Nord Stream's Online Magazine*. https://e-facts.nord-stream.com/app/article/index.cfm?fuseaction=OpenArticle&aoid=840&lang=EN Accessed February 2010.

Nord Stream. (2010a). *Nord Stream: The New Gas Supply Route for Europe*. Moscow: Nord Stream. http://www.nord-stream.com/fileadmin/Dokumente/1__PDF/3__Background_Infos/General_Background/Nord_Stream_White_Paper_General_Background_eng.pdf Accessed February 2010.

Nord Stream. (2010b) *Nord Stream and Cultural Heritage*. Moscow: Nord Stream. http://www.nord-stream.com/fileadmin/Dokumente/1__PDF/3__Background_Infos/Cultural_Heritage/Nord_Stream_White_Paper_Cultural_Heritage_eng.pdf Accessed February 2010.

Nord Stream. (2010c) *Nord Stream and Munitions in the Baltic Sea*. Moscow: Nord Stream. http://www.nord-stream.com/fileadmin/Dokumente/1__PDF/3__Background_Infos/Munitions/ Nord_Stream_White_Paper_Munitions_eng.pdf Accessed February 2010..

Nord Stream. (2010d) Gazprom. *Nord-Stream*. http://www.nord-stream.com/our-company/shareholders/gazprom.html Accessed November 2010.

Paarlberg, R. (2004) Knowledge as Power. *International Security* 29(1): 122–151.

Rodgers, J. (2009) Strategy Behind Europe's Gas Game. *BBC News*. http://news.bbc.co.uk/2/hi/7828471.stm Accessed October 2010.

Saunders, N.J. (2001) Matter and Memory in the Landscapes of Conflict: The Western Front 1914–1999. In B. Bender and M. Winer (eds), *Contested Landscapes: Movement, Exile and Place*, 37–53. Oxford: Berg.

Saunders, N.J. (2004) Material Culture and Conflict: The Great War, 1914–2003. In N.J. Saunders (ed.), *Matters of Conflict: Material Culture, Memory and the First World War*, 5–25. Abingdon: Routledge.

Shabanov, V. (2011) Germany does not need Gazprom's Nord Stream pipeline. *Pravda*. http://english.pravda.ru/business/companies/21-07-2011/118557-nord_stream_germany-0/ Accessed 23 July 2011

Smith, K.C. (March 2008) *Russian Energy Policy and Its Challenge to Western Policy Makers*. Washington, D.C.: Center for Strategic and International Studies.

Thulin, J. and Andrushaits, A. (2003) The Baltic Sea: Its Past, Present and Future. In *Proceedings of the Religion, Science and Environment Symposium V on the Baltic Sea*. Athens: Religion, Science and the Environment. http://www.rsesymposia.org/themedia/File/1151679536-Thulin__Andrusaitis.pdf Accessed October 2010.

Wingfield-Hayes, R. (3 January 2009) Russian Gas Theories Abound. *BBC News*. http://news.bbc.co.uk/2/hi/7809131.stm Accessed October 2010.

Afterword

Paul Cornish

I suppose it is apt that this collection of papers of such cross-disciplinary reach, having been introduced by an archaeologist and anthropologist, should conclude with a contribution from someone raised in the disciplines of History and Curatorship.

Historians have traditionally failed to engage with objects as a potential research source – even at the most prosaic level. For example, the failure of most military historians to engage physically with the weapons and equipment about which they write has led to the transmission and multiplication of errors and mis-apprehensions too numerous to list. Having spent 20 years in a profession where I was in a position to make such material available for study, I can count the number of historians who have taken advantage of this facility on the fingers of one hand.

If this is the case with regard to a simple analysis of the functionality of objects, we cannot be surprised that the record of historians when it comes to incorporating the fruits of conflict archaeology and material culture studies into their own intellectual universe is, with honourable exceptions, even worse. This may be because many are wedded to an outmoded conception of this alien discipline – seeing it simply as what has been characterised above as 'Battlefield Archaeology'. Consequently they ask: 'what can this tell me that written records cannot tell me more efficiently?' This is of course particularly the case with warfare of the 'Supermodern' era – for which mountains of documentary evidence are available. Actually, any battlefield excavation can probably tell them something: about burial practices perhaps, or about units ending up in unplanned and unrecorded locations.[1] However, as is made plain in this volume, this would be to merely scratch the surface of an incredibly rich seam of evidence.

There is every hope, however, that this situation will improve. The history of war and conflict has, in recent years, been freed from the damaging and artificial division into History (worthy) and Military History (slightly suspect). Historians are thankfully now aware that what we call 'peace' cannot be understood without knowing what went on in wars, any more than wars can be comprehended in isolation. A new generation of scholars are looking at warfare in more holistic way than has previously been the case. Moreover they are investigating areas in which a multi-disciplinary approach, with due weight being accorded to material culture as evidence, is likely to be profitable.

My own current interest is in the First World War and the twenty-first century has witnessed exciting developments in the field of First World War Studies. That curious lacuna in historiography – the lack of a modern and scholarly single volume history of the war – has been multiply filled, with several thought provoking and academically rigorous works appearing.[2] Importantly for Anglophone history, the study of the war has become more consciously internationalist in its approach, and no longer so closely focused on Britain's war effort. Furthermore, historians have begun to apply themselves to that most interesting area of study at the juncture between war and culture – how our culture was changed by the war, and how our memory of the war has developed.[3] As much of this culture manifested itself in material ways, the potential value of material culture studies to this new wave of war history is obvious.

For example, a major current historical debate centres on the balance between consent and coercion in maintaining the war effort. In my view, the archaeological remains of the war – which can be as widely differing as a patriotic trinket in a museum collection, or a soldier's shelter clinging to the side of a mountain in the Julian Alps (we should ask why a man should willingly put himself in such a place) – can speak eloquently for a subject for which written evidence does not give a complete picture. Collective mourning is another subject which is increasingly becoming the focus of investigation. In this case the primary evidence consists of material reifications of loss – ranging from the monumental memorials of the Western Front, to personal mementoes, or even the less concrete (but nonetheless artefactual) consolations to the grief-stricken which emanated from the post-war boom in spiritualism.

In the museum world, a fuller engagement with conflict archaeology and material culture has already been in evidence in some places. At Péronne, on the Somme, in France, the Mémorial de la Grande Guerre has, from its inception, concentrated on the material culture of conflict – the relationship the war, people, and their things. The In Flanders Fields Museum at Ieper, in Belgium, broke new ground with its 2006 exhibition 'The Last Witness' in which conflict archaeology and the material culture of landscape were combined. A variant of this concept looks likely to be a permanent feature of the museum when it re-opens in 2012 following redevelopment

I am happy to report that my own place of work, the Imperial War Museum in London, has become aware of the potential value of material culture studies in discharging its remit. By taking on board the concept that objects have 'social lives' the museum will be able to exploit its abundant collections in a new way. The IWM is unique in being concerned with the causes, course, and consequences of all wars in which Britain has been involved since 1914. Material culture studies and modern conflict archaeology are perfectly adapted to creating links, through objects, between the before, the during, and the after of wars.

This perspective will, henceforward, inform the museum's education programme. It will also be consciously employed in the creation of a new First World War gallery – to open in 2014. Objects with 'stories' have always featured heavily in IWM displays; but only as straightforward objectifications of a person or an event. A grasp of the concept of material culture gives those of us engaged in creating the new gallery the opportunity to use artefacts in ways which are simultaneously more subtle and more powerful.

One of the main considerations in designing this new exhibition is a problem which our predecessors did not have to face; namely a dwindling familiarity with the social and material context of the war. No longer can we, or any other museum, expect young visitors to be primed with information by parents or grandparents for whom the war was part of their world.

This is a generational thing. The material surroundings of my own youth are now unfamiliar to people in their twenties. The latter are still further removed from the material world of the early twentieth century. Objects can help bridge this chasm. Obviously, it is relatively simple to make, for example, a parallel between a silver cigarette case and an iPhone as objects of desire then and now. More than this, however, the relationships which people have formed with artefacts now held in our collections give us the opportunity to engage with less tangible concepts. A material culture studies approach can open a way into the minds of our forebears allowing us to understand their patriotism, their religiosity, their sense of social deference, their pleasures and their pains. With equal facility it can be used to track the changes which wars wrought in this world view.

The First World War was but the first of the wars of *matériel* which blighted the twentieth century; to all of which the application of this approach is appropriate. In short, material culture studies and modern conflict archaeology offer both historians and museums the opportunity which they offer to renegotiate the way in which their audiences view war in the 'Supermodern' era.

Notes

1 Both types of information might be considered to be exemplified by the excavation of a mass grave of 10th Lincolnshire Regt soldiers at Arras in 2001 (Defossés, Y., Jacques A. and Prilaux, G. (2008) *L'archéologie de la Grande Guerre*. Rennes: Éditions OUEST-FRANCE).

2 For example: Stevenson, D. (2004) *1914–1918*. London: Allen Lane; Beckett, I.F.W. (2004 and 2007) *The Great War*. London: Longman; Strachan, H. (2004) *The First World War*. London: Simon and Schuster.

3 For example: Audoin-Rouzeau, S. and Becker, A. (2002) *1914–1918*. London: Profile; Todman, D. (2005) *The Great War. Myth and Memory*. London: Hambledon Continuum; Kramer, A. (2007) *Dynamic of Destruction*. Oxford: Oxford University Press.